Perfect Days in...

VENICE

Travel with Insider Tips

D0420033

www.marco-polo.com

Contents

For chapters: see inside front cover

Not to be missed!

Our top hits – from the absolute No. 1 to No. 10 –

help you plan your tour of the most important sights.

★1 ST MARK'S SQUARE ➤ 54

Loved by Napoleon, this piazza boasts no fewer than 5 of the city's highlights: the Basilica San Marco, the Campanile, the Torre dell' Orologio, the Palazzo Ducale, the Museo Correr and the historic cafés.

★2 SAN GIORGIO MAGGIORE ➤ 56

This Benedictine Abbey, built by Andrea Palladio, is the final resting place of two Doges. Don't miss the view from the Campanile.

★3 PONTE DI RIALTO ➤ 118

The world-famous Ponte de Rialto bridge lies in the heart of the old trade district.

★4 MERCATO DI RIALTO ➤ 120

With its artfully arranged fruit and vegetables, freshly caught fish and seafood, the Rialto market is a true feast for the senses.

★5 ACCADEMIA ➤ 136

Discover 800 works by Bellini & Co. spanning five centuries on the south bank of the Grand Canal.

★6 COLLEZIONE PEGGY GUGGENHEIM ➤ 140

Wild parties were held in this palace on the Grand Canal before its owner – art-lover Peggy Guggenheim – transformed it into a home for creations by such painters and sculptors as as Giacometti, Magritte, Picasso and Pollock.

★7 SANTI GIOVANNI E PAOLO ➤ 82

The largest Gothic church in the city serves as the final resting place of no fewer than 27 Doges.

★8 MURANO ➤ 154

Artistic glass has been blown on this lagoon island for 1,000 years. Several "Fornaci" show visitors how a vase or piece of jewellery can be created from raw glass in just a few minutes.

★9 BURANO ➤ 156

Burano's colourful houses used to show fisherman the safe route home, even when thick fog hung over the lagoon. The place is also famous for its richly decorated bobbin and needle lace. The women in the Museo del Merletto show how this delicate material is produced.

★10 IL GHETTO ➤ 100

All other ghettos take their name and form from this walled-off Jewish quarter in the Sestiere Cannaregio. With its kosher shops, restaurants, Torah schools and synagogues, the Ghetto is flourishing again today.

THAT VENICE

Find out what makes Venice tick, experience its unique flair – just like the Venetians themselves.

AN OMBRA IN A BACARÒ

Treat yourself to what Venetians call a "shadow" (ombra) – a small glass of wine enjoyed in a cosy bàcaro accompanied by tramezzini or cichetti, typical Venetian antipasti. At over 500 years of age, Do Mori, with its copper pots dangling from the ceiling, is considered the oldest place to enjoy these tasty delicacies.

STROLLING IN THE SESTIERI

There are at least two sides to Venice: the tourist side with its heavily trampled routes (all of which lead to St Mark's!), and the side enjoyed by locals. You'll only dis- cover the latter by chance if you make a sudden turn, go down a narrow alleyway, saunter along a Sottoportego (a passage through a building) and arrive at some of the most beautiful, best-hidden corners of the city. Simply stroll through the passageways of Cannaregio, Castello, San Polo and Santa Croce, take a break in such tranquil squares as the Campo Zanipolo and lose yourself in the city on stilts.

CANAL CRUISE

Gondola or vaporetto? The cheapest, most authentically Venetian option is to take one of the traghetto ferries rowed by two Gondolieri (e.g. from the San Tomà jetty). Whichever way you decide to travel, however, a trip through the city's canals in an absolute must! If you go early in the morning you'll see vegetable producers bringing their wares to the Rialto market and piling large barges high with bags upon bags of rubbish. In the evening, the illuminated palazzi are reflected in the waters and give Venice a real sense of fairy-tale magic.

GUZZLING GELATO

According to locals, for the last eight decades the best ice cream has been sold at the Gelateria Nico on the Zattere – a quay named after the rafts (ital. "Zattere") that used to land there – in the Sestiere Dorsoduro, the southernmost part of Venice. Enjoy their homemade gelato on a sun-kissed pontoon or take a stroll along the waterfront promenade down to the Punta della

FEELING

The best of Venice: Love, luxury, and a cooling ice cream in the heat of the midday sun

That Venice Feeling

Dogana with its magnificent views of St Mark's and the islands in the lagoon.

VIVALDI IN VENICE

The music of the Baroque composer Vivaldi is inextricably linked with Venice, and his creations are played year round in churches and concert halls by local orchestras of very varying quality. You're guaranteed to have a truly exceptional listening experience if you go and see the Venice Baroque Orchestra or the La Fenice Orchestra, two of the best in the whole of Italy.

A BOAT TO THE BEACH

When the sun's out, it's time to go to the beach. Take the *vaporetto* to the Lido with the locals and you'll really be spoilt for choice. If you fancy a bit of exclusivity and elegance, head to the Lido beach for a dip in the Adriatic. And if natural beaches and dunes are more your thing, catch the bus (Line B) to Alberoni and enjoy a day in the Bagni di Spiaggia.

The Piazza San Marco at night…

ART ON THE CANAL

During the Biennale, the work of contemporary artists takes over the city's quays, churches, parks and *palazzi*. The rest of the time, a handful of museums and collections invite you to discover typical Venetian art from the middle ages to the modern day. The Vaporetto dell'Arte (www.vaporetto arte.com) sails to exhibitions on the Grand Canal – the boat ticket is also your ticket to get in!

BELLA FIGURA

Traditionally conservative Venetian society places great importance on looking good to make a good impression. Help comes in the form of such Italian fashion designers as Roberto Cavallo, Armani, Prada, Gucci & Co., whose boutiques crowd the San Marco fashion district around the Calle Vallaresco and the Calle larga XXII Marzo.

UNFORGETTABLE NIGHTS

A night on the Piazza San Marco, when the day's tourists have long left the city, is something really special. The Campanile, the cathedral and the Doge's palace are softly lit, a light breeze picks up the sounds of the coffee house orchestra, and couples dance between the rose sellers and street artists. The best place for a last drink is on the rooftop terrace of the Molino Stucky Hilton Hotel, where you can have a cocktail and enjoy the view out over the Serenissima under a sky bedecked with stars.

The Magazine

'O SOLE MIO' –

Getting around in Gondolas

Venice is the best place in the world for simply messing about in boats. Originally decorated with bright colours, gondolas had to be painted black from 1562 to put a stop to the overly ostentatious gaudiness with which the noble families were beautifying their vessels.

There is a specialist boat for every purpose and occasion – mail, goods and rubbish barges, hearses, fire engine, ambulance and police boats, sleek fast taxi boats, private pleasure craft and the *vaporetti*, the public transport boats (▶ 33–34). Travelling through Venice's canals in a gondola is a real luxury (unless you're on board one of the traditional *traghetti*).

Black, Streamlined and Fit for Purpose

It's unclear exactly when the gondola's unique form was developed. What is certain is that their long, slim shape and low draft – making them perfect for the city's narrow, shallow canals – had come into being by the 11th century. Gondolas measure in at 10.87m (35.66ft) in length and 1.42m (4.66ft) at their widest point. To counteract the weight of the Gondolier at the

back, all the boats are equipped with a "ferro" at the prow, a heavy metal plate with a curve representing the Doge's cap and six teeth in honour of the Sestieri: San Marco, Giudecca island, San Polo, Cannaregio, Castello and Santa Croce. The "felze" – a wooden cabin with a semi-circular roof that sheltered passengers from the summer sun and the elements in winter – can only be admired in historical paintings today. That this gondola cabin doesn't completely fall into obscurity is down to "El Felze", a society for the preservation of gondola culture. This association unites all of the tradespeople involved in building a gondola from 280 individual pieces in less than

A gondola ride under the Rialto Bridge

The jetty on the Grand Canal: Room for one more…?

four months: the Squerarioli (boat builders), the Ottonai and Fonditori (metal workers), the Intagiadori (woodcarvers), the Remeri (forcola carvers), the Tapessieri (upholsterers), the Caleghieri (shoemakers), the Fravi (ferro makers), the Indoradori (gilders), the Bareteri (milliners) and the Sartori (tailors).

A Woman in a Man's World

Since it was founded in 1094, none of the 425-strong membership of the exclusive Association of Gondoliers had ever been female – at least not until 23 year-old mother of two Giorgia Boscolo bucked the trend in 2009. Giorgia is the daughter of a Gondolier who – although proud of her – doesn't support her ambition. He's believes that "the work of a Gondolier is not suitable for a woman." Many Gondoliers share this opinion, at least partially due to a sense of financial self-interest: steering gondolas is a lucrative tradition, with the men bringing home 5,000 Euros a month.

Do It Standing Up

Venetians love rowing, and enjoy getting together in clubs to train the whole year round in readiness for the regattas in the summer. Each sestiere (city quarter) has its own club, its own roster of rowing heroes, and its own fans who pack themselves into the best vantage points to cheer on their teams. Gondolas are steered using the "forcola" at the back. How this undulating oar mount is cut from cherry or walnut wood in such a way that its curves and bulges allow the boat to be propelled at a total of seven tempi (ranging from docking mode to top speed) is a well-guarded trade secret among those in the know.

The State of the
NATION
SECURING THE FUTURE

In the first decades of the 21st century, Venice faces huge problems right across the board, but there are signs that everything possible will be done to secure the city's future.

A Vicious Circle?

At the end of World War II, around 170,000 people lived in the Centro Storico, the old part of Venice. Only about 60,000 live there today. The city's population is shrinking and ageing, in large part due to the lack of affordable, good-quality housing. Living in Venice is complicated, time-consuming and expensive – factors that have caused an exodus to the conveniences and lower costs of a drier lifestyle on the mainland. Depopulation is a vicious circle; as residents move out,

> "As public housing is scarce, many Venetians struggle with the upkeep of ancient buildings"

local shops and services close, and fewer people choose to live in an area. Meanwhile, public housing is scarce, so many Venetians struggle with the expense of the upkeep of ancient buildings, whose only foundations are wooden piles driven into mud. Any building work is not only has to comply with the labyrinthine regulations common to the whole of Italy and seen at their worst in Venice, but, like everything in the city, has the high add-on costs caused by the expense of transporting materials by water.

Life On and Around the Water

Venice depends on the tides and the lagoon, and the lagoon itself is sustained by a delicately balanced ecosystem. Following World War II, this balance was destroyed as deep-water channels were excavated to allow access to Mestre-Marghera, a vast petro-chemical works and industrial complex on the edge of the lagoon. Elsewhere, new man-made islands

World Heritage in Danger: Air pollution is damaging stonework and buildings

replaced nearly a third of the wetlands, while there was indiscriminate tapping of the lagoon-bed aquifers. By the 1970s, as 3.5 million tonnes of waste were dumped daily into the lagoon, pollution levels and health problems rocketed. As the lagoon changed, Venice, delicately balanced on its wooden piles, sank faster than ever before. Today, the city is 123cm (48in) lower in the water than in 1900 and *acqua alta* (a high, flooding tide) hits the city on an average of 130 days a year, causing immense damage to the city's buildings. These are further at risk from pollution blown

Canals are sealed off for repairs

by westerly winds from Mestre. Humidity and salt combine with acids in the atmosphere to eat away at the city's artistic treasures; it's estimated that the surface 6 per cent of marble and stone, 5 per cent of frescoes and 3 per cent of paintings on canvas and wood have been disappearing annually. Industry is still a major source of contamination.

Saving Venice

By the 1990s, there was widespread realisation that something had to be done to halt the destruction caused by constant *acqua alta*, exacerbated by climate variability. In 2003, the government voted the necessary funding for a scheme to build 79 inflatable seabed floodgates at the lagoon entrances to control high incoming tides. That very same year, building work began on the MOSE Megaproject (MOdulo Sperimetale Elettromeccanico), the cost of which was then estimated at around 4.3 billion Euros. Ten years later, in August 2013, fourteen people involved in the project were arrested under suspicion of criminal dealings. Nevertheless, the gates – built in spite of opposition from ecologists – will begin combating high water levels as early as late 2014. In addition to this feat of engineering, the city's pavements (sidewalks) and quaysides are being raised and side canals dredged to help halt the harm done by flooding, while steps have been taken to limit the damage to the underwater piles on which the city stands by limiting the speed of motor-powered boats. There are signs of

Dredging the canals and replacing piles is an ongoing task

restoration and improvement projects all over the city as buildings are put under wraps while they're strengthened using state-of-the-art techniques.

The Right Balance

How Venice plans to live sustainably on and around the water over the years to come will be shown when the lagoon city acts as an outpost for Milan's World Fair in 2015. By the time EXPO 2015 comes around, the old waterways leading to Milan will have been made navigable again at a cost of 2.4 billion Euros. One of Venice's biggest problems is the number of tourists it attracts: more than 60,000 tourists visit the city every day (22 million a year). What's more, 439 cruise ships dock at the quays and – as there is no shore-based power supply – emit just as many fumes as all the industry on the mainland put together. The movements of the ships also shake the foundations of the city, a place that is becoming ever more dependent on tourism.

The majority of visitors come as day-trippers, spend little, but put a huge strain on the city's infrastructure. In addition, the council must address the problem of attracting people back to live in the historic centre as well as tackle the ongoing challenge of saving the fabric of the city. Only Venice itself can decide whether the city should strive to remain a viable, living, thriving entity or survive as a theme-park fantasy land with World Heritage status, a travesty of its former self.

THE RISE AND FALL OF
VENICE

Venice was an independent power for more than a 1,000 years, and its political and financial clout made it admired and feared all over the world.

Legend dates the founding of Venice to 25 March 421, although this can not be confirmed by historians. The city's origins arose when the Teutons invaded northern Italy during the Barbarian Invasions that marked the beginning of the end for the western Roman Empire. The inhabitants of the Italian mainland took refuge in the impenetrable maze of islands in

The Bronze Horses of San Marco became the symbol of the Serenissima

the Venetian lagoon (latin: *lacuna,* "pond", "pool"). The first settlers took root on the islands of Malamocco (called the Lido today), Torcello and Murano, clearing and draining their partially marshy new homes. They eked out a rather meagre existence as fishermen, coastal skippers, salt workers and vegetable growers. Attila the Hun (452) and later the Lombards (from 568) triggered further waves of exodus and colonisation.

A Refuge Amid the Waters

By 697, when the Venetians elected their first Doge (from lat. *dux,* "Duke") to oversee the ever-expanding city, necessity had made them into master ship-builders. From its origins as a loose band of several lagoon islands, the settlement developed into a tightly organised maritime and trading power that even marched against Constantinople during the fourth Crusade in 1204. As the new Mediterranean superpower – long-term challenger Genoa

The Magazine

The most beautiful side of Venice, complete with the Doge's palace: Town hall, court and living quarters of the Doge

was wiped out for good at Chioggia in 1378 – the Serenissima enlarged its kingdom on terra firma, where Palladio designed palace-like estates in Padua, Vicenza, Verona, Bergamo and Brescia for the Venetian nobility. Such merchants as Marco Polo brought home silk and velvet, emeralds and rubies, spices and other luxury goods from Arabia, India and China; Arabic merchants, slaves and Jews added a pinch of exoticism to city life. Bellini and Vivarini turned the lagoon city into a centre of the arts, and the Arsenale was considered the best shipyard in the world, where up to 16,000 men worked on the galleys that the seafaring Republic used to secure its power. The Palazzo Ducale functioned as the centre of politics and law, and its halls were decorated by Titian, Tintoretto and Paolo Veronese. These stars of the 16th-century art world immortalised the most important events of the city's history in their monumental paintings.

The Glory Days

By the 15th century, rich and powerful Venice was one of the largest cities in Europe. Dazzling buildings adorned the place, while the citizens were famous for their opulent clothes and jewels and their hedonistic lifestyle. At one time, more than 10,000 courtesans are thought to have lived in this cosmopolitan trading city. The Serenissima provided them with an official red light district in the sestiere San Polo. You could see them sitting at the windows with their breasts exposed just a few steps from the Rialto bridge. The "Ponte delle Tette" (the "Bridge of Breasts") over the Rio Terrà delle Carampane was famous for this visual spectacle. Although the life of courtesans was restricted by law – they could only stroll through Venice on Saturdays, for instance – their "connection" to prestigious, high-standing individuals nevertheless meant that they often became some of the most influential people in Venetian society.

The political system, based on complicated layers of checks and balances that ensured no one section of the political elite had excessive power, generally, worked. The Major Council, Minor Council, Senate, Council of Ten, heads of the supreme courts, committees, clerks, spies and backroom boys all kept the delicate equilibrium, while the Doge, elected for life and privy to all secrets, presided over all.

> "The citizens of Venice were famous for their opulent clothes and hedonistic lifestyles"

The aristocrats, nominally involved in government through the Major Council, were able in reality to concentrate on serious retail therapy and maintaining a lavish lifestyle.

Venice's Changing Fortunes

Venice, rich, stable and respected, was the envy of the world. True, there was the odd blip. Conspiracies and plots occasionally threatened the State, plague struck with monotonous regularity, notably in 1348 when the Black Death killed around 60 per cent of the population, and, in 1450, syphilis arrived, affecting as many as one in five Venetians. In 1453, Constantinople fell to the Turks and Venice's access to the eastern trade routes was blocked. In 50 years, Venice lost her trade monopoly on which her economy depended and the writing was on the wall, though, cushioned by centuries' worth of booty, few realized the gravity of the situation. As the state coffers emptied, Venice re-invented itself as the party capital of Europe, a mecca for sybarites.

The End of the Republic

In 1789, Lodovico Manin was elected the 120th Doge. Rather than interrupt the *Carnevale*, his election was barely announced. Eight years later, in 1797, the young Napoleon swept into the city and deposed Manin. He went quietly, removing his Doge's cap, the 1,000-year old symbol of the Republic, and handing it to his valet with the words, "Take this, I shall not be needing it again."

VENICE:
MECCA FOR THE ARTS

The city of Venice is a fragile work of art made up of bridges and canals, palaces with peeling plaster, churches boasting shimmering gold mosaics, impressive Titian Madonnas and Tintoretto Last Suppers. What's more, it's also a real hotspot for anyone who loves modern and contemporary art.

Almost nowhere in the world knows how to put itself on show quite as well as the Serenissima. After the last Doge stepped down, it was mainly thanks to the efforts of one man, Teodoro Correr (1750–1830), that not all of Venice's artistic treasures left the city. He jammed the 20 rooms in his Grand Canal *palazzo* floor to ceiling with the art that forms the basis of the Museo Correr today. The City Elders founded the Venice Biennale in 1895, and Klimt, Renoir and Courbet were the first international artists to be exhibited there in 1910. The biannual show has long taken over the Arsenale, the old shipyard complex, and art has also crept into the city's *palazzi* and other groups of buildings. Aside from the Biennale, Venice offers a mammoth selection of art from two millennia in its 40 museums, meaning that you can admire the Bellinis and Titians in the stately "Accademia" and stroll over to the Rococo splendour of the Ca' Rezzonico, before checking out the flirtatious mix of Pop, Minimalism and the Baroque magnificence of Giorgio Massari in the Palazzo Grassi.

Patrons of the Arts

The city has been lucky time and time again with rich benefactors. Fiat boss Giovanni Agnelli bought the Palazzo Grassi in 1984, for example. He commissioned architects Gae Aulenti and Antonio Foscari with its restoration and opened it two years later as a cultural centre in a fabulous location on the Grand Canal. After the CEO's death, this veritable jewellery box was put up for sale. Taking his his cue from the motto "it's good to spoil yourself sometimes", French industrialist and art collector François Pinault spent 29 million Euros to open a major exhibition there with 200 works from the likes of Andy Warhol, Gerhard Richter and Maurizio Cattelan in

The Biennale attracts visitors every other year from mid-June to mid-November

April 2006 after five months of alterations. As if that wasn't enough, Pinault then started work on the Punta della Dogana, the former customs post at the mouth of the Grand Canal (which the Guggenheim foundation also had their eye on). He had it remodelled following plans by Tadao Ando and opened a permanent exhibition of contemporary art there in 2009.

The unfinished Palazzo Venier dei Leoni on the Grand Canal has also been turned into a temple of art. It was bought in 1910 by the Marchesa Luisa Casati, who dedicated herself to becoming "a living work of art", a quest that led the lover of poet D'Annunzio to squander her fortune in just a few years. She held wild parties and walked two leopards around the Piazza San Marco on diamond encrusted leashes. That alone would have made the Marchesa the talk of the town, but the capricious noblewoman also enjoyed going stark naked under her cosy fur coat. Casati fled her immense debts and went to London in 1932, and her estate was acquired in 1949 by Peggy Guggenheim, an equally well-heeled hedonist who also knew a thing or two about the good life herself. Addicted to acquiring images and fascinated by all modern art's movements, she collected work by the Cubists and Surrealists, action painters and abstract artists. Venice's visitors can still enjoy the fruits of her passion to this day.

INSIDER INFO

You'll find the **Palazzo Grassi** on the Grand Canal (Campo San Samuele, San Marco 3231; www.palazzograssi.it, Wed–Mon 10–7). It's best to buy a combined ticket for the Grassi and the Punta della Dogana (€20, €15 one venue only). The **Punta della Dogana** is in Dorsoduro (▶ 145 for details). You can get information about the **Biennale Internazionale d'Arte** – celebrating it's 120th anniversary in 2015 – at www.labiennale.org (there's also an app you can download from the website). You'll need to allow a couple of days to see everything.

CARNEVALE
Behind the Mask

Venice's masked celebrations hold their very own special fascination – even though you have to share the Carnival experience with hundreds of thousands of fellow visitors annually. Luckily, a great deal more festivals are held throughout the year.

In the Middle Ages, all Europe celebrated *Carnevale* (ital. *carne vale*, "meat, farewell"), a free-for-all, pre-Lent party, the last chance for fun and games before enduring the long and penitential weeks leading up to Easter. Venice was no exception. The city's Carnival isn't quite as traditional as it might look, however – at least not in the form it takes today. Despite being first mentioned in the writings of Doge Vitale Falier as far back as 1094, Venice stopped having a Carnival altogether from 1797. Napoleon forbad the celebrations because he feared (not without good reason!) that the Venetians might be up to no good behind their masks and costumes. The present-day Venetian Carnival as experienced by hundreds of thousands of visitors a year was reintroduced in 1979 as a marketing ploy to try and liven up the less popular winter months.

Judging from the event's success, it's a plan that certainly seems to be working.

Fireworks and Human Pyramids

The wildest of the earlier Carnivals boasted puppet theatres, fireworks being shot into the skies, young men building human pyramids, and a myriad of exotic animals. The highlight of the celebrations was the "Flight of the Angel", however, during which an acrobat walked on a rope from the Campanile down into Saint Mark's square. This tradition has been revived today, with celebrities (carefully secured with ropes!) playing the part of the "angel". In the 18th century, people liked to dress up as characters from the *Commedia dell'arte*, going as Pantalone or Colombina, Pulcinella or Harlequin. A variety of traditional types of mask were available, and a whole industry sprung up to make them, creating jobs for the *maschereri* (mask makers) who are still hard at work today.

Celebrations and Commemorations

If you can't make the *Carnevale*, there are other festivals throughout the year, many of them dating back to the days of the Venetian Republic. Heading the list are the rowing regattas, the Vogalonga, held in May on the first Sunday after the feats of the Ascension, and the Regata Storica, on the first Sunday in September. The Festa del Redentore (Redeemer), in late July, celebrates the deliverance of the city from the plague of 1575–77. A pontoon bridge is built across the wide Giudecca canal to the church, and the week ends in a huge party and firework display. Another temporary bridge goes up for the 21 November, across the Grand Canal, when the 1630 plague deliverance, which resulted in the building of the church of the Salute, is commemorated.

INSIDER INFO

The precise date of *Carnevale* depends when Easter falls but it's usually a 10-day period between **mid-February** and **early March**. You can get details from the tourist information office APT (Piazza San Marco 71f, tel: 041 5 29 87 11; www.carnevale.venezia.it). There are sumptuous theatrical **costumes** for hire at Atelier Pietro Longhi (San Polo 2580, Calle dei Saoneri, tel: 041 71 44 78, www.pietrolonghi.com), and you can buy a **genuine papier-mâché mask** made by hand from MondoNovo (Dorsoduro 3063, Rio Terrà Canal, tel: 041 5 28 73 44, www.mondonovomaschere.it) or Tragicomica (San Polo 2800, calle dei Nomboli, tel: 041 72 11 02, www.tragicomica.it). If you're coming, book well in advance for accommodation.

Insider Tip

STONE AND PAINT
A STUNNING VISUAL IMPACT

Venice's urban landscape is incomparably beautiful. It may be enough just to soak it all in; but to make sense of what you see, a little background information may come in handy.

Byzantine Influence

The city's close relationship with Constantinople had a marked influence on the development of art in Venice. San Marco, the official house of worship for both the State and the Doge, was based on the five-domed Church of the Holy Apostles in Constantinople. Byzantine mosaicists worked with Italian assistants on the building's imagery. Although the church's iconography displays a strong influence from the east, its expressive composition of surfaces and figures and its stylised representation of folds differ from the formal approach of Byzantine art. This combination of western stylistic elements and eastern prototypes is the defining characteristic of Venice's Romanesque art.

Architecture

The architecture of Santa Maria Assunta on Torcello displays important features of Romanesque design. The triple-aisled, timber-ceilinged columnar basilica without a transept is towered over by a high campanile. The exterior is generously decorated with blind arches, and the interior walls above the narrow arcades are undecorated, emphasising their flatness. Santa Fosca on Torcello was built on a Byzantine ground plan (late 11th c.). The central structure with its cupola contains octagonal, cruciform and round shapes that intertwine unconventionally to create a square interior space. The building's octagonal external shell is dominated by high-pillared, slender arcades.

Murano's cathedral, Santi Maria e Donato, displays a combination of Romanesque and Byzantine influences. This triple-aisled columnar basilica without a transept boasts a mighty east façade that is both wide and extremely impressive. The building also includes a two storey arcade with rows of double columns that surround niches on the lower floor and enclose a

The Grand Canal sparkles at night

GREAT ARTISTS AND WHERE TO FIND THEM

Tintoretto's ceiling panel, *The Triumph of Venice*, in the Palazzo Ducale

Paolo Veneziano (before 1333–58): Gallerie dell'Accademia

Gentile Bellini (c1429–1507): Gallerie dell'Accademia

Giovanni Bellini (c1437–1516): Gallerie dell'Accademia, Frari, Santi Giovanni e Paolo

Vittore Carpaccio (c1455–1526): Gallerie dell'Accademia, Scuola di San Giorgio degli Schiavoni

Giorgione (1478–1510): Gallerie dell'Accademia

Titian (Tiziano Vecellio, c1488–1576): Frari, Santa Maria della Salute, Gallerie dell'Accademia

Tintoretto (Jacopo Robusti, 1518–94): Scuola Grande di San Rocco, Madonna dell'Orto, Gallerie dell'Accademia

Veronese (Paolo Caliari, 1528–88): Gallerie dell'Accademia, San Sebastiano

Giambattista Tiepolo (1696–1770): Scuola Grande dei Carmini, Ca' Rezzonico, Gesuati

Canaletto (Giovanni Antonio Canal, 1697–1768): Gallerie dell'Accademia, Ca' Rezzonico

Francesco Guardi (1712–93): Gallerie dell'Accademia, Ca' Rezzonico,

Pietro Longhi (1702–1805): Fondazione Querini Stampalia

broad walkway above. Running between the arcades are two friezes, one of which is made from various types of marble. The relatively protuberant arcades – which help lend the building a sense of verticality – are a characteristic feature of pre-Gothic secular buildings in Venice.

Painting in Venice
The first Venetian pictures are mosaics – 11th- and 12th-century narrative images telling religious stories to a largely illiterate population, their brilliant

ARCHITECTURE'S BIG FOUR

Mauro Coducci: 15th-century Early Renaissance master; see his work on the cemetery island of San Michele and the churches of Santa Maria Formosa and San Giovanni Crisostomo.

Jacopo Sansovino (1486–1570): born in Tuscany, he came to Venice from Rome. Between 1536 and 1537, he designed three major buildings around the Piazza San Marco – La Zecca (the Mint), the Biblioteca Marciana (Library) and the Loggetta, at the foot of the Campanile.

Andrea Palladio (1508–80): his major works in Venice are the churches of San Giorgio Maggiore and Il Redentore.

Baldassare Longhena (1598–1682): Venice's home-grown baroque virtuoso made his mark from the 1620s. Don't miss Santa Maria della Salute or the huge *palazzo* of Ca' Pesaro on the Grand Canal.

colours contrasting with a gold background. These artists were seduced by the richness of the textiles pouring into Venice from the East, and incorporated them into their pictures, laying the foundation for the preoccupation and theme of Venetian art – colour and texture.

By the Renaissance, as perspective and architectural composition were mastered, figures in paintings became more spatially rooted. One hundred years later, the invention of oil paint allowed artists to scale new heights in the handling of light and colour. At the same time, better understanding of human anatomy, coupled with technical expertise in painting perspective, brought every element together. By the 16th century, this synthesis of native-born genius, medium and technical ability had united to produce the luminous and exciting works typical of Venetian painting.

TOP ARCHITECTURAL STYLES

Byzantine: San Marco, Santa Maria Assunta, Santa Fosca
Medieval: San Nicolò dei Mendicoli
Gothic: Palazzo Ducale, Ca' d'Oro, Frari, Santi Giovanni e Paolo
Early Renaissance: San Zaccaria, San Michele, Santa Maria dei Miracoli, Palazzo Loredan (a town house on the Grand Canal with arched first-floor windows supported by slim columns)
High Renaissance: Biblioteca Marciana, Procuratie Vecchie, San Giorgio Maggiore, Il Redentore, Rialto Bridge
Baroque: Santa Maria della Salute, Santa Maria del Giglio, San Moisè
Neo-classical: La Pietà, Ala Napoleonica

The Magic of GLASS

Since 1291, Venetian glass manufacture has been centred on Murano, where traditional techniques and working practices produce glass of museum quality.

From the Middle Ages, Venice was the western world's main glass-producer, guardian of the secret magic that transformed sand quartz, sodium and potassium into delicate and useful products. The Venetians probably learned their skills from descendants of the Roman refugees who fled to the lagoon islands after the fall of Rome. Trade routes with the East brought them further ex-pertise, and local sand and marine vegetation provided the raw ingre-dients. By the late 12th century, local glassblowers had mastered the techniques of making windowpanes and mirrors, and the state realized there was big money to be made. In 1291, the furnaces were moved to the island of Murano (► 154) where the glass-workers could be

It's amazing what you can make out of glass

kept under the watchful eye of the Republic's officials. Any worker who attempted to take his knowledge elsewhere was ruthlessly pursued. By the 15th century, dazzling technique ensured the Murano glass-blowers were the acknowledged world masters.

Their glass was recognisable by its intricate colour and design, epitomized by the Venetian chandelier, which has remained an integral part of all Venetian glass manufacture to the present day. By the 1600s, glass-makers' fake jewels could hardly be distinguished from the real ones, and a law was passed forbidding their manufacture. There was a decline in the 19th century, but the 20th century saw a revival in both design and technique. Today, Murano produces large quantities of glass, mostly from small concerns, where master blowers still hand on their secrets to their apprentices.

Glass for the Modern Age

Every piece of true Venetian glass is marked and guaranteed as such and is of a technical and aesthetic quality that can command high prices in thousands of Euros. Since the pioneering work of Archimede Seguso in the 1950s, Muranese high-end glass has emerged as an art form in its own right. Designers work hand-in-hand with the *maestri* who make the glass; firms such as Barovier e Toso, Venini and Fratelli Toso all come into this category. Some designers are involved in every stage of the production process, and none more so than Luigi Camozzo and Michele Micheluzzi. Camozzo incises and etches his big pieces so they more resemble stone or marble than glass, while Micheluzzi specializes in cold carving, etching sinuous rhythmic patterns on to monochrome, plain forms.

Everything is geared towards glassmaking on Murano

A TASTE
OF VENICE

To find food and drink that is truly Venetian, seek out the places frequented by the locals and visit the Rialto markets to see the range of superb produce that comes into the city.

Kick off your gastronomic exploration by heading for a *bàcaro* (➤ 44), a traditional wine bar where you can have a glass of wine and something to eat without. You can stand at the bar, or tuck into a plate of risotto or pasta at long wooden tables at the back of the *bàcaro*. Most will knock you up a *spritz*, a mix of white wine, soda and Campari, the Venetians' favourite tipple that packs a bit of a punch.

Shells, Scales and Fins
Make a point of tracking down a top-range fish restaurant during your stay, even if it means stretching the budget. The variety of seafood is dazzling, with crustaceans you've probably never tasted, such as *granseola* (spider crab), *capelonghe* (razor shells) and *schie* (miniature prawns), cooked quickly. Also

> "You can stand at the bar, or tuck into a plate of risotto or pasta at long wooden tables…"

look for traditional dishes, such as *sarde in saor*, marinated sardines made to a traditional recipe. If you fancy a snack, try the soft, white, triangular sandwiches called *tramezzini*. You can get them in a wide range of varieties, filled with such accompaniments as shrimps and mayonnaise, tuna and tomatoes or hard-boiled eggs.

Trattorias and Osterias
If you look beyond the tourist grub found at the city's biggest sights, you'll discover trattorias and osteria that base their fare on local recipes. That's a good thing: Venetian cuisine has a diverse heritage and produces some of the most exciting food in Europe. The region's cooking is a true melting pot, combining spices from their eastern trade routes with produce

Elegant canal-side dining in San Marco

and recipes from the Greek islands they ruled for centuries (e.g. braised beef with onions). What's more, the Venetian mainland and the foothills of the Alps provide the city with such typical produce as Treviso radicchio, yellow asparagus and air-dried goose breast. Lagoon seafood and delicate spring vegetables from Sant'Erasmo and other small islands are also added into the mix. Finally, *cucina veneziana* gets its own unique twist thanks to the Jewish recipes that introduced artichokes and aubergines to European cooking.

A Spoonful of Sugar

Venetians head for a *pasticceria* (pastry shop) for their sugar fix. For interest, try the two classic biscuits known as *baicoli* and *busolai*, hard cookies flavoured with aniseed, vanilla and lemon. For some of the best *pasticcerie* you're ever likely to eat, head for Bar Pasticceria Ballarin (Cannaregio 5749), where you can buy all the delicacies that no proper breakfast table should be without: filled *cornetti* (croissants) dusted in icing sugar and feather-light *briosca* (brioche).

Insider Tip

ECOLOGY
Caring for the Lagoon

Italy's second largest wetland habitat (after the Po delta) is a similar size to the Isle of Man. Neither water nor land, it's an in-between realm of marshes, canals, sand banks and tiny islands – some of which are only visible at low tide. Twelve of the islands are inhabited.

The Lagoon – an Inland Sea

Venice sits like a jewel in the lagoon, a crescent shaped inland sea that is approximately 40km (25mi) in length and 15km (9.3mi) across at its widest point. It covers a total area of around 215mi². The "living" part of the lagoon, the *laguna viva*, is regularly awash with salt water at high tide. In contrast, the *laguna morta*, which represents about half of the lagoon, only occasionally feels the salty tang of seawater. The canals near the harbour range from 15 to 20m (49 to 65.5ft) in depth. Elsewhere, however, the bottom is only 50cm (20in) away, and the water is more or less brackish, depending on the tide. The lagoon, the meeting point for currents of fresh

and salt water, provides magnificent conditions for plants, water birds and fish. While the south of the lagoon has the *valli da pesca* (fish ponds) where people breed fish, mussels *(cozze)* and clams *(vongole)* using tell-tale nets hung between poles, the north is a protected natural area, and remains an almost completely unspoilt island world. This unique landscape was created in a prehistoric age when Alpine sand and rock was deposited here by rivers like the Brenta, Sile and Piave as they flowed down to the Mediterranean Sea. Changing watercourses, high and low tides, storms and the constant power of the surf formed the rubble into sandbanks *(litorali, barre)* and sandy shores *(lidi)* around 20km (12.5mi) off the original coastline. The Italian lagoons have disappeared wherever people chose not to intervene (at Ravenna, for example). As early as the 14th century, the inhabitants of the lagoon began to redirect the largest rivers to counteract the progressive drying up of the waterways that was seriously damaging their trade and their ability to defend themselves. Only three large outlets *(bocche)* remain in the lagoon today: the 900m (3,000ft) wide Bocca di Lido, the 470m (1,500ft) wide Bocca di Malamocco and the Bocca di Chioggia, which measures in at almost 500m (1,650ft) across. The Adriatic floods through these *bocche* into the lagoon twice a day, allowing seawater to flush out the canals before flowing back out again. The bocche are kept open with a great deal of technical effort to make sure that no hindrance stops either this 'natural' method of sewage disposal or the movement of ships in the area.

Burano, viewed from the bell tower of the Basilica di Santa Maria Assunta on Torcello

The Magazine

Death(s) in Venice – The Cinematic Lagoon

Melancholy, mysterious, morbid – three characteristics that are often attributed to the lagoon city. If you've ever seen Venice in the fog, when it's raining, or even during a flood *(acqua alta)*, you'll easily be able to understand why. It's no wonder that Venice's unconventional charm has inspired writers and filmmakers alike to create dark stories that send shivers down your spine. There are some films that do use the city as a cheerful, romantic or exotic backdrop for holidays, carnivals, colourful thrillers and spy adventures. One movie in this vein came from Oscar-winning director Florian Henckel von Donnersmarck, whose secret agent flick "The Tourist" with Johnny Depp and Angelina Jolie included such scenes as a riveting boat chase through Venice's canals. The archetypal Venetian movie is an altogether much darker affair, however. The most famous example of the genre is Luchino Visconti's "Death in Venice", the film adaptation of Thomas Mann's novella. Visconti's movie sees Aschenbach, a composer, becoming completely obsessed with a beautiful boy in the city. Nicolas Roeg's Thriller "Don't Look Now" (1973) also deals with obsession and death. A couple of English artists come to Venice to try to forget the accidental demise of their child, only to be haunted by the terrible memories the city uncovers. Finally, Paul Schrader's 1990 thriller, "The Comfort of Strangers", based on a novel by Ian McEwan, shows a couple coming to Venice to rekindle the diminishing flame of their romance – a love affair that began in the city itself. Their plans go awry too, however: they lose their way and walk straight into the clutches of a man (Christopher Walken) who ensnares them in a game that – are you seeing a pattern in Venice movies by now? – can only lead to ruin.

Acqua alta: **A perennial symbol of the "cinematic" sinking of Venice**

Finding Your Feet

First Two Hours

No matter how you travel to Venice, the nature of the city can make arriving a little more challenging than some other destinations. Day visitors should use the multi-storey car parks round the Piazzale Roma (opposite the station) and on the island of Tronchetto. Although open round the clock, they're expensive and often congested. Below are some pointers to help make your journey as smooth as possible.

Aeroporto di Venezia Marco Polo

Venice's own airport (tel: 041 2 60 92 60, www.veniceairport.it) handles domestic and international flights.

■ There are **flights direct to Marco Polo** from London Heathrow, London Gatwick, Bristol, Liverpool and Nottingham East Midlands.

■ There is **one daily flight direct from both New York and Philadelphia;** US passengers arriving in Rome or Milan can transfer to a flight to Marco Polo.

■ Some charter and budget-price flights arrive at **Aeroporto di Treviso Antonio Canova** (tel: 042 2 31 51 11, www.trevisoairport.it), 30km (18mi) to the north.

Best Bets for Airport Transfers

Marco Polo lies 10km (6mi) from Venice at Tessera. The services below all leave from outside the terminal building.

■ *Taxi acquei* **or water taxis** (tel: 041 72 31 12) are the fastest and most expensive (around €100) means of reaching central Venice. Follow the signs from the terminal to the water's edge, then agree the price to your destination before boarding. Journey time is 25 to 40 minutes. You'll get a ten per cent discount if you book a water taxi from Consorzio Venezia Taxi online (www.veneziataxi.it).

■ **The Società Alilaguna** (tel: 041 5 41 65 55/041 2 96 03 81; www.alilaguna. it) runs an **hourly boat service** from Marco Polo to the city. There are five lines: Blu, Arancio, Giallo, Oro and Red, serving different areas of the city and the lagoon islands, though you may find that you will have to connect with an ACTV *vaporetto* for the last stages. Children under six travel completely free. Single tickets to Venice, the Lido and the cruise ship terminal cost €13 (€27 for a return trip). Blu line services start at 6:10am and run hourly until 12:10am; Oro at 9:30am and run hourly until 5:30pm and Red from 9:15am and run hourly until 6:15pm. The Arancio and Giallo lines serve Murano and the north of the city. Tickets cost €13 and can be bought on board; the journey time is 75 to 90 minutes.

■ ATVO **buses** go from the airport to the city from 7.50am to 10.20pm, and from the city to the airport from 5am until 8.50pm. The direct 20-min bus journey on the *Servizio Aeroporto* costs €6, while a return trip costs €11 (www.atvo.it). The ACTV line 5 AeroBus runs from 4.08am right through until 1.15am. The half-hour trip costs €6 each way, it's €11 for a return ticket, and it costs €12 for the AeroBus plus a boat ride (90 mins from the moment you validate your ticket).

■ Beware: you may be offered a passage to the lagoon by **private launch**; note that the *vaporetti* service (➤ 38) is excellent and much cheaper.

■ **Taxis** will take you to Piazzale Roma for around €40. For official tariffs, route info and booking, visit www.radiotaxivenezia.com.

Aeroporto di Treviso Antonio Canova

■ **Charter and budget flights** arriving at Treviso Angeli (tel. 0422 31 51 11) connect with Venice's Piazzale Roma by **ATVO buses** (www.atvo.it), which are scheduled to coincide with flights. Central Treviso (including the train station) is served from the airport by bus No 6.

Arriving by Train

■ Venice's **Santa Lucia station** is reached from the mainland by a rail causeway. Don't be tempted to get off at Venezia Mestre.

■ Some trains run only as far as Mestre. **You'll have to change to a local train** for the final hop across the lagoon; these leave about every five minutes.

■ **Steps outside the station concourse** lead down to the Grand Canal and the *pontile* (*vaporetto* stop). Take No 1 or 2 for the Grand Canal or 5.1 or 5.2 to encircle the city. You can also pick up a water taxi or a gondola here.

■ **Tip:** The buffet in the Santa Lucia railway station is a good place to wait for your train. As so often is the case in Italy, you pay for your food first at the till before taking your *scontrino* (receipt) to the bar (daily, 6.05am–10.55pm).

Arriving by Road

Apart from the Lido, Venice is totally car-free. If you're driving, travel to the lagoon city over the nearly 4km-(2½mi)-long "Bridge of Freedom" (Ponte della Libertà).

■ The nearest city centre **car park** is at Piazzale Roma (Autorimessa Comunale, tel: 041 2 72 72 11, www.asmvenezia.it), which gives access directly to the Grand Canal. This is often full, so it may be better to head for the huge car park on the island of Tronchetto (Venezia Tronchetto Parking, tel 041 5 20 75 55, www.veniceparking.it), from where the "People Mover" cable car (www.peoplemover.avmspa.it) whizzes over to the Piazzale Roma in just three minutes (adults, €1).

■ **Cheaper parking** can be found at **Fusina** on the mainland, from where boats travel to the city centre around thirty times a day (Zattere, line 16, €8; €13 return).

■ **Short-stay parking costs** €6–€8 for two hours, **Day Tickets:** Autorimessa comunale €26, online €24.40; Tronchetto €21, Fusina €15.

■ Car parks are open 24 hours a day; parking can be reserved online.

Car Rental

There are car rental offices at Marco Polo Airport and Piazzale Roma.

Avis
✉ Piazzale Roma 496G ☎ 041 5 23 73 77
✉ Arrivals hall, Marco Polo Airport ☎ 041 5 41 50 30

Hertz
✉ Piazzale Roma 496E ☎ 041 5 28 40 91
✉ Arrivals hall, Marco Polo Airport ☎ 041 5 41 60 75

Europcar
✉ Arrivals hall, Marco Polo Airport ☎ 041 5 41 56 54

Finding Your Feet

Tourist Information Offices

APT (Azienda di Promozione Turistica) ☎ 041 5 29 87 11; www.turismovenezia.it

⊠ Piazzale Roma ⏰ Daily 9.30–3.30pm

⊠ Santa Lucia station ⏰ Mon–Sat 8–6:30

⊠ Piazza San Marco ⏰ Daily 8–6:30

⊠ Venice Pavilion (Ex Giardini Reali, San Marco) ⏰ Daily noon–6

⊠ Aeroporto Marco Polo ⏰ Daily 8–6:30

⊠ Venezia Tronchetto Parking ⏰ April–Sep, 9–2:30am

⊠ Lido di Venezia (Viale S.M. Elisabetta 6a) Cwww.lidodivenezia.it ⏰ June–Sep, 9–12:30, 3:30–6

Getting Around

In Venice, there's no option other than walking or taking a boat. When crossing the city, it's often quicker to combine walking with water transport, rather than take frustratingly slow boat journeys. If you're visiting in winter, however, be prepared for *acqua alta* (high water) by bringing suitable footwear.

Water Transport

■ The transport system is run by **ACTV** (Azienda del Consorzio Trasporti Veneziano), Piazzale Roma, www.actv.it, 7:30–8), which operates **boats** in the city and lagoon and **buses** on the Lido and mainland. Services run from 5am to midnight, after which a **night system** operates hourly.

■ There are **three types of boat** – *vaporetti*, large and fairly slow, sometimes with front outside seats and plenty of standing and luggage room; *motoscafi*, smaller and faster with a few outside seats at the back; and *motonavi*, double-deckers that ply the lagoon routes, though even the Venetians tend to refer to them all as *vaporetti*. Pick up a **timetable** and **route map** from one of the main ACTV ticket booths.

■ All *pontili* (**departure quays/wharfs**) have clear timetables and route maps and the *vaporetti* themselves are numbered on boards on their sides.

■ The **main routes** you'll probably use are the No 1, which runs down the Grand Canal from Piazzale Roma and continues to the Lido, and the No 2, which follows a circular route from Piazzale Roma down the Grand Canal, on to the Lido and back via the Giudecca and Tronchetto.

■ There are several **circular routes** (*giro città*) around the outside of the city: of these, no 41 and 42 include stops at Murano, while 5.1 and 5.2 run to the Lido. The main **lagoon routes** are LN and T (Burano and Torcello).

■ The *traghetti* (**gondola ferries**) which ply back and forth at different points across the Grand Canal will save you time if you are far from one of the four bridges that span the canal. These are operated by gondoliers and generally run from 8am to 1pm or 6pm. Boarding points are marked by green signs. Pay as you board (locals, €0.70; tourists, €2). It's customary to ride standing up.

■ Several companies run the extremely expensive and fast **water taxis**, which can be summoned by phone (tel: 041 2 40 76 11/041 5 22 23 03). The starting price is €15, rising to €20 if they come and pick you up. Metered fares cost around €2 a minute on city routes. There's a €10 night-time supplement from 10pm to 6am. The fixed prices set for many routes in the city are sometimes cheaper than the metered fares. The city council publishes the official tariffs (*tariffe taxi acquei*) as a PDF on www.comune.venezia.it.

■ There are gondola stands all over the city or you can call **Calle Vallaresso** (tel: 041 5 20 61 20); **Ferrovia** (tel: 041 71 85 43); **San Marco** (tel: 041 5 20 06 85); or **Rialto** (tel: 041 5 22 49 04). The hire charge is €100 for six people for 40 minutes; most Gondoliers will demand upwards of €100 for 30 minutes, however – make sure to settle the price before you get in, and only pay at the end! Most *gondolieri* only work from April to October.

Island Buses

■ **Buses** serve the Lido: routes A and B serve the north and south respectively. The island of Pellestrina is served by the No 11 bus (hourly from Viale Santa Maria Elisabetta on the Lido), which drives on to the ferry to Pellestrina, then connects with the ferry to Chioggia.

Travellers with Disabilities

■ Contact **Informahandicap** (Ca' Farsetti, San Marco 4136, ground floor, tel: 041 2 74 81 44, Thu 9–1, 3–5). Enquiries can also be dealt with by the city council (cittapertutti@comune.venezia.it), who also make an **Accessible Venice map** available to download.

■ **Routes suitable for wheelchairs** are marked on detailed free tourist maps.

■ Some bridges have **automated ramps**; access keys from APT offices.

Tickets and Travel Cards

■ ACTV issues a **range of tickets** including single-journey tickets, group tickets and return tickets. The good-value **travel cards (*biglietti a tempo*)** are valid on all ACTV water and land routes for periods of 12 hours (€18), 24 hours (€20), 36 hours (€25), 48 hours (€30), 72 hours (€35) and seven days (€50). All tickets are sold at ACTV booths, the ACTV offices at Piazzale Roma or Tronchetto, *tabacchi* (tobacconists), or online at www.veniceconnected.com. Further information is available via the call centre or online (tel: 041 24 24; www.hellovenezia.com).

■ **Tickets should be validated** for every journey by passing them in front of the imob ticket sensors found on every pontile.

Accommodation

To look out on to a canal, or over one of the beautiful campi or the flowered gardens of a Venetian *palazzo*, is a great experience – and one that can often be costly. As with everything else in Venice, hotel rooms cost proportionately more than their counterparts on the mainland, and you can expect to pay much more for a room with a canal view. Generally speaking, the further you are from St Mark's and the Rialto bridge, the more unique the accommodation and guest houses will be.

Tips

■ Always **book hotels well in advance**, especially in peak season (Carnival, Easter, June–Sep, Christmas). Although there are more than 350 hotels and guesthouses equipped with around 22,000 beds in the historic centre alone, the total of 3 million overnight guests a year means that bed shortages do sometimes still occur.

■ Many hotels offer **dramatic reductions off-season** – enquire when booking or browse www.hoteldiscount.com

Finding Your Feet

Insider Tip

- **If you are budget conscious**, consider staying in Mestre (on the mainland), on the Lido and travelling into Venice by the 24-hour bus and *vaporetto* service.
- **Prices within the same hotel can vary greatly**, depending on the view, so be clear what you are getting when booking; most hotels give better prices for online reservations.
- **A few hotels still offer half-board** (*mezza-pensione*) rates with one meal per day included, but you may prefer to eat out in the evening.
- It is best to **confirm bookings by email**. A credit card number is usually required to hold a room. This does away with the need to reconfirm. For security reasons, you should only give out your credit card number over the phone – don't send it by email.
- When travelling to Venice, don't forget that **you may have to walk some distance** carrying your luggage: there are no door-to-door taxis.
- Baggage can be delivered to your hotel by porter service, **at a price per piece** that depends on its final destination. Book in advance: **Cooperativa Trasbagagli** (tel: 041 71 37 19, www.trasbagagli.it).
- If you are travelling with children, or prefer to be slightly removed from the mass of tourism in the centre of Venice, **consider staying on the Lido** (➤ 150); it has a more laidback atmosphere, has some wonderful hotels and is close to the beach.

Information

- For a full catalogue of Venice accommodation, contact the **Venice Tourist Promotion office (APT)** (➤ 38), which publishes a complete list: **Azienda Promozione Turistica Venezia**, tel: 041 5 29 87 11; www.turismovenezia.it
- The **VeneziaSì** booking centre run by the Associazione Veneziana Albergatori (AVA) hotel union can also help individual travellers find rooms (call centre, tel: 041 5 22 22 64; 8am–11pm daily, www.veneziasi.it). Their Venice offices can also help: find them at the Piazzale Roma (Garage Comunale, Garage S. Marco), in S. Lucia station, at Marco Polo airport and at the Villabona Sud/Marghera motorway roundabout. More accommodation addresses: www.venicehotels.com.
- **Bed and breakfast**: Associazione Vacanze in Famiglia, via Orlanda 105, tel: 041 90 03 85; www.vacanzeinfamiglia.it
- **Private apartments**: Venetian Apartments, 271 Regent Street, London W1B 2ES, tel: 020 31 78 41 80, www.venice-rentals.com, www.nicevenice.it or www.holidayrentals.co.uk
- You won't just find information about local Italian courses on the website of the Istituto Venezia language school (www.istitutovenezia.com/en). They also provide tips for finding reasonably priced accommodation: in a Palladian convent, for example, or with a Venetian host family.
- Full listings of accommodation available in **Padova**, **Chioggia**, **Verona** and **Vicenza** is available from local tourist offices (➤ 170, 171, 174, 176).

Grading

- Accommodation ranges from simple lodgings to luxurious hotels. A private bathroom can be expected in rooms in all but the most basic establishments. Even in the smartest hotels, however, bathrooms may have only a shower (*doccia*) and no bath (*vasca da bagno*).
- Always ask to see a selection of rooms: you may be shown the worst first.
- Venice has had a tourist/visitor's tax *(tassa di soggiorno)* for the last few years. It varies between €2 and €4, depending on the category of hotel.

Accommodation prices

Prices are per night for a double room with private bathroom.

€ under €100   €€ €100–€220   €€€ €220–€380   €€€€ over €381

Ai Tolentini €€

This simple, good value hotel is just a few minutes walk from Piazzale Roma, and a good option for budget travellers. The immaculately clean rooms are on the small side, but the beds are comfortable, bathrooms quite adequate and some rooms have canal views.

➕ 200 C1 ✉ Santa Croce 197, Calle Amai
☎ 041 2 75 91 40; www.albergoaitolentini.it
🚏 Piazzale Roma

Alex €/€€

This traditional, family run and friendly little hotel, located just round the corner from the Frari and ideal for exploring, is a good choice. It offers clean, comfortable, simple accommodation.

➕ 201 E1 ✉ San Polo 2606, Rio Terà dei Frari
☎ 041 5 23 13 41; www.hotelalexinvenice.com
🚏 San Tomà

Al Ponte Mocenigo €€/€€€

Accommodation-wise, Santa Croce is a peaceful area off the beaten track where your money will go further. Cross the Mocenigo's private access bridge and you'll find a tranquil courtyard, a cool oasis in summer for breakfast or an evening drink. Inside, the theme is 18th-century Venice, and the high-ceilinged bedrooms come complete with terrazzo floors, painted armoires and Murano glass chandeliers.

➕ 201 F2 ✉ Santa Croce 2063, Calle Mocenigo
☎ 041 5 24 47 97; www.alpontemocenigo.com
🚏 San Stae

Becher €/€€

Pleasant three-star hotel not far from the Teatro Fenice. Half of the 17 rooms have canal views.

➕ 206 B4 ✉ Calle del Frutariol 1857
☎ 041 5 22 12 53, www.hotelbecher.com
🚏 Giglio

Bucintoro €€€

With wide views over the Bacino and set on one of the quietest stretches of the Riva, this four-star hotel is themed around its name; the Bucintoro was the Doge's state galley during the days of the Republic. Every room is named after an historic sailing vessel and the design features nautical details in restrained good taste. All 20 rooms are a good size, those at the front have superb views, as does the breakfast room and terraced tables outside.

➕ 208 A3 ✉ riva San Biagio, Castello 2135/a
☎ 041 5 28 99 09; www.hotelbucintoro.com
🚏 Arsenale

Ca' Dogaressa €€

This is a good choice in Cannaregio, where so many hotels are on the busy stretch leading from the station. The Antenori family's hotel is right on the Canale di Cannaregio, and front rooms have waterside views. The style, as you would expect in this 18th-century *palazzo*, is traditionally Venetian, with beamed ceilings, brocade, Murano glass chandeliers and a rooftop *altana* (Venetian terrace).

➕ 201 E3 ✉ Cannaregio 1018,
Fondamenta di Cannaregio
☎ 041 2 75 94 41; www.cadogaressa.com
🚏 Tre Archi

Ca' Pisani €€€

The millennium saw the advent of the boutique designer hotel in Venice, and Ca' Pisani led the way. This is a stylish hotel, a far cry from the traditional Venetian glitz and gloom, where clean lines and minimalist décor are inspired by art deco. Each room, with its sybaritic bathroom, is individually designed, public rooms are elegant, and the

Finding Your Feet

hotel restaurant serves Venetian cuisine.

🏨 205 E3 ✉ 979/a Dorsoduro, Rio Terà dei Foscarini ☎ 041 2 40 14 11; www.capisanihotel.it 🚏 Accademia

Casa Querini €€

Eleven small, but clean rooms, each with a bath, in a converted private house in a quiet residential neighbourhood not far from the centre. Friendly atmosphere. Breakfast included.

🏨 207 D4
✉ Castello 4388, Campo San Giovanni Novo
☎ 041 2 41 12 94; www.locandaquerini.com
🚏 San Zaccaria

The Gritti Palace €€€

The Gritti Palace, a legendary hotel on the Grand Canal, has shone with renewed magnificence since reopening in 2013 after 15 months of renovations costing 35 million Euros. This Starwood luxury hotel with 61 sumptuous guest rooms and 21 comfortable suites is situated in a Gothic palace built right on Venice's main canal by the Pisani family in 1475. Doge Andrea Gritti made the palace his private residence in 1525. It was turned into a luxury hotel in 1895, and became the well-loved luxury retreat of the foremost political, literary and artistic figures of the age. Writers such as Ernest Hemingway and Somerset Maugham were guests here for many years and helped make Harry's Bar – still one of the most famous bars in the world – a true household name.

🏨 206 A3✉ Campo Santa Maria del Giglio, San Marco 2467 ☎ 041 79 46 11; www.thegritti palace.com 🚏 Santa Maria del Giglio

Hotel Cipriani €€€€

An oasis within the Venetian panorama, Hotel Cipriani sits in verdant luxury, looking back at San Marco from across the water. Step out of the Cipriani launch (always on call from the San Marco pier) and find lush gardens, exquisitely decorated rooms, a world-class restaurant, a giant pool – and an atmosphere that is relaxing yet stimulating, formal yet intimate.

🏨 206 C1
✉ Giudecca 10, Fondamenta San Giovanni
☎ 041 5 20 77 44; www.hotelcipriani.it
🚏 Zitelle

Hotel Colombina €€€

Named after the Carnival character, this charming small hotel, 150m from San Marco at the Ponte del Remedio, has exclusive views of the Bridge of Sighs, with 17 of its 32 rooms looking out on to the canal, where there is a private boat landing. The atmosphere is friendly in this ancient *palazzo*, which has been completely redecorated with tasteful Venetian furnishings, including Murano chandeliers and damask textiles. Air-conditioning and private bathrooms throughout.

🏨 206 C4 ✉ Castello 4416, Calle del Remedio
☎ 041 2 77 05 25; www.hotelcolombina.com
🚏 San Zaccaria

Hotel Danieli €€€€

What can one say about one of the world's most famous hotels? It offers a cultural experience as much as luxurious surroundings: an ornately decorated, theatrical setting. The rooms are opulently furnished, the halls hung with great paintings, the service is formal and abundant, the views spectacular, the restaurants glamorous, the guests mostly foreign, and the prices suitably high (►88).

🏨 207 D4 ✉ Castello 4196, Riva degli Schiavoni
☎ 041 5 22 64 80; www.danieli.hotelinvenice.com
🚏 San Zaccaria

LaGare Hotel €€€

Opened in a former nineteenth-century glass factory in 2013, this four-star hotel complete with 118 comfortable rooms unites hi-tech with history, art and design.

🏨 203 north of F5 ✉ Riva Longa 27, 30141 Murano ☎ 041 7 36 25 03; www.lagarehotelvenezia.com 🚏 Murano Faro

Accommodation

Locanda ai Santi Apostoli €€

Two of this hotel's 11 rooms overlook the Grand Canal, and all are tastefully decorated, featuring beamed ceilings and pretty fabrics. Public areas are furnished with chintz and antiques. The hotel is approached through a courtyard.

➕ 202 B2 ✉ Campo Santi Apostoli, Cannaregio 4391 ☎ 041 5 21 26 12; www.locandasantiapostoli.com 🚊 Ca' d'Oro Locanda

Locanda San Barnaba €€/€€€

A small, attractive hotel, in a converted 16th-century *palazzo*, on the narrow street between Campo San Barnaba and the Ca' Rezzonico *vaporetto* stop. Each of its 14 rooms has a theme and is decorated with antiques and parquet flooring. Some overlook a garden. Air-conditioning and private baths in all rooms.

➕ 205 B3 ✉ Dorsoduro 2785, Calle del Traghetto ☎ 041 2 41 12 33; www.locanda-sanbarnaba.com 🚊 Ca' Rezzonico

Molino Stucky Hilton €€€€

The Hilton Group have done a fabulous conversion on this 19th-century flour mill on the island of Giudecca, resulting in Venice's slickest and most international hotel, where elements of the building's industrial past blend with 21st-century opulence. There are two restaurants, terraces and bars, and non-residents should make a point of enjoying a drink in the Skyline Bar, with its rooftop pool and fabulous city and lagoon views. Deals and packages are available online.

➕ 204 B2 ✉ Giudecca 810 ☎ 041 2 72 33 11; www.molinostuckyhilton.com 🚊 Palanca; hotel has private launch service to San Marco

Novecento €€€

The multi-talented Spanish artist and fashion designer Fortuny (1871–1949) was the inspiration for much of the décor in this stunning boutique hotel, where rich colours and textures are combined with traditional old furniture to place this hotel well up with the best of the city's designer lodgings. The Philippe Starck bathrooms are a joy, as are the tiny courtyard, honesty bar and charming breakfast room. Expect a relaxed yet attentive ambiance, shown in the attitude of helpful staff.

➕ 205 F3 ✉ San Marco 2683, Calle delle Dose, Campo San Maurizio ☎ 041 2 41 37 65; www.novecento.biz 🚊 Giglio

Palazzo Stern €€/€€€

For a room with a view on the Grand Hotel, this is one of Venice's prettiest Gothic *palazzi*. Public areas and bedrooms are rich in colour, tiling and mosaics, and there are carvings and elaborate plasterwork, columns and pillars, making a stay here a truly unique experience. The breakfast terrace is set right on the canal.

➕ 205 E9
✉ Dorsoduro 2792/A, Calle del Traghetto
☎ 041 2 77 08 69; www.palazzostern.com
🚊 Ca' Rezzonico an Zaccaria

Insider Tip

Pensione Accademia Villa Maravege €€€

Regular Venetian visitors have been patronising this long-established hotel, housed in a 17th-century villa that was once the Russian Embassy, for decades. Tucked down a narrow *calle*, and right on the Grand Canal, the hotel is surrounded by shady gardens, while the breakfast terrace overlooks a canal. Bedrooms are comfortable, while public rooms are beautifully decorated and furnished with antiques, making the Maravege an oasis of calm in the city centre. Such pleasures attract clients year after year, so it's essential to reserve well ahead.

➕ 205 E3 ✉ 1058 Dorsoduro, Fondamenta Bollani ☎ 041 5 21 01 88; www.pensioneaccademia.it 🚊 Accademia

Pensione La Calcina €€/€€€

John Ruskin (1819–1900) stayed in this inn in 1876; today it retains all of its old-world charm. The hotel overlooks the Giudecca canal, with a terrace on the waterfront for break-

Finding Your Feet

fast and on the roof for sunbathing. The 32 rooms have been renovated, using original furniture and parquet flooring, but with modern new bathrooms and air-conditioning. Many rooms have canal views.

➕ 205 E2 ✉ Dorsoduro 780, Zattere ai Gesuati
☎ 041 5 20 64 66; www.lacalcina.com
🚤 Zattere

San Clemente Palace €€€/€€€€

Around 100 million Euros were invested on San Clemente island to turn this former cloister – parts of which are nearly 900 years old – into a top-class luxury hotel complete with precious antiques and the highest levels of comfort. The resort, just 10 minutes from St Mark's by motorboat, boasts three gourmet restaurants, a 108,000ft² spa with an open-air pool, tennis courts and a small golf course.

➕ 206 south of A1 ✉ Isola di San Clemente 1, San Marco ☎ 041 2 44 50 01, www.sanclementepalacevenice.com 🏨 hotel has private launch service to San Marco

San Sebastiano Garden €€€ *Insider Tip*

Tucked away on a quiet canal and opposite the church of San Sebastiano, this attractive and comfortable hotel is housed in a thoughtfully renovated old *palazzo*. All is space and calm in the public areas, while the bedrooms are well-appointed and comfortable. The chief draw perhaps, is the garden, one of Venice's "secret gardens" that is ideal for whiling away late summer afternoons.

➕ 204 C3 ✉ Dorsoduro 2542, Fondamenta San Sebastiano ☎ 041 5 23 12 33; www.hotelsansebastianogarden.com
🚤 San Basilio

Food and Drink

Venice offers a wide range of eating options, from stand-up snacks to elegant restaurants. When the cuisine is at its best, you will be treated to fresh lagoon fish, seasonal vegetables and local staples such as polenta and rice, cooked lovingly using traditional recipes. At its worst, you will encounter the same anonymous frozen fast food now on offer all over the globe.

■ For somewhere uniquely Venetian, **go to a *bàcaro*** (➤ 46). They often still sell such regional specialities as *brodeto* (Adriatic fish soup), *baccalà mantecato* (fine dried-cod mousse on slices of toasted bread), or *mo'leche* (also called *mojecche*) cooked in hot fat. The latter are crabs that have shed their shells in the spring and autumn. By the time they're brought to the kitchen, their new armour plating is so soft they can be eaten whole (in contrast to normal crabs, whose meat usually only comes from the legs).

■ Some restaurants have one system of pricing for residents and a higher one for foreign visitors. To combat this, a group of 14 of the most serious restaurants in Venice have formed an association called **Ristoranti della Buona Accoglienza** (Warm Welcome Restaurants; www.veneziaristoranti. it) which aims to provide well-cooked, fresh food, a friendly and professional service and an honest quality–price ratio. These restaurants are highlighted in the book.

When and What to Eat

■ Lunch is between 12:30 and 2:30 (few restaurant kitchens open after that); dinner is from 7:30 to 9:30. With the onset of tourism and fast food, hours have become more flexible.

Food and Drink

- **Don't expect to be served a meal** in the mid-afternoon, except in a snack bar.
- Italians **traditionally eat three or four courses** at each meal: *antipasto* (hors d'oeuvres), *primo* (rice, pasta or soup), *secondo* (meat or fish main course with a *contorno*, or side serving, of vegetables) and *dolce* (dessert). However, it is now usually acceptable to have just one or two courses.
- If you want a full meal, some establishments offer a **menù degustazione, or tasting menu**. In a good restaurant, this can be great value, offering a chance to taste dishes in each category at a predetermined price.

Venetian Food

- Since the 17th century, **maize-flour polenta has been the main staple** in the Veneto, whether of ground white or yellow kernels, and today it still features in every restaurant in Venice, served hot and creamy or sliced and grilled.
- **The Veneto is famous for its *risotti***, flavoured with seafood or vegetables. ***Risi e bisi*** is a wonderful Venetian springtime dish of fresh peas and rice.
- Pasta is traditional: try ***pasta e fagioli***, a hearty soup of pasta and beans, and ***bigoli in salsa***, large, handmade *spaghetti* in anchovy or sardine sauce.
- The Venice lagoon also produces a **wide range of tasty vegetables**, such as artichokes – small and bitter (*castraure*), or large (usually only the heart is eaten of these); *zucca* (pumpkin or squash), and *radicchio* in its many forms.
- The Venice lagoon and Adriatic and Tyrrhenian seas offer **an extraordinary assortment of sea creatures** to taste.
- **Local molluscs, fish and crustaceans include** *schie* (minute prawns the size of a fingernail); *sarde* (fresh sardines, nothing like their tinned cousins); *gamberi* (bigger prawns or shrimp); *canocie* (mantis shrimp); *seppie* (cuttlefish); *calamaretti* (squid); *capesante* or *canestrelli* (scallops); *granseola* (spider crab), best served in the shell, just-cooked, and drizzled with fine olive oil; *moleche* or *moeche* (soft-shell crabs, only in season for a few weeks); *caparozzoli* (warty Venus clams); *capelonghe* (razor-shell clams); *peoci* (mussels); *polipo* (octopus); *tonno* (tuna); *San Pietro* (John Dory); *gò* (black goby); *branzino* (sea bass); and *sfogi* (small sole).
- **From northern Europe comes *baccalà* or salt cod** (in the Veneto, incorrectly, the term refers to stockfish) which is popular in Venice as *baccalà mantecato* (creamed cod).
- Add to these the spices brought to Venice by the great traders, and you have a **rich palette of ingredients** to produce a cuisine that extends from humble country recipes to noble and exotic dishes fit for the Doges.

What To Drink – Ombra, Spritz and Wines

- ***Un'ombra*** (ital.: "a shadow") is an unassuming glass of wine – closer to plonk – served primarily in the *bàcari*. Around 50,000 of these *ombre* are said to be drunk in Venice every day – adding up to a total of around

Finding Your Feet

5,000 litres of wine shared out in small glasses. Venetians like to start drinking them at around 11am: that's when you stand at a bar and enjoy the day's first small glass of wine. When it's hot, you can also try a *spritz:* white wine from the Veneto with mineral water and a shot of Aperol.

■ If you want to taste some of the **best local wines from around Venice**, try those from the Veneto and Friuli-Venezia Giulia regions, including Bardolino, Bianco di Custoza, Breganze, Pinot Grigio, Prosecco di Conegliano-Valdobbiadene, Recioto, Ribolla Gialla, Soave, Tocai and Valpolicella.

Where to Eat

We've already mentioned the ***bàcari*** that sell wines (mostly *sfuso*, from the barrel) to accompany a tapas-like selection of light bites (*cichetti*) and extremely tasty *tramezzini* (multi-layered sandwiches on white bread). But that's not all – Venice has a great deal else to offer if you're looking for somewhere to eat. You'll find our carefully selected tips on the "Where to…" pages in this book.

Bars

Bars sell **coffee, drinks and snacks**; some even serve simple meals. They sell *caffè, espresso, ristretto* (brewed with less water), *caffè macchiato* (*espresso* "stained" with a dash of cold or hot milk), *caffè corretto* (*espresso* "corrected" with a dash of brandy or grappa), *caffè lungo* or *americano* (*espresso* "lengthened" with hot water), and *cappuccino* (*espresso* with hot, frothy milk). Drinks are cheaper at counters than sitting down – you'll pay the highest prices if you relax on a terrace.

Gelaterie

What could be better than a cold ice cream in a hot city? The principal ***creme*, or "creamy" flavours**, are: *cioccolato* (chocolate), *caffè* (coffee), *nocciola* (hazelnut), *gianduia* (chocolate and hazelnut) and *crema* (an egg-yolk enriched "cream" flavour). The Gelateria Nico (Zattere ai Gesuiti, www.gelaterianico.com) has a legendary reputation. People go crazy for their "Gianduiotto da passeggio": hazelnut and chocolate ice cream is generously scooped into a tall glass, the space is filled with whipped cream, small biscotti are placed on the top and the whole thing is crowned with yet more more cream. The magnificent view of Giudecca from the Dorsoduro sun promenadecomes at no extra cost.

Osterie and Enoteche

Traditionally, *osterie* were the **oldest drinking establishments** serving wine, beer and spirits and usually **a menu of simple or rustic home-cooked dishes**, often at wooden tables topped with butcher's paper mats. An *enoteca* is a wine bar; **many serve food** and some **sell bottles to take away**.

Ristoranti

Book ahead at the best restaurants: they are popular. The Italians **always dress well** when going out to dinner: jackets and ties for men are expected at the fanciest restaurants.

Trattorie

Trattorie are quintessentially Italian, **family-run restaurants** and the cooking is **usually popular local fare**, served in abundance.

Shopping

Venice is world-famous for its masks, artistic Murano glass, fine lace from Burano, and its unusual textiles. There are shops catering for foreign visitors at every turn, many selling the same selection of stock souvenirs, often at hefty prices. If you're prepared to seek them out, the city also offers wonderful artisan and handmade objects, and typically Venetian or Italian gifts. And the very best of Venice comes for free – the experience of the city itself.

What to Buy

- **Carnival masks:** many artisans still hand-paint works in papier mâché.
- **Paper:** fine, hand-printed papers covering notebooks, gift boxes, etc.
- **Murano glass**: the range on offer includes inexpensive Murrine (glass beads and jewellery), decorative wine glasses, one-off museum-quality objects, and very expensive antique glass. Going to Murano's factories to buy modern glass might not be the cheapest option. If you're interested in costly glass pieces, research prices carefully before buying.
- **Gondola paraphernalia:** everything from hats to hand-carved oar-locks.
- **Kitchen equipment:** bring home an espresso pot, an olive-wood Parmesan grater, a pasta rolling pin or an Italian tea- or tablecloth.
- **Italian food:** bottles of fine extra-virgin olive oil, freshly roasted coffee beans, Italian vegetable seeds to plant in the garden, handmade pasta, hunks of vacuum-packed Parmesan, jars of local honey, tins of traditional Venetian biscuits – many food items make great gifts to take home.
- Also look out for the **velvet slippers known as** *friulane* that come in a rainbow of different colours, and whose soles are recycled bicycle tyres. They are inexpensive (€22–€30) and guaranteed not to slip – the Venetian equivalent to espadrilles. They are sold throughout Venice.

Food Markets

- The streets around Campo San Giacomo di Rialto and Campo della Pescaria are home **to colourful, vibrant fish, flower, fruit and vegetable markets**, open Mon–Sat 7–1 (fish markets closed Mon), *vaporetto*: Rialto.
- There are also **individual fruit and vegetable stalls** set up in several main squares such as Campo Santa Maria Formosa, Campo Santa Margherita, San Leonardo and Via Garibaldi, and on the boats moored by the Ponte dei Pugni on Fondamenta Gherardini, and Rio della Tana.
- You'll find an overview of all the markets on this website: www.comune. venezia.it/flex/cm/pages/ServeBLOB.php/L/IT/IDPagina/46626.

Buying Food

- **Fruit and vegetables** are **sold by weight**: *un chilo* = one kilo (2 pounds 3 ounces); *un etto* = 100g (3.5 ounces) or by the piece (*il pezzo*).

High Fashion – *Alta Moda*

- Most of the **brand-name Italian designer shops** are clustered in the streets around Piazza San Marco (➤ 75 for addresses).

Department Stores

- Many of the **department stores** are on the mainland (in/around Mestre)..
- **COIN** (www.coin.it; Salizada San Giovanni Crisostomo, near Campo San Bartolomeo) has a modest branch in Venice.

Entertainment

Venice is not known for its nightlife, but there are after-dinner options, from concerts to piano bars and clubs. Some of the nicest evening activities are free (or almost) – a walk through the traffic-free streets, stopping for a drink or an ice-cream, are unforgettable experiences. So is a night ride down the Grand Canal or out to the Lido and back on the *vaporetto*, at unbeatable value.

Information

■ *Venezia News* (www.venezianews.it), the Venetian listings magazine, is available at news-stands; or check the *Spettacoli* listings in local papers.

■ *Un Ospite di Venezia* (*A Guest in Venice*) is a **free brochure in English and Italian,** available in most hotels giving listings; available online at www.unospitedivenezia.it. Or *Events & Manifestazioni*, free from the APT.

■ The internet now offers a range of **Venice-tourist sites**, including: www.provincia.venezia.it/aptve, www.comune.venezia.it, and www.turismovenezia.it.

■ For **advance bookings**, specialized agencies include: Intras City Service, Santa Croce 13036, tel: 041 2 75 07 83; Agenzia Kele & Teo, San Marco 4930, Ponte dei Bareteri, tel: 041 5 20 87 22. Many events can be booked via www.hellovenezia.com.

Events

■ The Mostra Internazionale d'Arte Cinematografica – **Venice Film Festival** – is one of the world's most important film festivals (end Aug, beginning Sep; www.labiennale.org/cinema).

■ In odd-numbered years, the **Biennale Internazionale d'Arte** takes place June to November in the Biennale Park, in the Giardini; information online at www.labiennale.org.

■ In even-numbered years, the **Biennale of Architecture** is held in Biennale Park (*vaporetto:* Giardini).

Casinò di Venezia

The Casinò's current homes are in Palazzo Vendramin-Calergi (➤ 112) and in the large new site near the airport (Via Pagliaga, Ca' Noghera, Mestre, www.casinovenezia.it).

Theatre and Concerts

The **Gran Teatro La Fenice** (San Marco 1965, Campo San Fantin, tel: 041 78 65 11, www.teatrolafenice.it) opened in its original form in May 1792. Since then, it's frequently been renovated in extravagant style following numerous fires. It's Venice's premier performance venue, staging opera, ballet and occasional concerts. You'll find day-by-day cultural listings in *Events & Manifestazioni*, available free at all APT offices.

Cinemas

Note that almost all foreign films are dubbed into Italian.

Gay and Lesbian Venice

Venice's gay scene is low key with no openly gay bars, restaurants or clubs. **Arcigay** is Italy's foremost gay and lesbian association. The nearest branch to Venice is in Padova (Via Garibaldi 41, tel: 049 9 90 08 27, www.tralaltro.it).

San Marco & San Giorgio Maggiore

Little Treats

 ### Panini Paradise
You'll find the best sandwiches in the city where Venice's workers go to sup their *caffè* or "Cappu'cho" from 5 in the morning: in the tiny **Bar Mio** (Via Garibaldi 1820, San Marco 1176, tel: 041 5 21 13 61).

Festa di San Marco
A **Gondola Regatta** from the isle of Sant' Elena to the Punta della Dogana celebrates the city's Patron Saint on the **25th of April**. Lovers give each other red roses.

Bella Vista
You usually have to pay a great deal for beautiful views in Venice. One exception is on the **roof terrace at the Gabrielli Hotel** (www.hotelgabrielli.it). Due to a lack of toilets or a lift to the top floor, it can't be used for commercial purposes. Instead, guests get drinks at the bar before enjoying a view of the lagoon from the terrace.

Getting Your Bearings

Venice's *centro storico*, the old town, has been split into six parts since the 12th century. These six sestieri are called San Marco, Castello, Cannaregio, Santa Croce, San Polo and Dorsoduro (the latter also includes the islands of Giudecca and San Giorgio Maggiore). San Marco, the heart of the city, is the most distinguished – but also most touristy – sestiere, and is characterised by its expensive St Mark's square cafés, luxury hotels, high-class boutiques, art galleries and museums. You can enjoy magnificent views of the Isola di San Giorgio Maggiore and its eponymous church from the Piazzetta and the Riva degli Schiavoni.

The big pulls are almost all clustered around the Piazza San Marco and its magical waterfront, from where the Grand Canal, lined with imposing *palazzi*, sweeps west to skirt the whole of one side of the *sestiere*. From the piazza itself, you can head on foot north to the Rialto through the tangle of shopping streets known as the Mercerie, or take the wider streets and bridges that run west to the Accademia. These lead to a clutch of Venice's most beguiling *campi* (squares), whose surrounding streets are crammed with tempting shops stocked with antiques, sumptuous fabrics, fine china and colourful ceramics, handmade marbled paper and smart clothes. To escape the crowds, board a boat and cross the Bacino di San Marco (St Mark's Basin), Venice's busiest stretch of water, to enjoy the contrast provided by the tranquillity and serene architecture of San Giorgio Maggiore.

Canal Grande

Sant'
Angelo

Palazzo
Mocenigo

Campo
S. Angelo

Palazzo
Grassi

Campo Santo
Stefano

Santo
Stefano

San
Samuele

18

Palazzo
Falier

Palazzo
Morosini

S. Maria
del Giglio

Morning atmosphere on the Piazzetta San Marco

Getting Your Bearings

TOP 10

⭐ Piazza San Marco & Campanile ➤ 54

⭐ San Giorgio Maggiore ➤ 56

Don't Miss

⓫ Basilica di San Marco ➤ 58

⓬ Palazzo Ducale ➤ 63

At Your Leisure

⓭ Museo Correr ➤ 69

⓮ Caffè Florian ➤ 70

⓯ Piazzetta San Marco ➤ 70

⓰ Torre dell'Orologio ➤ 70

⓱ Mercerie ➤ 71

⓲ Campo Santo Stefano ➤ 71

⓳ Harry's Bar ➤ 72

Looking across Bacino di San Marco at dawn

The Perfect Day

If you're not quite sure where to begin your travels, this itinerary recommends a practical and enjoyable day exploring San Marco and San Giorgio Maggiore, taking in some of the best places to see. For more information see the main entries (➤ 54–72).

🕘 9:00am

Arrive early in the ⭐**Piazza San Marco** (➤ 54) to view its glories before the crowds arrive, then take the lift up the **Campanile** (➤ 54) for great views of the city, the lagoon and its islands.

🕙 10:00am

Stroll across to the ⑪ **Basilica di San Marco** (ill. right; ➤ 58), one of Italy's architectural masterpieces and a Venetian-Byzantine treasure-house of mosaics and goldwork. Take in the Galleria, a superb vantage point with a close-up view of the famous bronze horses.

🕚 11:00am

Make your way through the piazzetta to the waterfront and the entrance to the ⑫**Palazzo Ducale** (➤ 63), and explore the fascinating interior of this sumptuous seat of the Venetian state and home of the Doge.

🕐 1:00pm

Head away from the piazza for lunch, unless you want to splash out at ⑭**Caffè Florian** (➤ 70) or Caffè Quadri (➤ 73), and walk towards the Accademia. There's plenty of choice on and around the Calle Larga XXII Marzo: try Vino Vino (San Marco 2007a, Calle del Cafetier, tel: 041 2 41 76 68; www.vinovinowinebar.com), one of the city's most authentic wine bars, which serves a range of typical Venetian snacks (*cichetti*). **Insider Tip**

🕝 2:30pm

Head back east to catch the *vaporetto* across St Mark's Basin to the island and serene Palladian church of ⭐**San Giorgio Maggiore** (➤ 56), the perfect antidote to the morning's architectural flamboyance.

🕓 4:00pm

After returning to San Marco, walk beneath the ⑯**Torre dell'Orologio** (below, left; ➤ 70) to head up the shop-lined ⑰**Mercerie** (➤ 71). You can escape the worst of the crowds here by heading west after a few blocks to

emerge in the Campo Manin. Take your time along the streets leading from here to **18 Campo Santo Stefano** (below; ► 71); you'll want to browse in the antique dealers, clothes boutiques and specialist paper shops.

🕕 6:00pm

Once you reach Campo Santo Stefano, one of the city's nicest squares, it's time for a refreshing drink or one of Venice's best ice-creams at Paolin, where you can sit outside, relax and indulge in some people-watching.

🕗 8:00pm

There's plenty of choice for dinner in the San Marco area, but make sure you return to the piazza after your meal, when the buzz of summer voices ensures the square lives up to Napoleon's description of it as "the biggest drawing-room in Europe". Late evening in winter, when the piazza is likely to be silent and empty, is one of the most evocative times to view this superb space.

⭐Piazza San Marco & The Campanile

Piazza San Marco, the heart of Venice, architectural showcase and world-famous square, is the one place everyone visits. It's here that you'll find the Serenissima's most famous buildings that bear witnesses to the glorious past of this UNESCO World Heritage site. Locals push their way laboriously through the crowds. Come here to get a feel for the soul of the city.

The very first glimpse will leave an unforgettable impression: The glittering bulk of the **Basilica di San Marco** (►58) rises up at the piazza's eastern end, and the **Palazzo Ducale** (►63) sits its south. On the other side, tucked away, is the Piazzetta dei Leoncini, a tiny square overlooked by the **Torre dell'Orologio** (►70).

Splendid lines of arcaded buildings run down the long sides of the piazza; they're known as the **Procuratie Vecchie**, to the north, and the **Procuratie Nuove**, on the opposite side. The Vecchie was built in the 16th century to house the Procurators of St Mark's, who were in charge of the maintenance of the basilica. A century later, the Nuove was constructed, its design inspired by the Biblioteca Marciana round the corner in the **Piazzetta San Marco** (►70). It became the imperial residence after the fall of Venice in 1797, and was linked by Napoleon to the

View of the Piazza San Marco: The Piazzetta with the lion of St Mark and the statue of St Theodore

Procuratie Vecchie with the construction of a further arcaded building, the Ala Napoleonica. This is now home to the **Museo Correr** (➤ 69). You can walk round three sides of the piazza under the arcades, passing a string of expensive shops and even more expensive historic cafés.

Venice's Famed Landmark
The **Campanile (Belltower)** stands opposite the basilica. There's been a bell tower here since the ninth century, though its present appearance, with its spire and gilded angel, dates from 1514. In July 1902, disaster struck when the entire tower subsided into

Evening is a good time to visit the piazza

a tidy heap of bricks and debris. No other building was damaged and the only casualty was the custodian's cat. It was rebuilt *"Com'era, dov'era"* – as it was, where it was – Sansovino's little Loggetta at the foot of the tower being pieced together from its fragments, found in the rubble. A lift whisks you to the top for marvellous views over the city, across the lagoon and north towards the Alps.

TAKING A BREAK
Take your pick of one of the piazza's three historic cafés – **Florian** (➤ 70), **Lavena** or **Quadri** (➤ 73).

➕ 206 C4 ✉ Piazza San Marco ☎ Campanile: 041 5 22 40 64
🕐 Nov–March daily 9:30–3:45, April–June and Oct 9–7, July–Sep 9–9.
Closed three weeks after Christmas for lift maintenance
🚤 1, 2, San Marco 🎫 Campanile: €8

INSIDER INFO

- Get to the piazza before 9 to **avoid the day trippers**.
- Choose a **clear day** to ascend the Campanile: heat haze or mist will reduce the visibility.
- Don't forget to check out the **tourist office** under the arcade at the southwest corner of the piazza (Piazza San Marco 71f, tel: 041 5 29 87 40, daily 8–6:30) for maps and information on sightseeing and events.
- If you have a drink at Florian, Lavena or Quadri, there's a **supplement** if a band is playing.
- Check out the **meteorological instruments** on the northern wall of the Campanile. There's a chronometer and thermometer as well as a gauge showing the times and heights of high tide.

⭐2 San Giorgio Maggiore

Facing the Palazzo Ducale across the waters of St Mark's Basin stands the great Palladian church of San Giorgio Maggiore, surely among the world's most beautiful. One of the most familiar of all Venetian images, its sublimely balanced façade is perfectly set off by the slender Campanile rising behind it.

As early as 982, Doge Tribuno Memmo donated a cloister and a church on the island to the Benedictine order of monks. The building that stands today was designed by Andrea Palladio – who worked on the island from 1560 – and was finished by Simone Sorella after the great architect's death. As with Palladio's other Venetian churches – San Francesco della Vigna (Santi Giovanni e Paolo) and Il Redentore (La Giudecca) – the façade is reminiscent of an antique temple, complete with colossal classical columns, niches and a triangular pediment. Palladio followed antique Roman architectural ideals in the white and grey interior by employing columns, pillars, pilasters and entablatures in a three-aisled basilica design that finishes in semi-circular transepts on each arm and boasts a central dome at the crossing. The building is completed in the east with a square chancel and an apsidal monks' choir. The real attention-grabber is the high altarpiece in the chancel (1591–93), a masterpiece by Girolamo Compagna, one of Sansovino's pupils.

The Grand Canal from San Giorgio Maggiore

The important paintings in the church include Jacopo Bassano's *Adoration of the Shepherds* over the first altar on the right, and two huge, dramatic works by Tintoretto: the *Last Supper* and the *Fall of Manna*. The artist's last painting, the *Entombment*, hangs in the **Cappella dei Morti**, behind the choir.

The Refuge of the Medici
Cosimo de' Medici (1389–1464) stayed here during his exile from Florence in 1433, building a library which was

The cloisters form part of the former monastery

elegantly replaced in 1641 by the baroque architect Baldassare Longhena. The 1790s saw the gradual confiscation of the monastery's property by the French; in 1806 the order was suppressed, and the monastery was used as workshops and barracks for the occupying Austrians during the 19th century. Industrialist Vittorio Cini purchased and restored it in 1951 and established the **Fondazione Giorgio Cini** in memory of his son, killed in a plane crash in 1949. The foundation conducts artistic and musical research, and runs a naval college and crafts school. The complex includes two **cloisters**: the one to the rear was built from 1520 to 1540, and the foremost was begun by Andrea Palladio in 1579 and completed by Baldassare Longhena. The latter also designed the early baroque staircase and the library (1641). The dormitory, measuring in at 128m (420ft) in length, was built between 1488 and 1521.

✚ 207 D2 ✉ Isola di San Giorgio Maggiore ☎ 041 5 22 78 27
🕐 April–Sep daily 9:30–12:30, 2:30–6:30; Oct–March 9:30–12:30, 2:30–4:30
🚢 2, San Giorgio
💶 Church: free, Campanile: €5

INSIDER INFO

- It's worth doing a bit of homework on *vaporetto* **timings** so that you're not stranded here longer than you want to be.
- There's no better place for a **summer concert** than the Teatro Verde on the island: ask at the main tourist office in San Marco for details of what's on.
- Guided tours by the Fondazione Giorgio Cini talk about the restoration and long military history of this island and show you artistic treasures from the school of Tintoretto. The **Borges Labyrinth**, a reconstruction of the maze designed by Randoll Coate in honour of the famous Argentinian writer, is also interesting (Oct–March Sat, Sun every hour 10-4, April-Sep, every hour 10-5, €10). *Insider Tip*
- Don't miss the **choir stalls**, decorated with scenes from the life of St Benedict, and some of Venice's finest wood-carving. They were created in the 1590s during the construction of the church.

①Basilica di San Marco

The 1,000 year-old Basilica di San Marco has served as the church of the Doge and the Venetian state, as a shrine to the city's Patron Saint, and as a cathedral since 1807. With its five domes, the ornate tracery on its arches and windows and its breath-taking interior, it's also one of the most beautiful medieval buildings in the world. The present basilica, the site's third, was built between 1063 and 1094.

The first church was built after St Mark's relics arrived in the city (▶ Venice and Saint Mark, right-hand side). The building was destroyed when the Doge's palace set alight in 976. It was rebuilt before being torn down again in the 11th century and replaced by the building we see today. The project was initiated by Doge Domenico Contarini (1043–70). The structure was designed on the previous church's ground plan, and took the form of a Greek cross with two side aisles, topped off with a large dome at the crossing and a smaller dome over each arm. The Basilica was consecrated in the presence of Holy Roman Emperor Henry IV in 1094 and was raised to the status of Venetian state church. After the Sack of Constantinople in 1204, the cupolas were raised, the northern portico was added and the building's western side was changed to a columnar façade. The sparsely decorated brick building was then

The façade of the Basilica di San Marco in all its glory

VENICE AND ST MARK

In 828, two Venetian merchants brought the bones of Mark the Evangelist to the lagoon city from Alexandria, then the second largest city in Egypt (after Cairo). They got away with blatantly stealing the relics by using a rather crude trick – they hid the bones underneath a mountain of cured pork, which their Muslim pursuers would of course not dare to touch. They also managed to have their theft "legitimised by God" in effect by invoking a religious legend, according to which the angel of Saint Mark was said to have spoken to him with the words "Pax tibi Marce Evangelista meus" ("Peace be with you, Mark, my Evangelist"), before prophesying that Venice would be his final resting place. Saint Mark subsequently became elevated to Patron Saint of Venice, the Basilica San Marco was built to house his relics, and the Evangelist's symbol, the winged lion, became the emblem of the city. You'll see the latter on top of a column at the entrance to the piazzetta. Next to it, you'll also spot a second column with a sculpture of the Greek Saint Theodore, who is traditionally represented standing with a crocodile at his feet. Both Saints were once revered in the city for a time, but Theodore slowly fell further and further into the background as Venice gradually became more and more independent of Byzantium.

richly ornamented inside and out with marble inlays, mosaics and countless pieces of plunder: a 1075 law by Doge Domenico Selvo decreed that every traveller returning home had to bring back a precious ornament for the "house of Saint Mark". This explains the many architectural pieces and jewels from the Orient and the rich variety of columns, reliefs, sculptures and goldsmithery on display.

Interior
The spatial impact of the triple-naved interior is created by the five domes that sit on massive pillars connected by wide barrel vaults. The magnificent mosaics, predominantly created in the 12th and 13th centuries, cover an area of 86,000ft². They were partially replaced following designs by such artists as Tiepolo, Tintoretto, Titian and Veronese between 1500 and 1750. The imagery's main themes develop between the apse and the exit, beginning with Christ as Ruler of the World (Christ Pantocrator) in the east and finishing with the Apocalypse in the west. Events from the Passion right through to the Ascension are depicted in between. The walls in the transepts are decorated with scenes of the Saints and the parents of Jesus.

The high altar, a composite of older parts, houses the bones of St Mark today. These used to be kept in the crypt, where they were visible through a window in the altar. The four relief-work columns on the baldachin are particularly deserving of attention: they show scenes from the life of Christ and the Virgin Mary.

The Treasury
The church's precious treasury predominantly consists of pieces of booty that the Venetians brought back to the lagoon city after the conquest of Constantinople in 1204: cups,

The Church of Gold

Topped by its five massive domes, the Basilica San Marco is one of the most impressive historical monuments the city on the lagoon has to offer.

❶ Portals: The church's round-arched portals are set deep into the western façade. They are adorned with mosaics, columns in precious multi-coloured marble, and – at the centre of the main entrance – stone carvings from the 13th century.

❷ Façade Mosaics: Merchants managed to get the earthly remains of Saint Mark to Venice from Alexandria by hiding it under a mountain of pork. The history of this "abduction" is represented in the mosaics over the portals on the west façade.

❸ Baptistery: Mosaics and reliefs on the baptismal font show scenes from the life of John the Baptist.

❹ The Tetrarchs: This mysterious 4th-century porphyry sculpture depicts four men in an intimate embrace.

❺ Tesoro: The spoils that the Venetians brought back after the Sack of Constantinople in 1204 form the basis of the treasury's collection today.

❻ The Miracle of the Pillar: St Mark's mortal remains were lost after a fire in the church in 976. The mosaic describes the miracle of their rediscovery.

❼ High Altar: The altar, itself a composite of assembled parts, boasts a magnificent baldachin resting on four columns.

❽ Domes: Visible from St Mark's square ever since they were raised after the Sack of Constantinople in 1204, the church's five domes lend the building an oriental flair.

The famous bronze horses of San Marco were created in Greece in the 4th c. BC. From there, they found their way to Rome, where they featured on Emperor Trajan's triumphal arch. They were transferred to Constantinople in the 4th c., before finally moving to Venice in 1204. The originals (left) stand in the Museo Marciano today; replicas are displayed on the balcony of St Mark's.

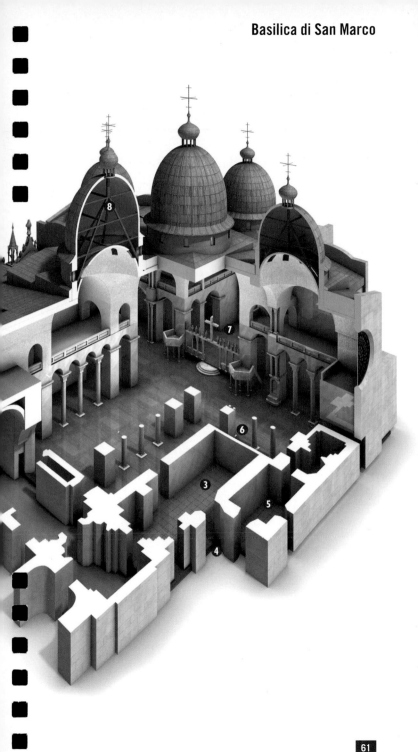

glasses, liturgical instruments, ivory work, icons, tapestries, and gold and silver reliquary shrines richly decorated and set with precious stones. One of the most important pieces is the "Throne of Saint Mark", a marble reliquary in the shape of a seat that, according to tradition, was given to the Patriarch of Grado by the Byzantine Emperor in 630. Another significant work is an incense burner in silver-gilt, cast in the form of a Byzantine church.

Mosaics with luminous gold backgrounds adorn the vaults and domes of the Basilica di San Marco

Viewing the Treasure House
For the best views, head to the gallery, accessed by steep stairs from the atrium.

TAKING A BREAK
Choose one of the cafés around the piazza or on the piazzetta – great views, high prices.

➕ 206 C4 ✉ Piazza San Marco ☎ Basilica, Pala d'Oro, Treasury and Loggia: 041 2 70 83 11, www.basilicasanmarco.it 🕐 Nov–Easter Mon Sat 9:45–5, Sun 2–5; Easter–Nov 9:45–5, Sun 2–5 (Pala d'Oro and Treasury close one hour earlier) 🚊 1, 2, San Marco 🎫 Basilica: free, Museo di San Marco: €4, Pala d'Oro: €2, Tesoro: €3

INSIDER INFO

- The side door, giving access from the Piazzetta dei Leoncini, **opens early** early so that the faithful can enter the Basilica to pray.
- In summer, **head directly up the stairs to the Loggia** on your way in; the roped route won't allow you to get back without queuing again.
- Give your eyes time to adjust to the low light levels.
- This is a church; remember to **cover your upper arms and dress modestly**.
- The Basilica has some wonderful **wonderful undulating floors** made of marble, porphyry and glass mosaics - make sure to have a look down as you walk around.

⑫ Palazzo Ducale

The Doge's palace was the centre of the Venetian Republic's power for over 1,000 years. Home to the Doge and the Serenissima's government, it was where the Chamber of the Great Council, the official rooms of state, the court, the prison, and the arsenal were all located. It's considered one of the most significant secular buildings in the world today.

The first Doge's palace stood on this spot as early as 814. This gloomy wooden structure with its massive defensive towers was protected by the lagoon in the south and canals on its three other sides. It was replaced with a new Byzantine-style building with loggias and arcades in the 12th century. By the mid 1300s, the Great Council had grown to over 1,000 members, necessitating a roomier assembly hall. As a result, construction began on the building that stands today.

The brightly lit Bridge of Sighs over the Rio di Palazzo – Casanova once crossed this bridge on his way to the Lead Chambers

Exterior
The building's 71 × 75m (233 × 246ft) ground plan consists of three wings arranged in a slightly trapezoidal form around an inner courtyard. The south wing, which faces the Molo, was built from 1340 to 1400. The west wing on the Piazzetta followed in 1424 to 1438. The final east wing, begun in 1483, was not completed until the 17th century. The palace's northern boundary is demarcated by the Basilica di San Marco. Although numerous fires have caused a great deal of damage to the palace, they have generally only effected the interior décor. The building's façade is derived from Venetian noble palaces of the 12th and 13th centuries. The open arcades on the ground floor are supported by low, baseless columns that sink nearly 40cm (15.7in) into the pavement (the square has been raised on numerous occasions). Above this is a loggia made up of narrower, more closely-spaced columns. The ogee arches and quatrefoils on this level proved extremely influential in Venetian ornamentation of the Late Gothic period. The marble-tiled walls above the loggia are interspersed with several pointed-arch windows. Ornamental crenulations round off the whole design.

Mauro Coducci designed the **east façade** on the Rio di Palazzo. Your eye is drawn here to the elegant Bridge of Sighs, which connects the Doge's palace with the Prigioni Nuove (the "New Prison"; 1589–1614) on the other side of the canal. Designed by Antonio Contin and built from

San Marco & San Giorgio Maggiore

Istrian marble in 1614, the bridge heralded the arrival of the Baroque style in Venice.

The eye-catching **south façade** is one of the oldest parts of the exterior. The balcony surrounding the central window, donated by Doge Michele Steno in 1404, is the only interruption in the façade's otherwise planar design. The Gothic window surround was created in Pierpaolo dalle Masegne's workshop; the finial on the balcony was rebuilt after a fire of 1577. The statue of Justice is the work of Alessandro Vittoria, while the figure of Saint George was created by Giovanni Battista Pellegrini (18th century). The sculptural decoration at the corners of the building dates from the 14th century.

Built from 1424 to 1438, the **façade nearest the Piazzetta** is the mirror image of the palace's older southern side. A lion of St Mark and a figure of Lady Justice stand above the balcony, which was added in the 16th century. This is where the Doge watched executions as they were being carried out on the Piazzetta.

The **Porta della Carta** provides the link between the architectural styles of the Doge's palace and St Mark's church. Along with the Ca' d'Oro, it is considered one of

The water approach to the Riva degli Schiavoni and the Palazzo Ducale, backed by the Campanile

DID YOU KNOW?

Approximately 20 million people visit Venice annually. Of these, it's been calculated that over 90 per cent head to the Piazza San Marco and spend less than €18. The city council therefore wants to reduce the incoming flow of day tourists and promote luxury and upscale cruise tourism instead.

the most significant works of Venetian Gothic architecture.
Giovanni and Bartolomeo Bon were entrusted with its
design between 1438 and 1442. Two large buttresses
frame both the entrance and the window above. Doge
Francesco Foscari is depicted over the gate kneeling
before the lion of St Mark, delete representing the individual's subordination to the interests of the State. St Mark
himself is shown over the window, and an allegory of
Justice accompanied by two lions sits further up the
structure. As petitioners were not allowed in the palace,
officials accepted written requests and petitions at this
gate, giving the Porta its name (the "Gate of Papers").

Inner Courtyard
The palace is entered today via the Porta del Frumento
next to the sea. The courtyard's highlights are the two
bronze fountains (mid-16th c.) and the Scala dei Giganti
by the east wing. When selected, a Doge would take an
oath of allegiance on the upper step of this "Staircase
of Giants". Designed by Antonio Rizzo from 1483, the
staircase takes its name from Jacopo Sansovino's colossal
statues of Mars and Neptune (1550) that embody Venice's
dominion over both the land and the sea.

Sala del Collegio und Sala dell' Anticollegio
Honoured guests were received in the State Council's
meeting room *(Sala del Collegio)*; Veronese's ceiling
paintings celebrate the might and glory of Venice.
The pictures in the waiting room for foreign emissaries
(Sala dell' Anticollegio) deal with mythological themes;

The Corridors of Power

Venice's administrative headquarters were moved to the Grand Canal and the first Doge's seat was built at the start of the 9th century. The Doge's palace, the Palazzo Ducale, stands on the site today.

❶ Balcony on the Piazzetta: The Doge watched executions taking place on the Piazzetta from this 15th-century balcony on the building's west façade.

❷ South Façade: The south façade is the oldest and most beautiful side of the Doge's palace. 14th-century statues stand on both corners of the building.

❸ Cortile: The palace's former entrance, the Porta della Carta, has been superseded by the Porta del Frumento on the waterfront façade today.

❹ Scala dei Giganti, Arco Foscari: The coronation ceremonies of the Doge took place on the Scala dei Giganti in front of the east wing. The richly decorated Arco Foscari triumphal arch stands opposite.

❺ Sala del Maggior Consiglio: This room was used for assemblies of the Great Council, selecting the Doge, and inducting politicians and high state officials into office. The wall paintings were created after a fire in 1577. A frieze with (predominantly invented) portraits of the first 76 Doges runs just beneath the ceiling. A black veil was painted over the picture of Doge Marino Falier, who was executed as a traitor in 1335. Tintoretto's *Paradise* hangs behind the throne.

❻ Appartamento Ducale: The Doges had to bring their own furniture when they moved into their living quarters in the east wing. It was cleared away again after their death.

❼ Sala dello Scrutinio: This room is where the elections for various state offices took place.

❽ Museo dell'Opera: Some of the 14th-century capitals, which used to adorn the palace's façades, are on show in this museum (copies stand in their place today).

❾ Ponte della Paglia: You get a good view of the "Bridge of Sighs" (Ponte dei Sospiri) from the "Straw Bridge" over the Rio di Palazzo (mid 14th-century). Prisoners crossed this bridge on their way to the Prigioni Nuove, the 16th-century prison that included the famous Lead Chambers in which Casanova was once held.

❿ Drunken Noah: The relief at the southeast corner of the palace (14th century) is thought to be a symbol of human weakness; statues of Adam and Eve can be seen on the corner in the Piazzetta.

The gilded ceiling paintings in the Sala del Maggior Consiglio were designed to impress foreign emissaries

6

3

5

10

9

2

San Marco & San Giorgio Maggiore

Veronese painted the ceiling's central fresco, entitled „Venice Distributing Honours".

Sala del Maggior Consiglio

The largest room in the palace was used by the Great Council to select members of government and high state officials. It was also where important decisions – including the dissolution of the Republic in 1797 – were discussed and made. Begun by Veronese, the eye-catching *Paradise* canvas behind the Doge's throne was the largest painting in the world when it was unveiled. Tintoretto – nearly 70 years old at the time – carried on after Veronese's death in 1588, finishing four years later.

Sala del Magistrato

The altarpiece by Hieronymus Bosch (*c*1450–1516) on display in this room is particularly impressive.

TAKING A BREAK

The stylish Culto Caffè Cioccolato, boasting magnificent views of St Mark's square, was opened on the palace's first floor in 2013.

✚ 206 C4 ✉ Piazzetta San Marco
☎ 041 2 71 59 11, palazzoducale.visitmuve.it
🕐 April–Oct daily 8:30–7; Nov–March 8:30–5:30;
last admission 60 minutes before closing
🚢 1, 2, San Marco
💶 €16; secret itinerary guided tour: €20

INSIDER INFO

- The main entrance for visitors is the **Porta del Frumento**, on the waterside of the palace.
- The **entrance ticket** to the palace is good for three months and is also valid for the Museo Correr, the Museo Archeologico Nazionale and the Biblioteca Nazionale Marciana.
- In high season, aim to **get there as the palace opens** to avoid the worst of the crowds of tourists.
- It's well worth investing in an **audio-guide**, available at the ticket office, to help you get the most out of your visit.
- Take time to read the excellent English-language **information boards** scattered throughout the building.
- Cool clothes in summer (it can be stifling and airless) and warm in winter (when it's freezing and draughty), plus **comfortable shoes**, make sense here.
- Don't be disappointed if some parts of the palace are **under wraps**: this is an ancient building and restoration work goes on almost non-stop.
- **The bookshop** has an excellent range of guidebooks, postcards, posters and quality museum gifts.
- There's a riveting 75-minute **secret itinerary guided tour** *(itinerari segreti)* of the palace. This gives you the lowdown on the inner workings of the State and takes you behind the scenes to the administrative offices and secret chambers. Tours in English leave daily at 9:55, 10:45 and 11:35, book two days in advance at the ticket office (tel:041 5 20 90 70).

At Your Leisure

Doge Giovanni Mocenigo by Gentile Bellini

🔢 Museo Correr

The doors that once divided the Museo Correr from the **Museo Archeologico (Archaeological Museum)** and the **Biblioteca Marciana (Marciana Library)** have been opened after years of negotiation, and visitors can explore the whole complex, which occupies the upper floors of the Procuratie Nuove and Sansovino's (►27) library building. The museum, based on the 18th-century collections of Teodoro Correr, is basically Venice's civic museum, telling the story of Venetian history and social life in the 16th and 17th centuries. There's much more besides, including a fine picture gallery on the upper floor. The itinerary leads through a hall devoted to the slickly perfect sculpture of Antonio Canova (1757–1822), to a series of stately

rooms overlooking the piazza. Here you can learn about the ducal elections and the workings of the Arsenale (►88), and admire miniature bronzes, coins, globes and robes. Upstairs, the Quadreria (Picture Gallery) traces the evolution of Venetian painting. The highlight is *Two Noblewomen* by Vittorio Carpaccio (*c*1460–1525), erroneously known for years as *The Courtesans:* these two bored and lonely ladies are actually awaiting their husbands.

The route then leads through the Museo Archeologico's collection of Greek and Roman art, before reaching the stunning state rooms of the Biblioteca Marciana. Here, manuscripts and early books are displayed beneath a magnificent ceiling of allegorical Mannerist paintings. Back in the Correr, there are enjoyable displays on festivals, games and pastimes and interesting information on the trade guilds.

➕ 206 B4 ✉ Ala Napoleonica, Piazza San Marco ☎ Museo Correr: 041 2 40 52 11; correr.visitmuve.it; Museo Archeologico: 041 5 22 59 78; Biblioteca Marciana: 041 2 40 72 11; marciana.venezia.sbn.it 🕐 April–Oct daily 9–7 (last entry 6);

Nov–March 9–5 (last entry 4) 🚊 1, San Marco 🎫 Combined ticket (Museo Correr, Museo Archeologico Nazionale, Biblioteca Nazionale Marciana and Palazzo Ducale): €16

San Marco & San Giorgio Maggiore

🔟4 Caffè Florian

The Caffè Florian was first opened in 1720 by Floriano Francesconi as a coffee house known as Venezia Trionfante. During the Austrian occupation, loyal Venetians drank here to escape the army officers in Caffè Quadri (➤ 73), across the square. The present building has a series of beautiful rooms dating from 1859, all frescoes, mirrors and polished wood. Marble tables and comfortable upholstered chairs spill on to the arcade and piazza,

Florian's – the epitome of café society

where an orchestra serenades patrons during cocktail-hour and throughout the evening. Have an *aperitivo*, a cocktail, a pot of tea or a sinfully rich *cioccolata calda con panna* (hot chocolate with whipped cream).

➕ 206 C4 ✉ Piazza San Marco 56
☎ 041 5 20 56 41; www.caffeflorian.com

🕐 May–Oct daily 10–midnight;
Nov–April Thu–Tue 10am–11pm
🚢 1, 2, San Marco

🔟5 Piazzetta San Marco

The Piazzetta San Marco, lying between the Basilica and the lagoon, was the state entrance to Venice in the glory days, where disembarking visitors would have gaped at the surrounding splendours.

Opposite the Palazzo Ducale is the **Biblioteca Marciana**, now part of the Museo Correr (➤ 69). It was built in 1537 to designs by Sansovino (➤ 27), just as Venice was making its mark as a centre for printing and book publishing. The columns near the water are 12th-century; the winged lion on the eastern one is Persian or Syrian; on top of the other column is a statue of St Theodore, the city's first patron, as always accompanied by his crocodile.

➕ 206 C4 ✉ Piazzetta San Marco
🚢 1, 2, San Marco

🔟6 Torre dell'Orologio

Crowds gather hourly beneath this superb Renaissance clock tower, which guards the entrance to the Mercerie (➤ 71) on the north side of the Piazza. The central tower was built between 1496 and 1499, the wings added in 1506. Mauro Coducci, the designer, placed a statue of the Madonna and a great golden lion on a star-spangled

---

👪 TRAVELLING WITH KIDS

- **The top attraction** if you've got kids in tow has to be exploring the eerie cells of the **Prigioni Nuove (New Prisons)** in the Palazzo Ducale. They're located just across the Bridge of Sighs.
- Every child visiting Venice should sit on the back of one of the **little marble lions** in the Piazzetta dei Leoncini.
- A trip up the **Campanile** is highly popular.
- Copy Venetian children and go to **the third column from the left** on the water façade of the Palazzo Ducale. Standing with your back against it, can you walk around it without your feet slipping off the marble pavement?
- Please beware: despite being great fun for young children, it's **forbidden** to **feed the pigeons** in St Mark's square!

blue background above the zodiacal gilt-and-blue clock face. Throughout the year, statues of Moors strike the hour, but at Epiphany and during Ascension Week, angels emerge from the side doors to lead the Magi in a procession to bow to the Virgin.

🕂 206 C4 ⊠ Piazza San Marco
☎ 041 5 20 90 70 (to book tours)
🕘 Guided tours only, in English Mon–Wed 10 and 11; Thu–Sun 1, 2 and 3 🚊 1, 2, San Marco/ Vallaresso, San Zaccaria 💷 €12

🔢 Mercerie

Since the Middle Ages, a chain of five streets has linked the Piazza San Marco with the Rialto (➤ 118). Collectively known as the Mercerie, perhaps after the haberdashers who once plied their trade here, the Mercerie has always been a shoppers' paradise, described by a 17th-century English traveller as "one of the most delicious streets in the world". Today it's a bizarre mix of big-name designers and emporia of outstanding kitsch. You'll have to battle to make progress along here, but the crowds and *mélange* of nationalities and languages hasn't changed much since medieval times.

🕂 206 C5 ⊠ Merceria dell'Orologio, Zulian, San Salvador, 2 Aprile
🚊 1, Rialto, 2, San Marco 💷 Free

🔢 Campo Santo Stefano

Lying on the well-worn route from the Accademia (➤ 136) to San Marco, this elongated and pleasant square has several bars, one of which – Paolin Gelateria (➤ 74) – serves some of the best ice-cream in Venice. It was the venue for Venice's bullfights until 1802, when several spectators were killed as a stand collapsed and the sport was banned. Niccòlo Tommaseo, a 19th-century Risorgimento ideologue, is commemorated by a statue. At the east end is the 13th-century

Statue of St Theodore in the piazzetta

Augustinian **Chiesa di Santo Stefano**, rebuilt in the 14th century and altered again in the 15th century. The interior of the church is an architectural treat, with a beautiful

San Marco & San Giorgio Maggiore

Summer living in the Campo Santo Stefano

ship's keel roof and multi-coloured marble columns, altars and flooring. Look out for the plaque to Doge Morosini – best known outside Venice for detonating the Turkish gunpowder stored in the Parthenon in Athens.

➕ 205 F4

Chiesa di Santo Stefano
✉ Campo Santo Stefano
☎ 041 2 75 04 62; www.chorusvenezia.org
🕐 Mon–Sat 10–5. Closed Sun, 15 Aug (holiday)
🚤 1, 2, Accademia 🎫 €3

WHAT'S IN A NAME

Each house's official **address** is simply the name of the *sestiere* (ward) followed by a number. Remember there's only one *piazza* in Venice – San Marco. All the rest are *campi* (singular *campo*), unless they're *cortile*, *campielli*, usually very small, or *piscine*, on the site of a filled-in boat-turning area. Streets are usually *calle*, unless they run beside water, when they're *fondamente*, or are important, when they're either a *ruga* or a *salizzada*. A street running beneath a building is a *sottoportego*, a wide *fondamenta* is a *riva*, and a street formed by filling a canal is a *rio terrà*. A canal is a *rio*, a bridge a *ponte*.

🔟 Harry's Bar

One of the most famous bars in Venice is tucked down a narrow street just a stone's throw away from the piazza. It's not much to look at outside, there's no terrace and the service can be offhand, but it's still high on the must-go list. In summer, sample one of Harry's cocktails, the legendary Bellini, a delicious mix of peach juice and sparkling *prosecco*, along with a snack, such as *polpette* (fried meat-balls). You can also choose from a three-course set menu or the *carte*. Ernest Hemingway spent a lot of time propping up the bar, and film stars and socialites still come here.

➕ 206 B3
✉ Calle Vallaresso, San Marco 1323
☎ 041 5 28 57 77 🕐 Daily 10am–11:30pm
🚤 1, 2, San Marco 🍴 Expensive

Where to...
Eat and Drink

Prices
Expect to pay per person for a meal, excluding drinks.
€ under €35   €€ €35–€55   €€€ over €55

BÀCARI, BARS AND GELATERIE

Acquapazza €€
You can sit outside overlooking one of San Marco's nicer *campi* and watch the world go by if you eat at this good, solid restaurant, where the accent is firmly on fish. Starters include prawns and rocket with a balsamic vinegar dressing, a simple, lemon-drizzled seafood platter and fresh anchovies; follow this with the catch of the day or a delicate fish risotto and round it off with a choice of home made desserts. They also serve good, crisp pizza if you're watching the budget.

206 B4 San Marco 3808, Campo Sant'Angelo 041 2 77 06 88; www.veniceacquapazza.com Tue–Sun 12–2:30, 7:30–9.30. Closed Jan Sant'Angelo

Antica Carbonera €€/€€€
The "Old Charcoalburner" has been in business since 1894, and everything about this quintessential Venetian restaurant reflects the owner's years of professionalism and hospitality. The dining room is lovely, with well-spaced tables, wood panelling, crisp linen and shining glass and silver. Service is impeccable, as a procession of elegantly presented, classic dishes, all cooked with care and attention to detail, are brought out. The wine list is long, too.

202 B2 San Marco 4648, Calle dei Fabbri 041 5 22 54 79; www.anticacarbonera.it Tue–Sat 12:30–2:30, 7:30–9:30. Closed 2 weeks Jan Rialto

Caffè Florian €/€€ (➤ 70)

Caffè Centrale €€
Venice's most stylish late-night restaurant and lounge is a restful minimal space, where tables are elegantly set with Venetian glass and service comes with flair. Expect superbly fresh ingredients served with a twist and beautifully presented dishes.

206 B4 San Marco 1659, Piscina Frezzeria 041 2 96 06 64; www.caffecentralevenezia.com Tue–Sun 6:30–2 San Marco

Caffè Quadri €/€€€
Caffè Quadri, another one of the great theatrical cafés in this most theatrical of squares, has been restored to its former grandeur. Its mirrored interior is hand-painted with monochromatic Venetian scenes. Upstairs, in the only dining rooms to overlook the Piazza, is the elegant and luxurious restaurant (member of Buona Accoglienza) where you can dine in style.

206 C4 San Marco 120, Piazza San Marco 041 5 22 21 05; www.quadrivenice.com Caffè: Tue–Sun 9am–midnight; restaurant: Tue–Sun noon–2, 7:15–10 San Marco

Osteria i Rusteghi €

Venice is famous for its *pannini* and *tramezzini* (filled rolls and sandwiches). This popular, long-established eatery offers well over 30 varieties that can be enjoyed with some wine from the extensive list. Sit inside or out on the *campo* and people-watch while debating the merits of the menu with delights ranging from scampi and rocket through egg and asparagus to porcini mushrooms and beef.

➕ 206 C5 ✉ San Marco 5513, Campiello del Tintor ☎ 041 5 23 22 05; www.osteriarusteghi.com ⊙ May–Sep Mon–Fri 10–9:30; Oct–April Mon–Sat 10–9 🚤 Rialto

Paolin Gelateria €

This is one of Venice's best and oldest *gelaterie*, with a fine palette of flavours, especially the summer fruits – apricot, melon, strawberry and lemon. Sit outside at one of the tables in the square.

➕ 206 B4 ✉ San Marco 2962/A, Campo Santo Stefano ☎ 041 5 22 55 76 ⊙ Summer 9am–11pm; winter Tue–Sun 8am–8:30pm 🚤 Accademia, San Samuele

E. Rosa Salva €

Come to Rosa Salva to join locals having a morning *cappuccino* with a light, sticky *brioche*, a piece of cake or an early *tramezzino*. Later in the day, people come to buy delicate little pastries or Venetian biscuits to take away. There are a number of branches in the city.

➕ 206 C4 ✉ San Marco 950, Ponte Ferai, Calle Fiubera ☎ 041 5 21 05 44; www.rosasalva.it ⊙ Mon–Sat 8–8 🚤 Rialto

Teamo €/€€

Trendy design and fabulous Fortuny textiles: this wine bar unites old and new in harmonious style. Choose from traditional *cicchetti* (snacks) or a range of one-plate dishes, or sample a simple but delicious plate of smoked meats and local cheeses.

➕ 206 A4 ✉ San Marco 30124, Ria Terà della Mandola ☎ 041 2 77 08 50 ⊙ Daily 8–10 🚤 Sant'Angelo/Giglio

Insider Tip

Da Fiore €/€€

Da Fiore offers a fabulous choice of *cicchetti* – fried sardines, salt *baccalà* (cod), assorted sausages, vegetables – which can be eaten at the stand-up bar with a glass of wine. For a full meal, sit at one of the tables for mixed fried fish (*fritto misto*), or spaghetti with seafood.

➕ 205 F4 ✉ San Marco 3461, Calle delle Botteghe ☎ 041 5 23 53 10; www.dafiore.net ⊙ Wed–Mon 11:30–2:30, 6:30–9:30 🚤 San Samuele, Accademia

Do Forni €€

Opt for a classy experience, all starched linen and elegant décor, or go for a more rustic style, with wooden tables and exposed beams, at this popular restaurant with two dining-rooms. Scampi in champagne served with tagliatelle is a perfect example of the chef's style.

➕ 206 C4 ✉ 457 San Marco, Calle dei Specchieri ☎ 041 5 23 06 33; www.doforni.it ⊙ Daily 12–3, 6–11 🚤 San Zaccaria

Harry's Bar €€€ (➤ 72)

Vini da Arturo €€

Known locally as *il vagone* (the railway carriage), the narrow, panelled interior is packed with diners enjoying some of Venice's finest meat dishes, including what is said to be the best fillet steak in town. *Antipasti* include imaginative salads, and among the desserts are a perfectly creamy tiramisu and wicked chocolate mousse. No credit cards.

➕ 206 A4 ✉ San Marco 3656, Calle di Assassini ☎ 041 5 28 69 74 ⊙ Mon–Sat 12:30–2:30, 7:30–10:30. Closed last 2 weeks Feb and Aug 🚤 Sant' Angelo/Rialto

Vino Vino €/€€ (➤ 52)

Where to...
Shop

The streets around San Marco offer everything from world-famous names in fashion to artisan shops selling Venetian specialities and others aimed at the day-tripper market. Take your pick, disembarking at San Marco unless otherwise indicated.

ARTS, CRAFTS AND ANTIQUES

Browse the stalls along **Giardini ex-Reali**, behind Piazza San Marco, where artists sell everything from charcoal sketches to watercolours and oil paintings. For something more classy, explore the antiques and art shops along **Calle delle Botteghe**, off the north end of Campo Santo Stefano. Here you'll find **Antiquus** (San Marco 313, Calle delle Botteghe, tel: 041 5 20 63 95), a treasure trove of antiques and old jewellery, including the Venetian Moor's head brooches and earrings. Nearby, **Gaggio** (San Marco 3441–3451, Calle delle Botteghe, tel: 041 5 22 85 74) sells hand-printed silk brocade velvet clothes, cushions, bags, hats and scarves, while San Samuele is home to **Livio de Marchi** (San Marco 3157/A, Calle San Samuele, tel: 041 5 28 56 94), creator of wooden sculpture in the form of everyday objects ranging from books and pencils to crumpled jeans. Knitters could visit **Lellabella** (San Marco 3718, Calle della Mandola, tel: 041 5 22 51 52, lellabellavenezia.com), where wool, cashmere and angora yarns lie alongside fur-trimmed and spangled cotton threads. Colour also shines at **Venetia Studium** (San Marco 2403, Calle Larga XXII Marzo, tel: 041 5 22 92 81; www.venetiastudium. co), where Fortuny-style pleated silk and figured velvet scarves, pillows and bags are piled high – they have branches throughout the city. On the same street, you'll find **Petra** (San Marco 2424, Calle Larga XXII Marzo, tel: 041 5 23 18 125), which sells rare books, antique prints, drawings and maps.

BOOKS AND PAPER STATIONERY

Legatoria Piazzesi (San Marco 2551, Campiello della Feltrina, tel: 041 5 22 12 02; www.legatoriapiazzesi.it) sells fine paper-covered items, as does **Ebrû** (San Marco 3471,

Campo Santo Stefano, tel: 041 5 23 88 30, www.albertovallese-ebru. com), whose range includes hand-marbled and stamped papers made up into books, albums and frames. For contrasting designs, head for **Carteria Tassotti** (San Marco 5472, Calle de la Bissa, tel: 041 5 28 18 81; www.tassotti.it), which specializes in paper and desk accessories featuring flora and fauna. For everyday stationery, try **Cartoleria Testolini** (San Marco 4744/46, Calle dei Fabbri, tel: 041 5 22 92 65), while **Libreria Studium** (San Marco 337/C, Calle Canonica, tel: 041 5 22 23 82) has maps, guidebooks and literature in English, including *Calli, Campielli e Canali*, a street map guide that shows every *sestiere* number.

FASHION

Emporio Armani (San Marco 9989, Calle dei Fabbri, tel: 041 5 23 78 08); **Laura Biaggiotto** (San Marco 2400, Calle Larga XXII Marzo, tel: 041 5 20 34 01); **Fendi** (San Marco 1474, Campo San Moisè, tel: 041 2 77 85 32); **Gucci** (San Marco 2413, Calle Larga XXII Marzo, tel: 041 5 22 91 19); **Bruno Magli** (San Marco 1302, Calle Vallaresso, tel: 041 5 22 72 10); **Mandarina Duck** (San Marco 193, Mercerie dell'Orologio, tel: 041 5 22 33 25); **Prada** (San

INSIDER INFO

Art and fashion come together in the work of **Fiorella Mancini** – Venice's Queen of Trash Culture and the most famous fashion designer in the city. Stars like Elton John and Mick Jagger love her provocative punk creations – the jackets, shirts, shirts, kimonos, and shorts that hang in her anarchic boutique are adorned with skulls, rats, mice and swastikas (Fiorella Gallery, San Marco 2806, Campo San Stefano, tel: 041 5 20 92 28, www. fiorellagallery.com).

Marco 1469, Salizada San Moisè, tel: 041 5 28 39 66), **Botteghe Veneta** (San Marco 1337, Calle Vallaresso, tel: 041 5 22 84 89), **Gianni Versace** (San Marco 1462), Campo San Moisè, tel: 041 5 20 01 76), **JB Guanti** (San Marco 4821, Salizada San Giovanni Crisostomo, tel: 041 5 22 86 33).

GLASS, BEADS AND JEWELLERY

Pauly (San Marco 1468, Piazza San Marco, tel: 041 5 20 31 18; www.pauly.it) creates handmade glass objects, while **Venini** (San Marco 314, Piazzetta dei Leoncini, tel: 041 5 22 40 45; www.venini.it), embraces modern shapes. For Venetian beads, head for **Perle e Dintorni** (San Marco 3740, Calle della Mandola, tel: 041 5 20 50 68; www.perle-e-dintorni.it), where they are sold strung or loose. Chrome and semi-precious stones are the hallmarks at **Nomination** (San Marco 4609, Calle Goldoni, tel: 041 5 20 13 44), while Campo Santo Stefano is home to **Ethnos** (San Marco 2958/A, tel: 041 5 28 99 88) where you'll find necklaces of glass beads, quartz and amethyst.

LINENS, HOUSE AND TABLEWARES

Stylish Italian linens can be found at **Frette** (San Marco 2070/A, Calle Larga XXII Marzo, tel: 041 5 22 49 14). Equally covetable, but less expensive, is **TSL Venezia** (San Marco 3324, Salizada San Lio, tel: 041 2 77 77 641), which also has branches at the Rialto and on the Strada Nuova. The best of Venetian cushions, throws and drapes are at **Luigi Bevilacqua** (San Marco 2520, Campo S Maria del Giglio, tel: 041 5 28 75 81; www.luigi bevilacqua. com), while **Domus** (San Marco 4746, Calle dei Fabbri, tel: 041 5 22 62 59) has Italian-style kitchen and dining-room requisites. There are Italian decorative ceramics at

Rigattieri (San Marco 3535/36, Calle dei Frari, tel: 041 2 77 12 23; www.rigat tieri-venice.it).

Where to…
Go Out

Piazza San Marco by night is the perfect place for a low-key evening out, when its great cafés compete with each other for musical attention and lights bathe its splendid buildings.

For serious culture, the winter season is the time to hear opera in the stunning setting of the **Teatro La Fenice** (San Marco 1965, Campo San Fantin, tel: 041 78 65 11, www.teatrolafenice.it, ➤ 42), while summer visitors could catch a performance in the verdant open-air setting of the **Teatro Verde** on San Giorgio Maggiore (tel: 041 5 28 99 00, www.cini.it).

Both the **Scuola Grande di San Teodoro** (San Marco 4810, Salizada San Teodoro, tel: 041 5 21 02 94; www.scuolagrandesanteodoro.it) and the **Ex-Chiesa di San Vidal** (San Marco 2862/B, Campo San Vidal, tel: 041 2 77 05 61, www. interpreteveneziani.com) have regular concerts of 18th-century Venetian orchestral music, sometimes performed by players in contemporary costume. The **Fenice**, **San Teodoro** and **San Vidal** can be booked online.

Jazz and modern music fans can enjoy good music with a drink at **Bàcaro Jazz** (San Marco 5546, Salizada del Fontego dei Tedeschi, tel: 041 5 28 52 49; www.bacaro jazz.com), or pop into **Torino@Notte** (San Marco 459, Campo San Luca, tel: 041 5 22 39 14) for a cold beer while listening to a selection of jazz and Latin American rhythms.

Insider Tip

Castello

Little Treats

Contemporary Art from around the World

The **Gervasuti Foundation's Artisans' Workshops** are some of the most exciting spaces for video installations and contemporary art around. (Via Garibaldi, Fontamenta Sant'Ana, Castello 995, gervasutifoundation.com).

Coffee and Art in Leafy Surroundings

Had enough of city life? This Art Deco glasshouse from 1894 is perfect for a **break in leafy surroundings** (Viale Giuseppe Garibaldi, Castello 1254, tel: 041 2 96 03 60, serradeigiardini.org).

Fantàsia

Italy's first gastronomic social project is also one of the **best Cichetterie in the city** (Castello 391, Localita Bragora, tel: 041 5 22 80 38).

Getting Your Bearings

Castello, stretching from San Marco and Cannaregio in the west to the separate islands of San Pietro and Sant'Elena in the east, is the largest *sestiere* (ward) of the city. Its name comes from the early *castello* (fortress) that once stood on San Pietro, the island that was the religious centre of the city until 1807, when San Marco replaced San Pietro as Venice's cathedral. Castello was the industrial heart of the Republic, where warships and merchant vessels rolled off the production lines at the great shipyards of the Arsenale. Today, it's an area of huge variety, packed with fine monuments, historic churches and museums, its remoter corners giving a true taste of everyday Venetian life.

The buzzing Riva degli Schiavoni, packed with visitors and lined with souvenir stalls, marks the start of Castello's long southern waterfront, which you can follow all the way to the quiet green spaces that front Sant'Elena. Towards this eastern section you'll find the Arsenale, still a military zone, its western side hedged by bustling narrow alleys, its eastern side opening onto the wonderfully vibrant working-class streets around the Via Giuseppe Garibaldi, one of Venice's most genuine areas. North of the Riva, narrow streets lead over bridges and through atmospheric *campi* (squares) via the great church of Santi Giovanni e Paolo to the Fondamenta Nuove, with its

views of the northern lagoon. Castello's museums and its other churches are linked with its history, and traditional and highly skilled artisans and craftspeople still have their businesses here, making exploring the area serendipitous indeed. In the evenings, there are fine restaurants to sample, while the Riva offers some of the best of the city's after-dark panoramas.

Guarding the Arsenale

**Part of the grand entrance
to the Arsenale**

Darsena
Grande

㉔ **Arsenale**

**San Giovanni
in Bràgora**

CASTELLO

San Pietro
di Castello

Isola di
San Pietro

**Museo
Storico Navale**
㉕

Arsenale

Via Giuseppe Garibaldi

Riva dei Sette Martiri

Canale di San Marco

Biennale
Internazionale
d'Arte

Giardini

㉖ **Giardini
Pubblici**

Darsena
di
Sant' Elena

Isola di
Sant' Elena

**QUARTIERE
SANT' ELENA**

Sant'
Elena

S. Elena

0   200 m
0   200 yards

Castello

The Perfect Day

If you're not quite sure where to begin your travels, this itinerary recommends a practical and enjoyable day out in Castello, taking in some of the best places to see. For more information see the main entries (➤ 82–91).

🕘 9:00am
Start your day with a walk along the broad sweep of the ㉔**Riva degli Schiavoni** (ill. above, ➤ 84), with its wonderful views over St Mark's Basin. Early morning, before the crowds arrive, is the best time for photographing the famous view of the Bridge of Sighs (➤ 85).

🕙 10:00am
Head north from the Riva through Campo Bandiera e Moro, with its church of ㉓**San Giovanni in Bràgora** (➤ 88), to admire the jewel-like Carpaccio paintings in the ㉑**Scuola di San Giorgio degli Schiavoni** (➤ 86).

🕚 11:15am
Cut back to the Riva and walk eastwards to the Via Giuseppe Garibaldi, left, a wide 19th-century street, which is the heart of Castello for locals. Look out for the statue of the eponymous hero at the top of the Viale Garibaldi, halfway down, before admiring the market stalls and vegetable barge moored at the far end.

🕛 12:00 noon
Beat the crowds of locals to lunch at the Trattoria dai Tosi (Castello 738, Secco Marina, tel: 041 5 23 71 02; www.trattoriadaitosi.com), a pizzeria-restaurant in this working-class area.

⏰ 1:30pm

Cut through to the **26 Giardini Pubblici** (ill. above, ➤ 90) for a quiet moment in this green oasis. Created by Napoleon, part of the gardens is the scene of Venice's renowned Biennale Internazionale d'Arte, a biennial exhibition of international contemporary art staged in odd-numbered years.

⏰ 2:30pm

Catch the *vaporetto* at the Giardini stop. This takes you round the eastern end of the Castello *sestiere* and past the islands of Sant'Elena and San Pietro, a district well worth exploring. Leave the boat at Ospedale Civile and walk south.

⏰ 3:30pm

Spend some time in the Dominican church of ⭐**Santi Giovanni e Paolo** (➤ 82), a huge structure which is the burial place of 25 Doges and contains some compelling monuments to Venetian heroes. The *campo* outside, with Verrocchio's equestrian statue of the mercenary Colleoni (➤ 82), is a great place to recover from all this culture with a drink.

⏰ 5:00pm

Take your time wandering back through Campo Santa Maria Formosa, **27 Campo San Zaccaria** (➤ 90) and **29 San Giorgio dei Greci** (➤ 91). It's easy to get lost in the surrounding maze of streets – one of the great pleasures of Venice.

⏰ 8:00pm

Treat yourself and splash out on one of the best fish dinners you're likely to find in Venice at the Corte Sconta (Castello 3886, Calle del Pestrin, tel: 041 5 22 70 24).

Castello

⭐ Santi Giovanni e Paolo

By the 13th century, it was too cramped in San Marco and the Rialto to build large churches for religious orders. Doge Jacopo Tiepolo therefore gave the Dominicans land to the north of the city. Called "San Zanipolo" by locals ("Zanipolo" for short), Santi Giovani e Paolo is, along with the Frari (► 122), one of the largest Gothic churches in the lagoon city today.

Alongside the adjoining Scuola Grande di San Marco (which still belongs to the hospital) and the Colleoni equestrian statue on the square outside, the imposing brick church forms part of an outstanding ensemble of Gothic and Renaissance architecture. Its façade reflects the Dominican ideal of poverty (the gable's stone decorations were a later addition), a fact that explains the building's lack of a bell tower. The church took 200 years to complete, most likely due to financing issues: the nave was finished in 1369, but the choir and dome were only completed in 1450. The marble portal is the work of Bartolomeo Bon (1460); the pillars that frame it originally belonged to an earlier church on Torcello.

Measuring in at 101.5m (333ft) long and 35m (115ft) high, Zanipolo impresses thanks to its sheer size alone. The triple-naved interior, subdivided by tall columns, is more boldly proportioned than that in the Frari. The lack of a choir screen allows clear views into the light-filled apse. The church is also known as the "Pantheon of Venice", as 27 Doges and many noble families are spending eternity here. The style of the grave monuments created for them by significant artists reflects the development of sculpture from the late Gothic to the Baroque via the High Renaissance.

Limpid light fills the vast interior of Santi Giovanni e Paolo

Colleoni Monument

The Colleoni monument on the square outside was designed from 1481 to 1488 by Florentine sculptor Andrea del Verrocchio, and cast by Alessandro Leopardi in 1496. In a new departure for the era, both horse and rider are shown shown in motion. statue bears little resemblance to the military commander Bartolomeo Colleoni himself (1400–75),

A noble rider with his trusty steed: Andrea Verrochio's equestrian statue of Bartolomeo Colleoni instead representing an ideal of a proud, powerful Condottiere. From 1448, Colleoni led campaigns on the mainland, allowing him to amass a vast fortune. He later bequeathed his wealth to the state under the condition that a monument be dedicated to him "in front of San Marco". His statue was actually put up next to the monastery of San Marco, however – he hadn't stated that it had to stand by the "church" of San Marco, after all…

Scuola Grande di San Marco

The Scuola right next to the church of Zanipolo was home to the rich confraternity of goldsmiths and silk merchants. It serves as the main entrance to the state hospital today. The lower part of its beautiful Renaissance façade was begun by Pietro Lombardo in 1490; his son Tullio created the reliefs and carved the two lions. Mauro Coducci completed the upper section around 1500.

TAKING A BREAK

There are plenty of bars on Campo Santi Giovanni e Paolo.

🕂 203 D2 ✉ Campo Santi Giovanni e Paolo ☎ 041 5 23 59 13;
www.basilicasantigiovanniepaolo.it 🕐 Mon–Sat 9–7, Sun noon–6
🚤 41, 42, 51, 52, 13, Fondamente Nuove; 41, 42, 51, 52, Ospedale 🎫 €2.50

INSIDER INFO

- Choose a **bright day** to visit, as the interior can be gloomy.
- Look for the **Marcantonio Bragadin monument**. In 1571, this hero was forced to surrender to the Turks at Famagusta. They cut off his ears, then flayed him alive, parading his straw-stuffed skin through the streets before taking it to Constantinople. It was eventually returned to Venice, and lies today in the urn on his monument.
- **You should definitely also take a look at the tombs of** Pietro Mocenigo, Morosini, Vendramin, and Nicolò Marcello, *St Vincent Ferrer* by Giovanni Bellini, the ceiling paintings by Veronese in the Cappella del Rosario and *St Antonius Pierozzi Giving Alms to the Poor* by Lorenzo Lotto.

⑳ Riva degli Schiavoni

The wide stretch of the Riva degli Schiavoni runs along the waterfront from the Ponte della Paglia (Palazzo Ducale) almost right down to the Arsenale. Ships belonging to Dalmatian merchants once landed where small passenger boats dock and hawkers peddle their wares today. The attractive promenade changes its name as it travels east-wards, becoming the Riva di Ca' di Dio, the Riva San Biagio and the Riva dei Sette Martiri.

Venetians and visitors alike throng Riva degli Schiavoni. The broad quayside is a transport hub where you can catch a *vaporetti*, buy a superlatively tacky souvenir or an overpriced ice-cream from one of the stalls, or simply marvel at one of the finest views in the city.

The Riva got its name from the Slavs, synonymous with slaves, who were landed here in the early days of the Republic. Until 1780, it was a narrow working water-front, busy – as it still is – with boats and gondolas. It was then widened and paved with Istrian stone, and quickly became Venice's favourite promenade.

Start at the shallow-stepped **Ponte della Paglia (Straw Bridge)**, so-called because primitive boats woven from

VIVALDI AND VENETIAN MUSIC

Antonio Vivaldi wasn't merely the most significant composer to come out of Venice – he also went down in the annals of European musical history by developing the concerto form. Reported to have been born during an earthquake in 1678 and given an emergency baptism, Vivaldi, a sickly lad, was destined for the priesthood, and became known as *il prete rosso*, the red priest – a name recalling both his red hair and his red frock coat. In 1703, he was appointed violin teacher at the Ospedale della Pietà, a charitable institution for orphaned and illegitimate girls. He wrote a string of musical pieces for the girls, which were performed during church services, thus reaching a wide audience. This made Vivaldi well-known, a status that allowed him to dedicate himself entirely to composing from that period on. As well as his 500 or so concertos (including 241 for solo violin alone) which stand out thanks to their nuanced instrumentation, their effective and affecting melodic construction, and their lively sense of rhythm, Vivaldi also penned over 90 sonatas, three oratorios and 46 operas, 21 of which still exist today. As his music began to lose popularity in his home city, Vivaldi went to seek his fortune in Vienna from 1740, where he hoped to gain the support of Holy Roman Emperor Charles VI. Charles died that October, however, meaning that Vivaldi could no longer make an entrance into the Viennese music scene. He died a year after arriving in the city on the Danube. His works have nevertheless stood the test of time: Vivaldi's style influenced many composers, including Johann Sebastian Bach, who transposed many of his violin works for the organ and harpsichord. The composer's *Four Seasons* is omnipresent in his home city today, and can be heard played at many concerts (www.chiesavivaldi.it).

INSIDER INFO

- Unless you enjoy heaving crowds of day-trippers, save your walk along the Riva for **early or late** in the day.
- If you're catching a *vaporetto* from the Riva, **check numbers and directions** carefully – several lines leave from here and stops are always crowded and busy.

straw once docked here. From here, there's a fabulous view of the **Ponte dei Sospiri (Bridge of Sighs)**, built in 1602 to link the Doge's Palace with the New Prisons (➤ 63).

Cross two more bridges and you'll come to the church of **Santa Maria della Visitazione**, better known as **La Pietà** or "Vivaldi's church". The famous composer initially worked as a violin teacher in the neighbouring Ospedale della Pietà (➤ panel opposite). The present building went up after the composer's death and wasn't finished until 1760. The facade was finally completed in 1906. As much a concert hall as a church, it's one of the major venues for Venice's series of baroque concerts. It's been closed for restoration since 2007.

TAKING A BREAK

Move away from the overpriced bars on the Riva and head for **Alla Rivetta**, an old-fashioned *trattoria* popular with locals (Castello 4625, Ponte San Provolo, tel: 041 5 28 73 02).

🔶 207 D4–F4

Stormy skies above the Riva degli Schiavoni

Santa Maria della Visitazione (La Pietà)
✉ Riva degli Schiavoni ☎ 041 5 22 21 71, www.pietavenezia.org
🕐 Tue–Fri 10:15–noon, 3–5, Sat, Sun 10:15–1, 2–5 🎟 Free;
Piccolo Museo Antonio Vivaldi (by arrangement only): €3

㉑ Scuola di San Giorgio degli Schiavoni

Hidden away next to a bridge over a side canal, the Scuola's building contains one of the most beautiful works by Renaissance painter Vittore Carpaccio (*c*1465–1525/26).

The *schiavoni* were the Slav inhabitants of Venice, whose homeland (modern Croatia) had become part of the Republic's possessions in 1420. There had been Slavs in the city from the earliest times, and as their community flourished they approached the State for permission to found their own confraternity, the only one that was to be based on ethnic origin. The Scuola was established in 1451 and a meeting hall built beside the Slav church of San Giovanni in Malta. In 1502, the Scuola commissioned Vittore Carpaccio (➤ 26) to decorate the building with scenes from the lives of the Dalmatian patron saints: St George, St Tryphon and St Jerome.

Scenes of the Patron Saints

Three panels are devoted to **St George**. Starting from the left wall, the first shows the saint on his charger, making short work of the dragon in a landscape scattered with the dismembered remains of the monster's victims. At the side, the princess looks on in rapture. Next we see the blond hero finishing off the beast in the town square before going on to baptise the princess's parents into the Christian faith. *The Miracle of St Tryphon* follows, behind the altar, where we see this saint liberating another princess from the clutches of the devil, alluringly disguised as a less than terrifying basilisk. Two paintings with no Slav links follow: *The Calling of St Matthew* and *Christ on the Mount of Olives*.

The right wall of the hall is devoted to scenes from the life of **St Jerome**, an early Christian father and compiler of the Latin version of the Bible. We first see Jerome leading a lion to his monastery while monks flee in panic all around; they had been terrorised by the beast, but the saint realized the problem was a thorn in the lion's paw. This he removed, and the lion became his loyal and constant companion. You can see the grieving animal in the background

The elegant Renaissance façade of the Scuola di San Giorgio degli Schiavoni

Scuola di San Giorgio degli Schiavoni

of the next panel, which shows the death of the saint. The final picture shows St Augustine in his study at the moment a vision tells him of the death of St Jerome; he sits surrounded by the accoutrements of Renaissance culture and scholarship, with his little white dog as a companion.

The scenes from the lives of the confraternity's three Patron Saints, created between 1502 and 1508, represent the most significant work created by Carpaccio, a Renaissance painter who managed successfully to combine detailed realism with a sense of decorative flair.

TAKING A BREAK

St George and the Dragon by Vittore Carpaccio (detail)

Have a traditional Venetian snack at **Alle Alpi da Dante** (Castello 2877, Corte Nuova, tel: 041 5 28 51 63), just north of here.

➕ 207 E5 ✉ Castello 3259/A, Calle dei Furlani
☎ 041 5 22 88 28 ⏰ Mon 2:45–6, Tue–Sat 9:15–1, 2:45–6, Sun 9:15–1
🚢 1, 2, 41, 42, 51, 52, San Zaccaria 💶 €6

THE SIGNIFICANCE OF THE VENETIAN SCUOLE

The confraternities, known as *scuole*, played an important role in the social structure and stability of the aristocratic Republic. These guilds, which gathered together the predominantly male members of various trades, began to form in the 12th century. They chose representatives, wrote corporate statutes, and fulfilled a number of social tasks, such as founding and maintaining hospitals and hostels for the poor. A costly club culture developed in the *scuole*, with members paying dues and providing men to march in the most important processions. An example of the *scuole's* significance can be seen in the ability of the Scuola Grande di San Rocco (➤ 124), to commission one of the most impressive painting cycles in the world. Even such small Scuole as the Scuola di San Giorgio degli Schiavoni are also surprisingly well decorated. Marco Polo and many great artists belonged to the *scuole*. The Republic's demise also marked their (temporary) end: Napoleon banned the *scuole*, just as he had outlawed the cloisters. They did rise again, however – the Scuola Grande di San Rocco reformed as early as 1797, with the others following in the early 1820s.

At Your Leisure

The Gothic façade of the magnificent
19th-century Hotel Danieli

22 Hotel Danieli

Thousands of tourists wander past
the Hotel Danieli (➤42); few are
lucky enough to stay in this oasis of
sybaritic living, where the rooms are
furnished with antiques, paved in
marble and hung with Fortuny fabrics. Founded in the 19th century,
the hotel originally occupied the
beautiful 14th-century Gothic
Palazzo Dandolo. Some say it's
named after this venerable Venetian
family; others accept that it's actually named after the hotel's founder
Giuseppe dal Niel, who attracted
some of the biggest names of the
19th century here. Dickens, Proust,
George Sand, Balzac and Wagner
were all among its habitués, along
with many of Europe's crowned
heads and leading politicians. Its
far-from-attractive annexe went up
in 1948, the first stone building on
this site since the 12th century.

➕ 207 D4 ✉ Castello 4196, Riva degli Schiavoni
☎ 041 5 22 64 80; danieli.hotelinvenice.com
🚋 1, 2, 41, 42, 51, 52, San Zaccaria

23 San Giovanni in Bràgora

A peaceful *campo* is home to San
Giovanni in Bràgora, a simple Gothic
building dating from 1475, on the
site of an earlier church. It's best
known as the baptismal church
of the composer Antonio Vivaldi
(➤84); you can still see his name
in the register. There are some fine
pictures by Alvise and Bartolomeo
Vivarini, and two by Cima da
Conegliano (*c*1460–1508) – his
lovely *Baptism of Christ*, with its
details of the landscape around
the artist's home town, hangs over
the high altar.

➕ 207 E4 ✉ Campo Bandiera e Moro
☎ 041 5 20 59 06; www.sgbattistainbragora.it
🕐 Mon–Sat 9–11, 3:30–5:30 Sun 9–11, 3:30–5
🚋 1, 41, 42, Arsenale ✋ Free

24 Arsenale

The Arsenale was Venice's industrial
powerhouse, where its galleys were
constructed and equipped by one
of the world's first production lines.
Ship-building started here in the
12th century; the yards soon became known as the Arsenale, from
the Arabic *Dar Sina'a*, the place of

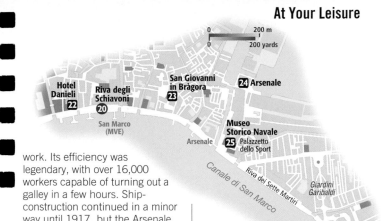

work. Its efficiency was legendary, with over 16,000 workers capable of turning out a galley in a few hours. Ship-construction continued in a minor way until 1917, but the Arsenale remains naval property, and strictly off-limits, though the vast Corderia (ropeworks) is used as an exhibition space during the Biennale. Venice's first Renaissance building, the 35m-(114.8ft)-high Porta Nuova, was designed as a crane

A glittering model of a ceremonial barge

tower by Gambello in 1460. It was converted into a culture and exhibition centre in 2011 as part of the EU's "Second Chance" project. Four lions stand sentry beside the gate, two of them looted from

Athens in 1687. Look for the markings on the sides of the larger beast: these are runic inscriptions gouged out by Norse Byzantine mercenaries in the 11th century. The **Ca' di Dio (House of God)** by the *arsenale pontile* (departure wharf) on the Riva gets its name from its function as a hostel for pilgrims embarking to the Holy Land in the Middle Ages.

✚ 208 A4 ✉ Campo dell'Arsenale
🎫 Corderia: during the Biennale for exhibitions 🚏 1, 41, 42, Arsenale
💰 Corderia: depends on exhibition

🖼 Museo Storico Navale

There's no better place to grasp the relationship between Venice and the sea than this museum of naval history, a four-storey treasure trove of things nautical, from model boats and naval instruments to uniforms, cannons and torpedoes. The museum originated in 1815, when the scale ship-building models used in the Arsenale were joined by

Castello

remnants of the Venetian navy and other ephemera. The collection moved to its present home in 1958. You'd need hours to examine everything, but look out for the gilded Bucintoro, a model of the Doge's ceremonial barge, used in his Ascension Day marriage to the sea; and an entire roomful of gondolas, including the last privately owned one in Venice, used by Peggy Guggenheim (➤ 140).

🕇 208 A3 🖂 Castello 2148, Campo San Biagio 🕿 041 5 20 02 76 🕓 Daily 10–6 🚤 1, 41, 42, Arsenale 🎟 €1.55

25 🚺 Giardini Pubblici

Don't judge the Giardini Pubblici, Venice's green lung, by the same standards you'd apply to the verdant, flower-filled parks of other cities. The gardens were created by Napoleon, who ordered an area of marsh to be drained and several churches demolished in order to provide the city with a green space. Much of the area is occupied by the pavilions of the Biennale, but the remaining grass is scattered with benches and shaded by trees, making it a splendid picnic spot with some of the best views in Venice.

🕇 208 C2 🖂 Giardini Pubblici 🚤 1, 2, 41, 42, 51, 52, Giardini 🎟 Free

26 Museo Diocesano d'Arte Sacra

The eclectic collection housed in the Museo Diocesano d'Arte Sacra (Diocesan Museum of Religious Art) is made up of artworks that need a temporary home – pieces that are perhaps awaiting restoration, collections from deconsecrated churches, stolen treasures that have been retrieved. It makes for an ever-changing and pleasantly interesting display of sculpture, silverware and other work, with changing exhibitions in the upstairs gallery. The museum's main draw is its superb 14th-century Romanesque cloister, once the focal point of the Benedictine monastery of

Giovanni Bellini's *Madonna and Child with Saints* in the church of San Zaccaria

Sant'Apollonia, and the only cloister of this period in the city.

🕇 207 D4 🖂 Castello 4312, Ponte della Canonica 🕿 041 5 22 91 66 🕓 Mon–Sat 10–4 🚤 1, 2, 41, 42, 51, 52, San Zaccaria 🎟 Free

27 San Zaccaria

Only a few steps from the bustling Riva, you'll find the lovely church of San Zaccaria, a beguiling and very Venetian blend of Gothic and Renaissance architecture. Founded in the ninth century to house the body of St Zacharias, father of John the Baptist (he's still here, under the second altar on the right), it was rebuilt several times. The final reconstruction was started in 1440, and continued for decades – years that saw huge stylistic changes, resulting in a Gothic interior and predominantly Renaissance façade. Scarcely an inch of wall space remains uncovered by paintings, mainly from the 17th and 18th centuries. Earlier in date is the main treasure, Giovanni Bellini's magnificently serene *Madonna and Child with Saints* (1505), which is on the second altar on the left. The right aisle gives access to the chapels of St Athanasius and St Tarasius, where there's an early Tintoretto and three beautiful, iconic 15th-century altarpieces by Antonio Vivarini (1415–76)

and Giovanni d'Alemagna. Eight early Doges are buried in San Zaccaria's permanently waterlogged crypt, a bizarre 10th- to 11th-century construction that was part of the first church on this site. If you want confirmation that Venice has sunk, look no farther. The Benedictine convent attached to the church of **San Zaccaria** was a favourite dumping ground for the surplus daughters of the Venetian nobility – it saved the expense of a dowry. Religious life did little to sanctify these ladies' lifestyles, and the nuns of San Zaccaria were renowned for their licentious behaviour and glittering salons held in the convent parlour. You can get a glimpse of convent life in Guardi's painting in the Ca' Rezzonico (▶142).

➕ 207 D4 ✉ Campo San Zaccaria
☎ 041 5 22 12 57
🕐 Mon–Sat 10–noon, 4–6; Sun 11–noon, 4–6
🚤 1, 2, 41, 42, 51, 52, San Zaccaria 🖐 €3

28 San Giorgio dei Greci

Greeks made their home in Venice from the 11th century, their numbers rising after the fall of Constantinople to the Turks in 1453. They were scholars, publishers, writers and merchants, and in 1526 were given permission to build their own church and college. San Giorgio degli Greci is the result, a canalside church whose tilting campanile is a Venetian landmark. This tree-shaded building contains a *matroneo* (women's gallery) and iconostasis (rood screen), elements essential to Orthodox churches. Icons adorn the incense-laden interior; many by Michael Damaskinos, a fellow Cretan and contemporary of El Greco.

To the left of the church are the **Hellenic Museum** and the **Institute of Byzantine Studies**, both housed in superb buildings by Baldassare Longhena (▶ 27).

➕ 207 E4 ✉ Fondamenta dei Greci
☎ 041 5 23 95 69 🕐 Wed–Mon 9–11, 2:30–4:30
🖐 Free 🚤 1, 2, 41, 42, 51, 52, San Zaccaria

The leaning tower of San Giorgio dei Greci

THE FLIGHT OF THE ELEPHANT

If you pass the church of **Sant' Antonin**, near the Scuola di San Giorgio degli Schiavoni, pause to reflect that this is the only church in Venice where an elephant has been shot. It escaped from a circus on the Riva in 1819 and trustingly took refuge in the church, where soldiers from the Arsenale pursued it and killed it.

Castello

Where to...
Eat and Drink

Prices
Expect to pay per person for a meal, excluding drinks.
€ under €35   €€ €35–€55   €€€ over €55

BÀCARI, BARS AND GELATERIE

Al Giardinetto €€
The Bastianelli family are justly proud of their lovely old restaurant, where classic Venetian dishes are beautifully prepared using seasonal and fresh ingredients. Sample favourites such as *sarde in saor* (sweet and sour sardines), *granseola* (spider crab), plump *canestrelli* (scallops) and exquisite mixed seafood antipasti dressed with lemon and celery, before moving on to risotto or pasta and grilled fish or meat. The vine-hung courtyard for summer eating is a real bonus.
✚ 207 D5 ✉ Castello 4928, Ruga Giaffo
☎ 041 5 28 53 32, www.algiardinetto.it
◉ Fri–Wed 12:30–3, 7:30–10 ▣ San Zaccaria

Osteria dal Pampo €/€€
Busy every day with locals enjoying straightforward pasta *primi* and meat and fish *secondi* dishes. Ask what's good that day and wash it down with some good red *sfuso* (cask) wine. In summer, tables spill out on the pavement.
✚ 208 off C1 ✉ Castello 24 ,
Calle Generale Chinotto ☎ 041 5 20 84 19
◉ Fri–Wed 12–2.30, 7:30–9 ▣ Sant'Elena

Enoteca Mascareta €
A popular wine bar belonging to Mascaròn (No 5525 at the end of the street), one of the best *osterie* in Venice. Their wine is drunk standing up accompanied with tasty cheeses and salami from various Italian regions or *crostini* with *lardo* and radicchio (toasted bread with chicory and bacon).

Venetians love coming here to visit Mauro, the owner, and set about quaffing a pre-dinner aperitif.
✚ 207 D5 ✉ Castello 5183, Calle Lunga Santa Maria Formosa ☎ 041 5 23 07 44 ◉ Mon–Sat 6pm–1am. Closed Dec 24–Jan 15 ▣ Rialto

OSTERIE, TRATTORIE AND RISTORANTI

Al Covo €€/€€€
This is one of Venice's most successful restaurants. In a series of little rooms that are unstuffy yet comfortable – with tables outside in fine weather – Al Covo presents a light, fresh rendition of the area's traditional seafood dishes. The menu includes *baccalà mantecato* (creamed salt cod) with cloud-soft white polenta, and the tempura-like *fritto misto* of deep-fried lagoon fish, polenta and vegetables. Pastas are home-made, as are the American-style desserts. The wine list features selections from the Veneto, Friuli and Trentino. There is a very economical three-course lunch option.
✚ 207 F4 ✉ Castello 3968, Campiello della Pescaria ☎ 041 5 22 38 12, www.ristorante alcovo.com ◉ Fri–Tue 12:45–2, 7:30–10 (kitchen). Closed 2 weeks in Aug, Dec 15–Jan 15 ▣ Arsenale

Alle Testiere €€/€€€
Alle Testiere belongs to the Venetian association of Buona Accoglienza restaurants (➤44). Seating 25, its ever-changing menu (unwritten) celebrates the clear, fresh flavours of the Mediterranean's fish and shellfish. These include *canestrelli* (scallops), *cozze* (mussels), *coda di*

92

rospo (monkfish), *granseola* (spider crab) and *moeche* (soft-shell crabs). All are delicately accented with fresh herbs, fruity olive oil and vegetables. Excellent wine list.

➕ 206 C5 ✉ Castello 5801, Calle del Mondo Nuovo ☎ 041 5 22 72 20; www.venezia ristorante.it ⏰ Tue–Sat 12–2:30, 7–10.30. Closed end July to mid-Aug, New Year 🚢 Rialto

Antica Trattoria Bandierette €€
This lovely, old-fashioned eaterie, tucked away near Santi Giovanni e Paolo has a welcoming ambiance that marries well with the carefully cooked and sourced menu. You'll find plenty of choice among the classic dishes, such as *sarde in saor* (sweet-and-sour marinated sardines), *spaghetti alle vongole* (pasta with clams), *fritto misto* (mixed fried fish) and grilled fish. They also serve meat dishes.

➕ 207 D5 ✉ Castello 6671, Barbaria delle Tolle ☎ 041 5 22 01 69 ⏰ Mon 12:30–3, Wed–Sun 12:30–3, 7:30–10 🚢 Fondamente Nove

Corte Sconta €€€
Nothing could be better on a summer's day than to eat a long, leisurely lunch in the shady garden off this wonderful, relaxed restaurant. Corte Sconta is justly famous for its *antipasti*: a slow, steady procession of little dishes, almost all fish-based, cooked with flair and care. Sample crabs and clams, fresh anchovies and miniscule shrimp, all cooked in pure, Venetian style. Pastas and gnocchi are home-made, light and flavourful; fish are fried, grilled or poached. A fine wine list enhances them all. Ask about the *degustazione*, or tasting menu.

➕ 207 F4 ✉ Castello 3886, Calle del Pestrin ☎ 041 5 22 70 24 ⏰ Tue–Sat 12:30–2, 7:15–9:30. Closed 7 Jan–7 Feb, mid-July to mid-Aug 🚢 Arsenale

Osteria Ale Do Marie €/€€
It may attract foreign visitors, but this remains a true Venetian neighbourhood restaurant, where the food is fresh, simple and seasonal. Fish

is bought daily and the changing menu reflects this – though classics such as *sarde in saor* (sweet and sour marinated sardines) and *spaghetti alle vongole* (pasta with clams) are staples. Good value tourist menu at lunchtime.

➕ 207 F5 ✉ Castello 3129, Calle de l'Olio ☎ 041 2 96 04 24 ⏰ Tue–Sun 12:30–3, 7:30–10 🚢 Celestia

Osteria Oliva Nera €€€
This laid-back restaurant, with its understated décor, is a perfect example of the new breed of Venetian eateries. Traditional dishes are given a confident and contemporary twist, and specialities include scallops cooked with wild *porcini*, lamb slow-braised with thyme, and desserts featuring copious amounts of mascarpone and *panna* (cream). Friendly and professional staff.

Insider Tip

➕ 207 E4 ✉ Castello 3417/18, Calle della Madonna ☎ 041 5 22 21 70, www.osteria-olivanera.com ⏰ Fri–Tue 12–2:30, 6:30–10 🚢 San Zaccaria

Where to...
Shop

Castello combines the bustling shops around San Lio, which provide everyday necessities for the locals, with quirkier artisan workshops and gift emporia, some of which are found in the eastern part of the sestiere. Thread your way gradually east from the Rialto vaporetto stop, or disembark at the Arsenale and head north and west.

Salizada San Lio is one of Castello's main shopping streets, and here you'll find **Ratti** (Castello 5825, tel: 041 2 40 46 00), Venice's top hardware and kitchen supply store, a great place to go for china and kitchenware of all descriptions.

Castello

Up the street from here at **Silvia** (Castello 5540, tel: 041 5 23 85 68) there's a great range of leather goods and shoes at keen prices, along with wools and haberdashery trimmings galore at **Resmini Passamanerie** (Castello 5784, tel: 041 5 23 51 41). Calle della Banda, at the bottom of the *salizada*, is home to a branch of **Il Papiro** (Castello 5275, tel: 522 36 48), where you'll find a wonderful range of marble and stamped paper goods such as visitors' books, notebooks, picture frames and folders, all beautifully made in jewel-bright colours.

The works of Klimt, Kandinsky, Tiepolo and Carpaccio provide the source of inspiration for the traditionally handmade masks sold at **Papier Mâché** (Castello 5175, Calle Lunga Sta Maria Formosa tel: 041 5 22 99 95), which can be reached over the Campo Santa Maria Formosa. On the same street you'll also find the **Libreria Acqua Alta** (Castello 5176, Calle Lunga Sta Maria Formosa, tel: 041 2 96 08 41), specializing in Venice-themed titles, and **Al Campanil** (Castello 5184, Calle Lunga Sta Maria Formosa, tel: 041 5 23 57 34), which sells unusual, delicate and pretty glass jewellery.

To the south lies **Anticlea Antiquariato** (Castello 4719/A, Calle San Provolo), a tiny treasure trove of antique beads and textiles, where the owner will make up necklaces and earrings while you wait. South from here, **Paolo Rossi** (Castello 4685, Campo San Zaccaria) has some of the best Roman and antique glass reproductions in the city. **Arabesque Barbieri** (Castello 3403, Ponte dei Greci, tel: 041 5 22 81 77) lies to the east, an elegant and tempting store selling scarves, stoles and pashminas in beautiful fabrics and colours. Heading east along the Riva you'll come to the more down-to-earth delights of the area around Via Garibaldi, home to a morning market where the produce is fresh and prices are low.

Where to... Go Out

Castello has a choice of two atmospheric locations for a leisurely after-dinner stroll and a drink – the lovely campo of Santa Maria Formosa, which often hosts live concerts in summer, and the Riva degli Schiavoni, where a string of bars have tables overlooking the lagoon.

You can enjoy early evening performances of 18th-century music in a 17th-century setting at the **Fondazione Querini Stampalia** (Castello 5252, Campiello Querini Stampalia, tel: 041 2 72 14 11, www.querinistampalia.it). There's also the chance to hear baroque music at the church of **Santa Maria Formosa** (campo Santa Maria Formosa, tel: 041 98 42 52), where the **Vivaldi** players perform on Monday, Wednesday and Friday from January to August.

Venetian music of a different type is found at **Ristorante Giorgione** (Castello 1533, Via Garibaldi, tel: 041 5 22 87 27, www.ristorante giorgione.it), where Lucio Bisutto often performs folk music, while on the waterfront, **Melograno** (Castello 1643, Riva VII Martiri, tel: 041 2 41 41 96) hosts live jazz on Saturdays.

The hottest nightspot is **Club 947** (Castello 4337, Campo SS Filippo e Giacomo, tel: 041 5 22 92 93, www.947club.com), a dining-dance club with an international, and expensive, clientele, or relax at **L'Olandese Volante** (Castello 5658, Campo San Lio, tel: 041 5 28 93 49), a student pub with tables on the *campo* and a wide selection of beers.

Insider Tip

Cannaregio & San Michele

Little Treats

New Perspectives

Ziva Kraus' **photo gallery** in the Jewish Ghetto includes a photography school that also offers workshops (Ikona Venezia, Campo del Ghetto Nuovo, Cannaregio 2909, tel: 041 5 28 93 87, www.ikona venezia.com).

Santa Lucia

Santa Lucia was a born and bred Italian. She lies in a crystal coffin in the **Chiesa di San Geremia**, only leaving the Grand Canal church for a procession on the 13th of December.

Mountain View

Locals sometimes need a break from living a (quite literally) insular life. That's when they take a stroll along the **Fontamenta Sacca San Girolamo** and enjoy the beautiful views of the Dolomite mountains.

Cannaregio & San Michele

Getting Your Bearings

The Canale di Cannaregio was named for the reeds that once grew here (ital. *canna*) before settlers came to this former marshland. Until the railway link to the mainland was built in 1846, the Canale was the main entrance to Venice, cutting through from the northern lagoon to the upper sweep of the Grand Canal, Cannaregio's southern boundary. The sestiere ends to the west at Santa Lucia, the 20th-century railway station, and its eastern limits lie in one of the oldest quarters of the city, while, to the north, the fondamente (lagoonside streets) look out to the northern islands, the nearest of which is San Michele, home to the city's cemetery.

Cannaregio is redolent with history and sprinkled with fine palaces and churches. To the east, Santa Maria dei Miracoli, a little Renaissance jewel of a church, contrasts with Ca' d'Oro, one of the city's finest Gothic *palazzi*, which lies just off the wide shopping street of the Strada Nuova. Laid out in 1871 as a fast track from the Rialto to the

Canale delle Sacche

Sant' Alvise

Ex Ospedale Psichiatrico Umberto I

SACCA DI S. ALVISE

SACCA DI S. GIROLAMO

Canale Colombola

Fondamenta della Sensa
32

CANNAREGIO

Tre Archi

Campo Ghetto Nuovo

Ponte della Libertà

Guglie

Il Ghetto **10**

Rio Terrà S. Leonardo

San Geremia e Lucia

San Marcuola

Canal Grande

Stazione Venezia Santa Lucia

Ferrovia

Stazione Ferroviaria Merci

Ferrovia

Piazzale Roma

Piazzale Roma

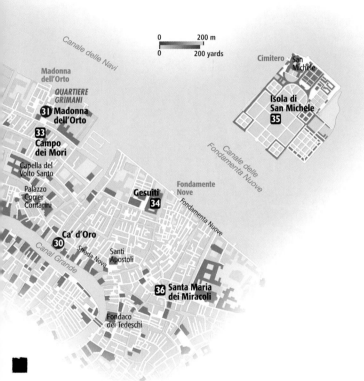

Left: Intricate stonework in Palazzo Giovanelli

station. North of here lies a series of wide parallel canals, linked by narrow streets lined with small shops, simple houses and busy workshops. This quiet and unpretentious area, with its lovely church of Madonna dell'Orto, has immense charm: only a ten-minute walk from the tacky souvenir stalls and immediately around the station, it's spiritually another world. On its edge lies the Ghetto, a former (cannonball) foundry (ital. *geto* = cast).

Perfect Days in...

The Perfect Day

If you're not quite sure where to begin your travels, this itinerary recommends a practical and enjoyable day exploring Cannaregio and San Michele, taking in some of the best places to see. For more information see the main entries (➤ 100–108).

🕘 9:00am
Arrive early by boat at the **30 Ca' d'Oro** (➤ 102), a museum whose art collections are seriously rivalled by the charms of the building itself – and don't miss the superb Grand Canal view from the upstairs loggias (ill. above).

🕙 10:30am
Walk up to the Strada Nuova, one of the main through-city routes, running from near the Rialto to the station. A huddle of narrow alleys was swept away when this wide shopping street was constructed in the 19th century.

🕚 11:00am
Time for a coffee on one of the wide *fondamente* overlooking the Canale di Cannaregio, Venice's only true canal aside from the Grand Canal. Then go through the alleyways to reach the Campo Ghetto Nuovo, set at the heart of the ⭐ **Ghetto** (➤ 100). Take a guided tour of the Ghetto area, one of the least visited, most fascinating and thought-provoking parts of Venice.

🕐 1:00pm

Head for lunch at Al Bacco (Cannaregio 3054, Fondamenta delle Cappuccine, tel: 041 71 74 93), an off-the-beaten-track *osteria*, with a pretty courtyard. They serve *pasta e fasoi* here, for example, a thick pasta soup made with Borlotti beans.

🕑 2:30pm

Digest your lunch as you wander along the **32 Fondamenta della Sensa** (➤ 106) and through the **33 Campo dei Mori** (➤ 106) to the Gothic church of **31 Madonna dell'Orto** (➤ 104), with its fabulous paintings by Tintoretto.

🕓 4:00pm

Board the *vaporetto* at Orto for the Fondamenta Nuove stop. If you have the strength to tackle another church, take in Santa Maria Assunta, known as the **34 Gesuiti** (right, ➤ 106), whose elaborate marble drapery is unique in Venice. From the Fondamenta Nuove, catch the boat for **35 San Michele** (➤ 107), the quiet cemetery island.

🕕 6:00pm

Back in the city, head southwest, keeping your eyes open among the many restaurants for one that takes your fancy for dinner. Fiaschetteria Toscana (Cannaregio 5719, Salizada San Giovanni Crisostomo, tel: 041 5 28 52 81, www.fiaschetteriatoscana.it) is a good bet, though to be sure of a table it's best to make a reservation in advance.

🕗 8:00pm

From mid-September to mid-June you could round off your day of culture and sightseeing with a visit to the **Casinò di Venezia** (➤ 112), wonderfully housed in a Renaissance *palazzo*.

⭐10 Il Ghetto

Although Shylock, Venice's most famous Jewish resident, was invented by William Shakespeare (*The Merchant of Venice*, 1596/97), the city's Ghetto really does exist. It's even the oldest ghetto in the world – all of the others across the the globe are named after this little island in Cannaregio.

From the 14th century, members of the Jewish community were only permitted to live in Venice for 15 years and to earn their livelihood through money-lending, second-hand trading and, later, as doctors and musicians. It was not until 1516 that they achieved the right to live permanently in the city – with many provisos.

Discrimination and Tolerance

The erstwhile iron foundry island was closed off from shortly after sunset till dawn by heavy gates across its access bridges. During these hours, no member of the Jewish community, except doctors visiting patients, could leave the Ghetto. By day they could move about freely, but had to wear a distinguishing badge. Their property rights were limited, and they were subjected to financial penalties. Despite this, they were more tolerated in Venice than elsewhere in Europe, and the Ghetto became the goal of Jewish people escaping persecution. Sephardic Jews from Spain and Portugal joined the Ashkenazim and Levantine Jews from the Ottoman Empire. Each wave of immigrants built its own synagogue; by 1575 there were five, two of which are still in use.

Overcrowding was a problem, even after the Jewish Venetians were allowed to spread outside the original Ghetto, Ghetto Nuovo (New Ghetto), to the Ghetto Vecchio (Old Ghetto). With limited space, buildings have as many as seven storeys. Generally, space could not be spared for the synagogues so they were incorporated into existing houses.

Only three or four families from Venice's 500-strong Jewish community still live in the oldest Ghetto in the world

Kosher baked goods in the Ghetto Vecchio's Panetteria Volpe bakery

After the Republic's fall in 1797, the Ghetto closed and Jewish Venetians gained citizenship in 1866. In 1943, 200 Jewish Venetians were deported and perished in the death camps. The population today is around 500, but it remains a spiritual, social and cultural centre for the community and is visited by thousands of Jewish people from all over the world.

Campo del Ghetto Nuovo

The **Campo del Ghetto Nuovo** is the heart of the Ghetto, a tranquil and spacious square approached by three bridges and enclosed by tall and narrow buildings. The **Museo Ebraico (Jewish Community Museum)** is here, along with a library, bookshop, Jewish bakery, nursery school and speciality shops. On a wall in one corner, you can see the series of reliefs which commemorate the Holocaust.

TAKING A BREAK

Grab a snack in the museum's kosher snack bar or head for Venice's only kosher restaurant, **Gam-Gam** (▶110).

✚ 201 D4

Museo Ebraico
✚ 182 B4 ✉ Cannaregio 2902b, Campo del Ghetto Nuovo
☎ 041 71 53 59; www.museoebraico.it 🕙 June–Sep 10–7; Oct–May 10–5:30
🚐 1, 2, San Marcuola; 41, 42, 51, 52, Guglie
🎫 Museum: €10; Guided tours to the synagogues: €10

INSIDER INFO

■ It's well worth taking the **guided tour** of the museum and synagogues – you'll see things you might otherwise miss. Make sure you arrive in good time if you want to take one of hourly tours – they can fill up pretty quickly.

■ You can buy such traditional Jewish delicacies as *empade* (almond pastries) and *pane azzimo* (unleavened bread) from the **Volpe Bakery** in Venice's Ghetto (Panificio Volpe, Calle del Ghetto Vecchio 1143, tel: 041 71 51 78).

■ The **old Jewish cemetery**, established in 1386, can still be seen near the church of San Nicolò (▶161) on the Lido.

Insider Tip

㉚ Ca' d'Oro

The Grand Canal is lined with beautiful buildings, but one that really catches the eye is the elaborate façade of the Ca' d'Oro (The House of Gold), one of Venice's finest and most flamboyant examples of a Gothic *palazzo*, and now housing the Galleria Franchetti. The interior has undergone numerous remodellings but still manages to convey some idea of its heyday as a great town house.

In 1420, the merchant patrician Marino Contarini commissioned a grand *palazzo*, all intricate Gothic tracery, windows, pinnacles and marble, whose design was very much influenced by the Doge's Palace. It was built between 1421 and 1431, when its **façade** was brilliantly decorated with the most expensive pigments available: vermilion, ultramarine and gold leaf – hence the name. Decline soon set in; it changed hands repeatedly and became semi-derelict. The worst moment came in 1847, when the Russian prince Troubetskoy purchased it as a gift for his ballerina mistress Maria Taglioni. His restorations included ripping out the open staircase, selling the original wellhead and tearing off the marble façade. All this took place under the horrified gaze of the art critic John Ruskin (1819–1900), who tried to sketch it before it was too late. Fortunately, salvation came at the end of the 19th century when Baron Franchetti, a 19th-century art enthusiast and collector, bought the *palazzo* and revitalized it, restoring the staircase and well, and filling it with his collections of paintings, sculptures and coins. He donated the building and its treasures to the state in 1916.

DID YOU KNOW?

Sebastian, the Patron Saint of plague victims, was a favourite subject for Renaissance painters. That's because the way he was martyred – by being pierced with arrows – gave them the chance to portray an almost nude figure and display their mastery of anatomical painting.

Visiting

The **ground floor**, with its main door opening on to the water, gives one of the few chances to understand how Gothic Grand Canal palaces functioned. Most of this floor was originally devoted to warehouse space, with a tiny garden, a courtyard with a well and an exterior staircase to the upper floors, where business was conducted and the family lived.

The Collection

A light and airy modern **art gallery** occupies the first and second floors; both floors have loggias overlooking the Grand Canal. The highlight of the collection is *Saint Sebastian* by Andrea Mantegna (1431–1506), painted towards the end of the artist's life. Look out, too, for the sculpture of a *Young Couple*, carved by Tullio Lombardo (c1455–1532), and the ghostly fresco fragments by Giorgione (►23) and Titian (►23). Among the displays in the cases of coins and medals, there's a portrait of Sultan Mohammed II by Gentile Bellini (►23).

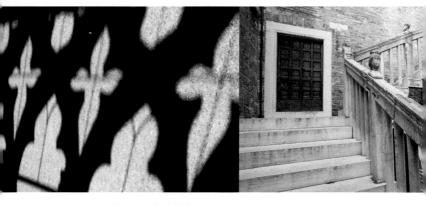

The Ca' d'Oro's façade is one of the Grand Canal's great landmarks

TAKING A BREAK

Have lunch at **Trattoria Ca' d'Oro all Vedova**, "The Widow's Place", situated on one of Venice's most atmospheric and long-established *bàcari*. They serve such traditional meals as squid with polenta (Cannaregio 3912, Ramo Ca' d'Oro, tel: 041 5 28 53 24).

➕ 193 E2 ✉ Cannaregio 3932, Ca' d'Oro
☎ 041 5 22 23 49; booking 041 5 20 34 54; www.cadoro.org
🕐 Mon 8:15–2, Tue–Sun 8:15–7:15 💶 Moderate 🚤 1, Ca' d'Oro

INSIDER INFO

- Visit in the morning and spend time on the balconies for a bird's-eye view of the delivery traffic on the Grand Canal.
- Entrance to the Ca' d'Oro is included on the **cumulative ticket** for the Gallerie dell'Accademia (►136).
- The **museum shop** has a better-than-average range of books, posters and cards about Venice for sale.
- Don't spend too much time on the Tintorettos and Titians: there are much finer ones elsewhere.

③ Madonna dell'Orto

Serene and lovely, the Gothic church of Madonna dell'Orto, lying hidden away in the north of Cannaregio, can truly justify its claim as "Tintoretto's church": the great artist (1518–94) lived near by and is buried here, and much of the interior is decorated with some of his most powerful works.

Founded in the 14th century, the church was originally dedicated to St Christopher, the Patron Saint of travellers, in the hope that he would keep an eye on the gondoliers who ran the ferry service to the northern islands from a nearby jetty. He was demoted in 1377 when a so-called miraculous statue of the Madonna and Child was moved here from a neighbouring *orto* (vegetable garden). This Madonna still stands in the **chapel of San Mauro,**

Tintoretto's great paintings dominate his burial church of Madonna dell'Orto

A cupola surmounts the church of Madonna dell'Orto

while St Christopher is over the main door. The whole church was rebuilt between 1399 and 1473, a light and balanced brick structure whose harmonious **façade**, topped by an onion-shaped **cupola**, is balanced by its slender **campanile**.

An Unlikely Tale

Tradition says Tintoretto (➤ 22,97) started his work here as a punishment for insulting the Doge by adding cuckold's horns, a traditional pair of goat-like horns said to be worn by all men whose wives proved unfaithful, to a portrait he had rejected: it's a good if unlikely story. In fact, these mighty paintings ooze religious passion and sincerity. Two huge canvases hang on the opposite **chancel** walls: the *Making of the Golden Calf* and the *Last Judgement*. Full of dramatic foreshortening, light and movement, they illustrate perfectly the artist's fiery style. The bearded man carrying the calf is said to be a self-portrait, and Signora

Tintoretto may have posed for the lady in blue near by. In the **apse,** hang the *Beheading of St Christopher* and *St Peter's Vision of the Cross*, both full of swirling, swooping angels. The mystical *Presentation of the Virgin in the Temple*, in the right aisle, provides a more peaceful contrast. If these aren't enough, the radiant blues in *St Agnes Reviving the Son of a Roman Prefect* in the **Contarini Chapel**, off the left aisle, should satisfy even the most fervent Tintoretto fan.

TAKING A BREAK

It's a five-minute stroll to the Rio della Sensa, where you can eat **Osteria Al Bacco** (Cannaregio 3054, Fondamenta delle Cappuccine, tel: 041 71 74 93).

➕ 202 A4 ✉ Campo Madonna dell'Orto
☎ 041 2 75 04 62 🕐 Mon–Sat 10–5. Closed Sun
🚤 41, 42, 51, 52, Madonna dell'Orto 💶 €2.50

INSIDER INFO

- Pause to admire the exquisite earlier **Renaissance masterpiece** by Cima da Conegliano in the first chapel on the right. Painted in 1494, it shows saints John the Baptist, Mark, Jerome and Paul.
- The first chapel on the left once contained a lovely **Madonna and Child** by Giovanni Bellini: it was stolen in 1993 when the priest forgot to turn the alarm on and has not, so far, resurfaced.
- **Tintoretto's tomb** is marked by a simple plaque in the chapel to the right of the chancel.
- *The Last Judgement* perfectly illustrates Renaissance artists' ability to integrate religion and myth: Charon, the classical god of the Underworld, can be seen busily ferrying the souls of the dead.

At Your Leisure

32 Fondamenta della Sensa

Three parallel canals cut through the quiet neighbourhood of northern Cannaregio. Along the Fondamenta della Sensa, which runs along the middle of the three to finish at the pretty Campo dell'Abbazia, you will see washing hung out to dry, peeling façades, and bars and restaurants which are patronized almost entirely by locals. There's a spacious feeling in this tranquil little backwater, and you are likely to see oarsmen practising their rowing technique in the weeks leading up to the big *regate* (➤ 23).

While you are in Fondamenta della Sensa, find the time to pay a visit to the other *fondamente* around here: the Fondamenta della Misericordia, which is lined with local food shops and busy with gossiping housewives, is a particularly appealing scene.

➕ 201 E4 ✉ Fondamenta della Sensa
🚤 41, 42, 51, 52, Madonna dell'Orto

33 Campo dei Mori

The oddly shaped Campo dei Mori probably gets its name from the three 13th-century stone figures of Moors set in its buildings, all suitably clad in flowing robes and wearing turbans. They are thought to be the Mastelli brothers, Greek merchants from the part of southern Greece once known as Morea, *mori* in dialect. One of the statues lost his nose at some time, and sports a replacement iron one; he is known as Signor Antonio Rioba and disgruntled and malicious citizens would leave their complaints at his feet overnight. A fourth Moor lurks round the corner on the *fondamenta* at No 3399, set into the stonework right outside the door of Tintoretto's house.

➕ 202 A4 ✉ Campo dei Mori
🚤 41, 42, 51, 52, Madonna dell'Orto

A statue of a Moor set into the wall of Tintoretto's house in the Campo dei Mori

34 Gesuiti

The Jesuits commissioned the church from Domenico Rossi in 1715. Just like Il Gesù, the Jesuits' Mother Church in Rome, the building's richly decorated Baroque façade reflects the confidence of the Order. The barrel-vaulted interior, complete with side chapels, transepts and a choir, impresses visitors with its lavish decoration. The space is filled with mighty columns, pilasters, green and white marble, gilding work, and a high altar complete with a baldachin and a sculptural retablo. The main attraction is Titian's *The Martyrdom of St Lawrence* in the first chapel on the left. Tintoretto's *The Assumption of Mary* in the left-hand transept and Palma Giovane's wall and ceiling paintings in the sacristy are also definitely worth a look.

➕ 202 C3
✉ Campo dei Gesuiti
☎ 041 5 28 65 79
🕐 Mon–Sat 10–noon, 4–6, Sun 4–6
🚌 12, 13, 41, 42, 51, 52, Fondamenta Nuove
💶 Free

Map labels:
Sant' Alvise
Madonna dell'Orto
Fondamenta della Sensa **32**
Sant' Alvise
31 Madonna dell'Orto
Isola di San Michele **35** →
Campo Ghetto Nuovo
CANNAREGIO
33 Campo dei Mori
S. Maria Valverde
Capella del Volto Santo
Ex Chiesa di Santa Caterina
Gesuiti **34**
0 — 200 m
0 — 200 yards

35 Isola di San Michele

A few minutes' across the lagoon from the Fondamenta Nuove lies the cemetery island of San Michele, encircled with rosy-red brick walls with spires of cypress trees rising behind. San Michele is far from melancholy: rather, it's a peaceful, well-tended and flower-bedecked city of the dead. Enter through the elegant Convento di San Michele in Isola, built in the 1460s for the Franciscans, with its lovely white Istrian stone church, Venice's first Renaissance church.

The cemetery is divided into sections according to denomination, so if you're on the hunt for celebrities, head for the Greek and Russian Orthodox sections, where Sergei Diaghilev (1872–1929), the legendary pre-Revolutionary Russian ballet dancer and his composer compatriot Igor Stravinsky (1882–1971) are buried. American poet Ezra Pound (1885–1972), who lived in Venice during his last

years, lies in the Protestant area. Nowadays, San Michele is only a temporary halt: after ten years or so bones are removed and buried elsewhere.

➕ 203 E4 ✉ San Michele
🕐 Oct–March daily 7:30–4:30; April–Sep 7:30–6 🚌 12, 13, 41, 42, 71, 72, Cimitero

36 Santa Maria dei Miracoli

The exquisite church of Our Lady of the Miracles, a little jewel of the early Renaissance, lies tucked away amid the narrow canals and alleys of eastern Cannaregio east of San Giovanni Crisostomo. It was built between 1481 and 1489 to house a miracle-working painting of the Virgin by Niccolò di Pietro. The artwork still hangs over the altar.

The church was designed by Pietro and Tullio Lombardo, who were also responsible for much of the interior sculpture and carving. Before you enter admire the exterior, with its subtly differing shades of

---

IN THE RIGHT LIGHT: THE ART OF TINTORETTO

Son of a *tintore* (silk-dyer), **Jacopo Robusti** (1518–94), nicknamed **Tintoretto**, "little dyer", was born, lived and died in Cannaregio. As well as creating large altarpieces, he painted a number of major works for secular buildings. Tintoretto wrote on his studio wall "the drawing of Michelangelo and the colour of Titian." His painting throughout his life bears witness to his success in creating a synthesis of these two formal and painterly ideals.

Tintoretto emphasised the plasticity of the moving figures in his compositions and arranged them in deep, precise perspectival spaces. Light gained particular significance as a means of conveying atmosphere, drama and vision in the work of his late period, making him one of the greatest masters of Mannerist art.

Almost all of his great paintings continue to hang in Venice – the city where they were created – to this day. His best work can be seen at the **Scuola Grande di San Rocco** (➤ 124), **Madonna dell'Orto** (➤ 102) and the **Accademia** (➤ 136).

Cannaregio & San Michele

The jewel-like Renaissance church of Santa Maria dei Miracoli

marble on each wall and graceful pilasters. Inside is some of the most delicate carving in Venice. Visit when the sun streams in through the windows, illuminating the rose, white and grey marble. The altar steps and balustrade are beautifully carved with figures and an Annunciation, while filigree stonework covers the columns below the nuns' choir. Overhead, the coffered ceiling is decorated with the portraits of around fifty prophets (Pier Maria Pennacchi, 1528).

➕ 202 C2

✉ Campo Santa Maria Nuova

☎ 041 2 75 04 62;

www.chorusvenezia.org

🕐 Mon–Sat 10–5. Closed Sun

🚢 1, 82, Rialto 🎫 €3

Where to...
Eat and Drink

Prices
Expect to pay per person for a meal, excluding drinks.
€ under €35   €€ €35–€55   €€€ over €55

BÀCARI, BARS AND GELATERIE

Bar Pasticceria Ballarin €
If you are out shopping in the Rialto area, then a good place to stop is the friendly Bar Pasticceria Ballarin, situated down the street from the Coin department store. Have a stand-up *espresso* coffee accompanied by a traditional Venetian *biscotto* or one of the superb selection of feather-light, mouth-watering *pasticceria*.
✚ 203 D2 ☒ Cannaregio 5794, Salizada San Giovanni Crisostomo ☎ 041 5 28 52 73
🕐 Daily 7:30am–8:30pm 🚊 Rialto

OSTERIE, TRATTORIE AND RISTORANTI

Ai Canottieri €€
This solidly traditional restaurant, with its terrazzo floor, wood panelling and simple table settings, is everything you could hope for if you're looking for a fine fish dinner. *Antipasti* include delicate raw fish dishes, such as slivers of marinated sword fish, while pasta *primi* range from a good *spaghetti alle vongole* (with clams and peperoncino) to *garganelli* (thick pasta) with a tomato, courgettes, basil and monkfish sauce. Bream and sea bass are served grilled, or you could try the crisp and light *frittura mista*. A limited, but good, wine list and homemade desserts round off the dining experience.
✚ 200 B4 ☒ Cannaregio 690, Fondamenta San Giobbe ☎ 041 71 79 99
🕐 Tue–Sat 12:30–2:30, 7:30–11, Sun, Mon 12:30–2:30 🚊 Tre Archi

(Insider Tip)

Al Bacco €/€€
A traditional neighbourhood eaterie with a cosy wood-panelled dining room for winter eating and an airy courtyard behind for long summer evenings. The fish-based menu is short and includes specialities like squid with polenta, excellent *spaghetti agli caparozzoli* (clams), and perfectly grilled fish. Crowded with locals, and run by a larger-than-life owner, the people-watching here is as good as the food.
✚ 201 D4 ☒ Cannaregio 3054, Fondamenta Capuzine ☎ 041 71 74 93
🕐 Tue–Sun noon–3, 7–10 🚊 San Marcuola

Algiubagiò €
Fosatelli with truffles, *capesante* with brandy, fine fish *carpaccio* and delicious lobster: Venetian cuisine that's worth its upscale price (a rarity in Venice!) is served under Murano chandeliers in an old boat house on the *vaporetto* jetty. The few seats on the waterside landing stage are sought-after in summer.
✚ 202 C3 ☒ Cannaregio 5039, Fondamente Nuove ☎ 041 5 23 60 84; www.algiubagio.com
🕐 Daily 6:30am–9pm 🚊 Fondamenta Nuove

Diana €€
With its tables ranged attractively beside the canal, this restaurant is a particularly nice place for lunch on a warm sunny day in spring or autumn. It serves meat and fish, though fish is probably your best bet, with a good *spaghetti alle vongole* and excellent grilled *orata* (bream). They have two different prices of tourist menu if you're watching the pennies.

Cannaregio & San Michele

➕ 202 A3 ✉ Cannaregio 2519f, Fondamenta della Misericordia ☎ 041 71 59 77 ⊕ Tue–Sun 12:30–3, 7:30–10 🚤 Orto

Fiaschetteria Toscana €€/€€€

Albino and Mariuccia Busatto run one of Venice's most respected restaurants. It gets its name from its original use as an unloading point and storage depot for wines coming in from Tuscany, but its cuisine is not Tuscan. The comfortable, smoothly run dining-room extends in summer to tables outside in the little square. The Fiaschetteria is a great place to sample traditional Venetian dishes, very well cooked, using fresh, seasonal ingredients – such as *sfogi in saor* (small local sole with onions, raisins and pine nuts in a vinegar-accented sauce) served with polenta, or pure *granseola* (spider crab), drizzled with light Ligurian olive oil. The menu favours seafood in all its forms, but excellent Tuscan beef is also available, and there is a great cheese board with over 30 varieties. Wine lovers will have plenty to keep them happy, too. End the meal with one of Mariuccia's delicious home-made desserts. The Busattos founded the Buona Accoglienza restaurant association (➤44) with the aim of offering reasonably priced, top-quality cuisine produced using regional ingredients to both locals and tourists alike.

➕ 202 A4 ✉ Cannaregio 5719, Salizada San Giovanni Crisostomo ☎ 041 5 28 52 81; www.fiaschetteriatoscana.it ⊕ Wed 7:30–9:30, Thu–Mon 12:30–2:30, 7:30–9:30. Closed 2 weeks in summer 🚤 Rialto

Insider Tip

Gam-Gam €

Venice's only kosher restaurant and bar, Gam-Gam offers a wide selection of Jewish and Israeli dishes that can make an interesting change from Italian food. The friendly, informal restaurant is located in a street at the edge of the old Jewish Ghetto; the décor is airy and modern, in light woods and pastel colours. The vegetable and salad assortment is particularly inviting: humous, falafel, coleslaw, roasted aubergine (eggplant), and other seasonal specialities. Main courses include grilled chicken, and the ever-popular schnitzels.

➕ 201 D4 ✉ Cannaregio 1122, Sottoportego del Ghetto Vecchio ☎ 041 71 52 84; gamgamkosher.com ⊕ 12–10pm. Closed Fri 2 hours before Shabbat; Sat (open Sat eve in winter) and all Jewish holidays 🚤 San Marcuola, Ponte delle Guglie

La Colombina da Fabio €/€€

This *enoteca* with food has been a hit since it opened, particularly among the many cooks and *sommeliers* in the city – the kitchen is open unusually late. The atmosphere is convivial and relaxed, and Chef Biba's dishes are home-cooked and delicious. She has carefully sought out great cheeses and *salumi*; many vegetables come from the family kitchen garden. Her husband, Alberto, is responsible for the enterprising wine selection from all over Italy, and Biba shares his enthusiasm for them. So, enjoy a glass of wine to complement your food, whether a *bruschetta*, a plate of pasta or some fresh fish. Book in advance for weekends.

➕ 201 E3 ✉ Cannaregio 1828, Campiello dell'Anconeta (Cinema Italia) ☎ 041 2 75 06 22 ⊕ Mon–Sat 6:30pm–2am (kitchen 8:30pm–1am) 🚤 San Marcuola

Osteria Anice Stellato €/€€

This fine family-run eatery, rustic-chic in style, is popular with Venetians from all over the city. The kitchen prepares pasta with fresh seafood every bit as well as it does a rare steak, yet the star anise of the restaurant's name suggests a pinch of exoticism to its repertoire. Fine wines, from the unpretentious to the big-named, are also available.

➕ 201 E4 ✉ Cannaregio 3272, Fondamenta della Sensa ☎ 041 72 07 44, www.osterianicestellato.com ⊕ Tue–Sun 12:30–2:30, 7:30–10 🚤 San Marcuola

Osteria l'Orto dei Mori €€/€€€

A justly popular Osteria in the north of Cannaregio, a region not otherwise known for having good restaurants. The interior looks as if it's been there for years, with warm panelling and shining glass, but the menu is decidedly 21st century, with Venetian specialities given a modern twist. Everything is superbly fresh, well-sourced and seasonal. The menu changes frequently, guaranteeing the best of the seasonal produce.

➕ 202 A4 ✉ Cannaregio 3386, Campo dei Mori ☎ 041 5 24 36 77 ⓘ Wed–Mon 12:30–3.30, 7:30–10 🚏 Orto

Trattoria Cea €

This Venetian local eating house, and there aren't many left, has been satisfying the neighbourhood for many years. There's an excellent value set lunch menu or go à la carte and choose from the short menu of mainly fish dishes. If you want to sample *baccalà mantecato* (creamed, dried salt cod), this is the place to try the real thing.

➕ 200 C4 ✉ Cannaregio 5422/A, Campiello Widman, ☎ 041 5 23 75 40; www.trattoriacea. com ⓘ Mon–Sat 12:30–3, 7:30 9:30 🚏 Fondamente Nove

Vini Da Gigio €€€

One of the best restaurants for authentic Venetian dishes, accompanied by an outstanding wine list – at honest prices. The setting is attractive, in a rustic, comfortable way: the intimate rooms have windows overlooking a canal. Seasonal dishes include sautéed *schie* (prawns), cold *polipetti* (baby octopus) and charcoal-grey *gnocchetti* with squid ink and crab sauce. The menu is seafood-based, but includes some meat dishes. The desserts are wonderful. It's always packed, so book ahead – it's part of the Buona Accoglienza Association (➤44).

➕ 202 A3 ✉ Cannaregio 3628, Calle della Stua, Fondamenta San Felice ☎ 041 5 28 51 40; www.vinidagigio.com ⓘ Tue–Sat noon–2:30, 7:30–10:30, Sun noon–2:30 🚏 Ca' d'Oro

Where to... Shop

The streets leading from the station down through Cannaregio to Santi Apostoli are known as Strada Nuova. It's a bustling area with market food stalls and shops selling everything from clothes, ironmongery and household goods to food.

Among the best of the latter is **Giovanni Volpe** (Cannaregio 1143, Calle del Ghetto Vecchio, tel: 041 71 51 78), an old-fashioned Jewish kosher bakery in the heart of the Ghetto.

Pick up some food for a picnic and get the rest of your supplies at **Billa**, Venice's best-stocked supermarket (Cannaregio 3659, Strada Nuova, tel: 041 5 23 80 46). The **Malefatte Boutique** sells a variety of products – including t-shirts, hand-sewn leather laptop cases and canvas bags – that are all created by inmates currently doing time in the men's and women's prisons in the city (Cannaregio 2433, Calle Zancan, tel: 041 5 21 02 72, www. rioteradeipensieri.org).

For footwear, **Mori e Bozzi** (Cannaregio 2367, Rio terà Maddalena, tel: 041 71 52 61) has some trendy numbers and designer-name copies, while *Virginia Preo* (Cannaregio 5800, Salizada San Giovanni Crisostomo, tel: 041 5 22 86 51) has delectable cashmere styled with Italian flair.

For something quirky, try **Papillon** (Cannaregio 4555, Salizada del Pistor, tel: 041 5 23 93 18), Venice's only outfitters to the service industry, where you'll find cotton trousers and jackets and cotton maids' dresses in checks and floral prints.

Then pop next door to **Peter's Teahouse** (Cannaregio, 4553/a, Santi Apostoli – Strada Nuova, tel: 041 5 28 97 76, www.peters-teahouse.com) to pick up one of its range of world teas.

Where to...
Go Out

Cannaregio, the only sestiere with a really active night scene, is nicknamed the New Bohemia. One long canal, Rio della Misericordia, which runs from Fondamenta della Misericordia to Fondamenta Coletti, is home to a string of bars, osterie, pubs and multi-ethnic restaurants.

The simple beauty of the **Al Timon** wine bar (Cannaregio 2754, tel: 041 5 24 60 66) can be seen on the Fondamenta Ormesini. Students and locals alike crowd in here at around 7pm to enjoy delicious *crostini* and *cichetti* served with Italian wines.

Pub Da Aldo (Cannaregio 2710, tel: 041 715 58 34, open Mon–Sat 11–3, 9–2) is the most popular joint, with a huge selection of decently priced beers, and a lot of noisy atmosphere; just one canal further on is **Sahara** (Cannaregio 2519, tel: 041 72 10 77, open Tue–Sat 7:30–midnight, Sun lunch), which offers the likes of couscous, falafel, *shawarma* kebabs and inexpensive *spritzes*, with live music on the barge moored outside.

Al Paradiso Perduto (Cannaregio 2540, tel: 041 72 05 81, open Mon–Tue, Thu–Sat 7pm–2am, Sunday lunch) started it all: crowded with tables, it's big, chaotic and fun, with cheap-and-cheerful Venetian food, and live music several times a week that ranges from reggae to jazz (via poetry readings and art shows).

If you fancy a good plate of pasta before going to listen to the music, **Trattoria Antica Mola** (Cannaregio 2800, tel: 041 71 74 92, open daily noon–1:30, 6:30–10, closed Aug) has a terrace in front and a garden at the back, with good home-cooking and fair prices.

Alla Bagatela (Cannaregio 2924, tel: 041 71 78 88, open Mon–Sat), doesn't open before 9pm, but it keeps going till late, offering satellite TV, computer games and drinks and snacks on the terrace.

On the canal bank, called Fondamenta delle Cappuccine, **Bea Vita** (Cannaregio 3082, tel: 041 71 81 98, open Mon–Sat) is the *in* place for a pre-dinner *aperitivo*.

Alle Due Gondolette (Cannaregio 3016, open for lunch Mon–Fri; tel: 041 71 75 28) is a simple *trattoria* with a little shaded garden.

Casanova Music Club (Cannaregio 158/A, Rio Terrà Lista di Spagna, tel: 041 2 75 01 99) is a lounge bar and disco club with special nights dedicated to different musical genres: mainstream, techno, house, hip-hop and Latino. There is a happy hour between 6pm and 8pm and an internet café which opens in the morning.

The **Casinò di Venezia** is world famous; its original headquarters are in the luxurious Palazzo Vendramin-Calergi (Rio Terrà della Maddalena, tel: 041 5 29 71 11, open: slot machines daily 11am; tables daily 3pm–2:30am, *vaporetto:* San Marcuola), with a branch also open near the airport, at Ca' Noghera. Go well dressed, and take your passport.

There are two excellent theatres, the **Malibran** (Cannaregio 5873, Calle dei Milion, box office tel: 041 89 99 09 090, www.teatro lafenice.it) and the **Teatrino Groggia** (Cannaregio 3161, Calle del Capitello, tel: 041 5 24 46 65). Both have occasional concerts or performances in English.

San Polo & Santa Croce

Little Treats

Great Cinema

The Arena di Campo San Polo shows the latest movies on the Campo San Polo during the Lido's **Film Festival** (end of July until beginning of Sept.).

Plaza Pleasures

On Tuesday evenings in summer, people dance the tango under the stars on the lovely **Campo San Giacomo dell'Orio**.

Gli ori di Venezia

In her small workshop, Christine Bedin creates thoroughly modern reinterpretations of traditional jewellery made from Murano glass beads (L'Opera al Bianco, Santa Croce 1239/a, www.operavenezia.com).

Getting Your Bearings

San Polo and adjoining Santa Croce, lying to the south of the upper stretch of the Grand Canal, get their names from churches that stood within their boundaries. These are busy, workaday areas, less well-endowed with famous sights than other parts of the city, but full of charm and atmosphere. Legend says that the first inhabitants of the city of Venice settled on the cluster of islands called the Rivus Altus, High Bank, later known as the Rialto. This ancient area is still the busiest part of San Polo.

The Rialto markets and surrounding streets are one of the city's big draws, a vibrant mélange of clothes boutiques, leather and gift shops, mouth-watering food stalls (stands), butchers and bakers. To the west lies the superb church of Santa Maria Gloriosa dei Frari, whose artistic treasures are splendidly complemented by the great cycle of paintings by Tintoretto in the neighbouring Scuola Grande di San Rocco. You can cut north from here through a maze of narrow streets and sunny squares to reach the topmost point of the Grand Canal, where its glories peter out beside the unalluring and fume-laden surroundings of Piazzale

Enjoy shopping in San Polo

Roma, with its garages and bus station. Better to stick to the back alleys and enjoy glimpses of everyday Venetian life, or follow the course of the Grand Canal, lined with dazzling *palazzi* such as the Ca' Pesaro, now the home of two eclectic museums. This is a good area to spend the evening: being close to the markets, San Polo has some of the city's most atmospheric and traditional bars and restaurants.

Perfect Days in...

The Perfect Day

If you're not quite sure where to begin your travels, this itinerary recommends a practical and enjoyable day exploring San Polo and Santa Croce, taking in some of the best places to see. For more information see the main entries (➤ 118–127).

🕓 9:00am

Start your day at the ⭐ **Rialto Bridge** (➤ 118), the only bridge over the Grand Canal until the 19th century, before heading for the ⭐ **markets** (ills. above and right, ➤ 120) and the surrounding streets, still named after the goods originally – and sometimes still – sold there. You could shop for a picnic to eat later, or pick up souvenirs ranging from a plastic gondola to a hard-to-tell-the-difference copy of a designer handbag.

🕓 10:30am

Spare a moment to pop into the church of San Giacomo di Rialto (➤ 121), reputedly founded on the same day in 421 as the city itself. Then it's time for coffee or a drink, either on the Fondamenta del Vin (➤ 119) or in one of the dozens of bars around the market.

🕓 11:00am

Thread your way northeastwards to take in the **40 Palazzo Mocenigo** (➤ 126), a sumptuous 18th-century palace where you may easily be alone to enjoy its lofty frescoed rooms. Then wander the maze of streets between the nearby church of San Stae and the station, finishing up in the leafy shade of the Giardini Papadopoli, once a private garden, on the edge of the Grand Canal.

🕓 12:30pm

Do some window shopping along the streets leading east to **41 Campo San Polo** (➤ 127), Venice's second-largest square.

⊛ 1:00pm

Rest your feet and enjoy a quick lunch in one of the many bars in the area – then follow it up with an ice-cream from one of the *gelaterie* near the Frari.

⊛ 2:00pm

On the Campo dei Frari, you'll find the great church of **㊲ Santa Maria Gloriosa dei Frari** (➤ 122), a cavernous Gothic building containing some superb works of art, including Titian's famous *Assunta* on the high altar.

⊛ 3:30pm

Tackle the glories of Tintoretto's masterpieces in the **㊳ Scuola Grande di San Rocco** (➤ 124), rated among the greatest of Venetian artistic treasures. If you're not sated, you'll find more paintings by the same artist in the church of San Rocco, which stands at right angles to the Scuola.

⊛ 5:30pm

Wander south to the Campo San Pantalon with its 17th-century church. San Pantalon lays claim to the world's largest art work on canvas; 40 *trompe l'oeil* ceiling panels by Fumiani tell the story of the saint's life.

⊛ 7:00pm

Take the *vaporetto* from San Tomà up the Grand Canal to the San Silvestro stop and have dinner at the Trattoria alle Madonna (San Polo 594, Calle della Madonna, tel: 041 5 22 38 24), a big and busy fish restaurant that's been popular with locals and knowledgeable visitors for many years.

★ Ponte di Rialto

Until the middle of the 19th century, the Ponte di Rialto was the only bridge over the Grand Canal. This was where the first Venetians settled at the start of the 9th century. The Rialto bridge is one of the four footbridges that cross the canal today – and it's known as an iconic symbol of Venice all over the world.

A wooden bridge was found at this site as early as *c*1180. This was later replaced by a drawbridge that collapsed under the weight of spectators who were watching a boat procession in 1444. A wooden bridge from this era has been immortalised in Vittore Carpaccio's painting *The Miracle of the Relic of the Cross at the Ponte di Rialto* which hangs in the Accademia. Such prominent architects as Palladio, Sansovino and (possibly) Michelangelo entered the competition that was held to find a designer for the current bridge. The single-arched solution proposed by Antonio da Ponte was crowned the winner in 1588. Constructed from Istrian marble, the bridge was opened three years later. Six thousand oak staves were driven into the muddy soil at each side of the canal to support the bridge's structure.

Three footways separated by two rows of shops selling leather, jewellery and

DID YOU KNOW?

The Ponte di Rialto (Rialto Bridge) has a single arch span 28m (92ft) wide and 7.5m (25ft) high – enough height for galleys to pass underneath. Until the first Accademia bridge was built in 1854, it was the only way of crossing the Grand Canal on foot.

souvenirs cross the mighty arch of the bridge. If you venture up to the edifice's upper platform, you'll be rewarded with great views of the hustle and bustle on the Grand Canal.

Medieval-style Wall Street

Throughout the Middle Ages, San Marco controlled trade between western Europe and the East, Rialto merchants acting as middlemen for the silks and spices craved by Europe. The offices of shipping, commerce and navigation were situated here, as were many of Europe's major banks and international trading companies. The good times came to an end in 1499 when news of Vasco da Gama's voyage around the Cape to India reached the Rialto, and the city merchants realized that the sea routes would spell the end of the Venetian overland monopoly to the East.

TAKING A BREAK

Head for the wonderfully atmospheric **Osteria Antica Dolo** (San Polo 778, Ruga Rialto, tel: 041 5 22 65 46, www. anticadolo.it) for delicious *cicheti* (snacks) or a full meal.

Insider Tip

Locals and tourists jostle in the Rialto's narrow streets

🗺 202 B1 ✉ Rialto
🚤 1, Rialto/San Silvestro/Rialto Mercato

⭐4 Mercato di Rialto

At 3am, when tired tourists are still sound asleep in their beds, the vegetable producers of Sant'Erasmo head for Venice. The milk delivery boats set sail half an hour later. Their first port of call is the big market on the Piazzale Roma to sell goods to Venice's vegetable shops and stalls. The largest and oldest market in the city is held at the Rialto. Apart from fruit and vegetables from the surrounding islands, you can also buy seafood from the lagoon and a great deal more besides. Even if you don't want to shop you're in for a treat: if you come early, the bustling atmosphere is unrivalled.

Jostle your way through bargain-hunting housewives, listen to the market traders' raucous shouts, enjoy the scents of fish, meat, fruit and vegetables, and lose your way in the labyrinthine *calle* that make up this ancient quarter. Nowhere else brings home more sharply the fact that this was a city whose wealth was founded on commerce. While merchants flocked to the Rialto from all over Europe, trading in precious stones, gold, silver, spices and silk, the citizens' needs were served by food markets, in streets named after the goods on sale. Market traders lived in the warren of tiny streets and did their drinking there – many still bear the names of ancient watering places. Gold-sellers still trade on the Rialto Bridge (► 118), but today's market is, above all, for food.

INSIDER INFO

- If you can, **get up at dawn** to see the delivery barges arriving and the stallholders setting up and getting ready for their customers.

- The label **nostrano** on fruit and vegetables – the word means "local" – indicates that produce usually comes from the market-garden island of Sant' Erasmo (► 162).

Insider Tip

SHAKESPEARE AND HUNCHBACK OF THE RIALTO

The Hunchback of Rialto can be found opposite the Gobbo di Rialto church on the Campo San Giacomo. The statue, hewn from Istrian marble by Pietro da Salò in the 16th century and restored in 1836, shows a naked man bent over by the weight of a small set of steps on his back. At one time, official proclamations were made and the names of criminals were read out from a small platform above. A common punishment in Venice – which seems rather "lenient" compared to being incarcerated in the Lead Chambers in the Doge's palace – saw wrongdoers being stripped naked and driven to this point with sticks from the Piazza San Marco. The offender then had to kiss the hunchback in order to avoid further humiliating treatment. It's thought that the figure of Old Gobbo, Shylock's father in William Shakespeare's comedy *The Merchant of Venice*, might have been inspired by this statue.

Head right on the San Polo side of the Rialto Bridge into **Campo San Giacomo**, the main fruit-selling area. This little square is home to one of Venice's oldest churches, **San Giacomo di Rialto**, founded, according to legend, on the same day as the city itself – 25 March 421. It still retains its Greek-cross ground plan and portico, and the shadowy interior has ancient Greek marble columns with 11th-century capitals.

Neighbouring **Campo Battisti** is home to more heaped fruit and vegetable stalls (stands). Beyond lies **Campo della Pescarìa**, the fish market, with some of the freshest fish and seafood you'll ever see. The surrounding streets are lined with bakers, *alimentari*, purveyors of fresh pasta, dried fruit and beans, cheese, tea, coffee and spices.

TAKING A BREAK

Buy a picnic from the market and mouth-watering food shops in the surrounding streets and eat it in a quiet *campo*. If this doesn't appeal, you'll find some of Venice's oldest *bàcari* in this area. Try **Da Pinto** (San Polo 367, Campo delle Beccarie, tel: 041 5 22 45 99).

➕ 202 B2 ⊠ Campo San Giacomo di Rialto, Campo Battisti, Campo della Pescarìa and surrounding streets ⏰ Market: 7:30–12:30
🚤 1, San Silvestro, 1, 2, Rialto

㉗ Santa Maria Gloriosa dei Frari

Usually called the "Frari" for short (a Venetian dialect word for "friars"), this Gothic church, built by the Franciscan mendicant order, is one of Venice's most important religious buildings. Packed with great paintings, monuments and sculptures, it's both the city's second largest church and the burial place of some of its most famous citizens.

The rear section of the **nave** contains an over-the-top 19th-century monument to Titian; opposite, a neo-classical marble pyramid, the design originally intended as a Titian memorial, contains the heart of Antonio Canova (1757–1822), the

Titian's glorious *Assumption of the Virgin*

TITIAN'S FASCINATING PAINTING

Titian (1488/90–1576) left the Cadore Valley in the Dolomites at the start of the 16th century and went to Venice, where he profited from the tutelage of Giovanni Bellini. Stylistically speaking, Titian stands somewhere between High Renaissance and Mannerist art. His extensive oeuvre – which wouldn't have been possible without his large workshop – includes altarpieces, mythologies, nudes, allegories, and numerous portraits. Titian's fascinating painting style is characterised by his use of harmonious colours, strong chiaroscuro contrasts, lively diagonal compositions and atmospheric background landscapes. His technique and breadth of compositional ideas blazed an artistic trail for centuries to come. When he died, he was the only plague victim to be buried within the city.

INSIDER INFO

- As you enter. **pause at the back** of the church to get your bearings and appreciate the scale of the interior.
- **You definitely shouldn't miss** seeing Titian's painted masterpieces *Assumption of the Virgin* and *Madonna di Ca' Pesaro*, Marco Cozzi's magnificent carved **choir stalls**, Donatello's sculpture of *St John the Baptist* and Giovanni Bellini's sumptuous gilt-framed triptych of the *Madonna and Child with Saints*.
- The former convent attached to the Frari and built around two cloisters has housed the **Archivio di Stato (State Archives)** since 1815. The 300-odd rooms contain the entire collection of official documents relating to the history of the Venetian Republic – a total of more than 15 million volumes and manuscripts.

greatest neo-classical sculptor of them all. His body rests in a mausoleum in his hometown of Possagno. A fine 15th-century carved marble **rood screen** stretches across the central nave; behind it lies the intricately carved **Coro dei Frati (Monks' Choir)**, 124 wooden choir stalls carved by Marco Cozzi in 1468, and worth examining for their city scenes. The composer Monteverdi (1567–1643) is buried in a chapel to the left of the high altar. *St John the Baptist* by Donatello (*c*1386–1466), in the chapel immediately to the right of the high altar, is the only work in Venice by the Florentine master. The Frari's greatest glories are its paintings: Titian's flowing and dynamic *Assumption of the Virgin* over the high altar, his captivating *Madonna di Ca' Pesaro* on the left-hand side of the nave and the sublime and tranquil triptych of the *Madonna and Child with Saints Nicolas, Peter, Benedict and Mark* by Giovanni Bellini, still in its original frame in the sacristy.

TAKING A BREAK

Head towards Campo San Polo for a pizza at **Da Sandro** (San Polo 1473, Campiello dei Meloni, tel: 041 5 23 48 94, www.basilicadeifrari.it); or try the restaurant of the same name opposite, run by the same team.

Take a good look at the carved wooden choir stalls

🚇 201 D1 🖂 Campo dei Frarl ☎ 041 2 75 04 82; www.chorusvenezia.org
🕐 Mon–Sat 9–6, Sun 1–6 🚤 1, 2, San Tomà 🎫 €3

㊳ Scuola Grande di San Rocco

The confraternity in honour of Saint Rocco, Patron Saint of plague victims, was originally dedicated to caring for the sick. The Scuola, which emerged from the "Battuti" flagellant brotherhood in 1478, became one of the richest confraternities in the city. Tintoretto, himself a member of the Scuola, won a competition to decorate the building in 1564 by entering a finished painting instead of a preliminary sketch. He painted until 1588, producing some of his most important work for what is one of the most extensive Biblical cycles in Italian art.

The Scuola's assembly halls were initially built under the direction of Bartolomeo Bon (1517). Antonio Scarpagnino carried on the work from Bon's death until the building's completion in 1549. The Scuola's Renaissance structure seems almost modest when compared to the mighty façade of the San Rocco church that houses the relics of the Saint.

Bartolomeo Bon's façade at the Scuola

Painting Cycle

Tintoretto's painting cycle begins with *The Annunciation* on the ground floor. It hangs on the long left-hand wall of the spacious columned hall where people once fed the poor and cared for the sick. The staircase, hung with images of the plague in Venice, leads to the 44 × 17m (144 × 56ft) assembly hall above. The wall paintings here show various scenes from the New Testament, including the Birth and Baptism of Christ, the Agony in the Garden, the Last Supper, and the Resurrection. One narrow side of the hall is occupied by the Rocco altar, which is framed by Girolamo Campagna's sculptures of Saint

THE VENETIAN SCUOLE

The *scuole* (schools) were devotional and charitable lay brotherhoods under the patronage of a saint-protector. They came under the authority of the state and existed to care for the interests of differing groups of citizens. By the 1500s, there were six *scuole grandi* (literally "big schools") and more than 200 *scuole piccole* ("small schools") each governed by elected officers. Each of the *scuole grandi* met in its own purpose-built halls, which normally comprised an entrance hall, a chapter hall and an *albergo* (boardroom), decorated with cycles of paintings celebrating the wealth of the *scuola* and the life of its Patron Saint. The Scuola Grande di San Rocco was not dissolved by Napoleon in 1806, and still meets annually.

The sumptuous main hall of the Scuola

The cycle of paintings Tintoretto created for the Scuola represents a highpoint in the artist's oeuvre

Sebastian and John the Baptist. The 21 ceiling paintings, designed to be seen from below, deal with scenes from the Old Testament. Perhaps Tintoretto's most moving work, *The Crucifixion*, hangs in the small meeting room for the Scuola's leaders.

TAKING A BREAK

Da Sandro (San Polo 1473, Campiello dei Meloni, tel: 041 5 23 48 94) is as convenient for San Rocco as it is for the Frari.

➕ 201 D1 ✉ Campo San Rocco ☎ 041 5 23 48 64; www.scuolagrande sanrococo.it 🕐 Daily 10–5 🚤 1, 2, San Tomà 💶 € (incl. audio-guide)

INSIDER INFO

- To view the panels in the order in which they were painted, **start your visit upstairs** in the Sala dell'Albergo, off the main hall.
- An **audio-guide**, available at the ticket office, helps make sense of the Scuola. Remember to pick up an English-language **plan and information leaflet**.
- Use the **hand-held mirrors** to take in the ceiling panels – you'll find them in the different rooms.
- **Not to be missed** The **panel paintings** by artists such as Titian displayed on easels in the ground floor hall.

At Your Leisure

THE OLDEST PROFESSION IN THE WORLD

The **Ponte delle Tette**, a bridge near Campo San Polo, acquired its bawdy name from the prostitutes who once attracted their clients by baring their breasts on the balconies. In 1509, there were over 11,650 courtesans in Venice, and Marin Sanudo, a Venetian historian (1466–1536), published a list containing the addresses and prices of 210 women plying their trade in the city.

Baroque at its finest – the Ca' Pesaro

39 Ca' Pesaro

The magnificent grandeur of the Palazzo Pesaro – often called simply the Ca' Pesaro – is due to Baldassare Longhena (▶27), who started working on this baroque palace in 1628, and Antonio Gaspari, who finally completed it in 1710. Since the early 20th century, it's been the home for two museums: the **Galleria d'Arte Moderna** and the **Museo d'Arte Orientale**. The former is a collection of superb late 19th- and 20th-century art. Japanese art of the Edo period (1600–1868), acquired by Count Enrico di Borbone during a late 19th-century world tour, is the focus of the Museo d'Arte Orientale.

🕂 201 F2 ✉ Santa Croce 2070, Fondamenta Ca' Pesaro ☎ 041 72 11 27; capesaro. visitmuve.it 🕓 April–Oct 10–6, Nov–March 10–5 🚤 1, San Stae 💶 €10.50

40 Palazzo Mocenigo

This splendid 17th-century palace was built for one of the Republic's most influential families, from whose ranks came seven Doges. The grandest rooms are found in the *portego*, the main salon, which runs the length of the building, and the red drawing-room, its walls hung with silk and glittering 18th-century mirrors. Reopened in 2013 following a programme of renovations, the Palazzo Mocenigo houses the **Museo del Tessuto e del Costume**. Stunningly embroidered and figured

Insider Tip

Leafy trees contrast with weathered stucco in the Campo San Polo

silks are widely used in the costumes, and there are stockings and corsets, as well as high-heeled shoes, proof of the long Italian love affair with the *bella figura*.

🔶 201 F2 ✉ Santa Croce 1992, Salizada San Stae ☎ 041 72 17 98; mocenigo.visitmuve.it ⏲ Daily 10–4 🚤 1, 2, San Stae 💶 €8.50

🕮 Campo San Polo

The biggest square on the western side of the Grand Canal, on one of the main routes from the Rialto to the Accademia, is a mellow, brick-paved space surrounded by *palazzi* and usually busy with local people and children. It's always been an important gathering place and in the past was used for religious ceremonies, festivities, bull-baiting and theatrical performances. In the summer it serves as an open-air cinema, attracting up to 1,000 people every night. Until 1761, there was a canal on the east side – you can trace its original course in the curving line of the *palazzi*.

Don't miss the two **Palazzi Soranzo**, a duo of lovely Gothic palaces, or the **Palazzo Corner Mocenigo**, an ornate 16th-century building. The church of **San Polo** faces Rio di San Polo, away from the square. It was heavily altered in the 19th century, but still has lovely 15th-century details. Look for the pair of stone lions at the base of the detached campanile, built in 1362. Inside, the *Oratory of the Crucifix* has a dazzling cycle of the Stations of the Cross by Giandomenico Tiepolo, son of Giambattista.

🔶 201 F1 Church of San Polo ✉ Campo San Polo ☎ 041 2 75 04 62; www.chorusvenezia.org ⏲ Mon–Sat 10–5 🚤 1, 2, San Tomà, 1, 2, San Silvestro 💶 €3.50

WELLS AND WATER

Before fresh water was piped from the mainland by aqueduct, every Venetian *campo* had a 5m (16ft) deep, sand-filled cistern with an impermeable lining. The brick-lined well-shaft stands at its centre, connected by tiny drainage holes to the sand. As rainwater drains into the cistern from cracks in the paving, it is filtered by the sand and passes into the shaft ready to be drawn up.

Where to…
Eat and Drink

Prices
Expect to pay per person for a meal, excluding drinks.
€ under €35   €€ €35–€55   €€€ over €55

BÀCARI, BARS AND GELATERIE

Antica Osteria Ruga Rialto €
The area around the Rialto market abounds with atmospheric *bàcari* where you can stand for an inexpensive, nutritious snack, or sit for a simple meal. Ruga Rialto offers a spectacular display of these typically Venetian *cicheti* (snacks) – such as *sarde fritte* (fried sardines) and *polpette* (meatballs). For lunch, have a plate of *spaghetti al nero* (with squid ink), and a glass of local wine.
✚ 202 A1 ✉ San Polo 692, Ruga Rialto
☎ 041 5 21 12 43 ⊙ Daily 11–3, 6–12
🚤 San Silvestro

Bottega del Caffè Dersut €
Huge windows allow a glimpse into the ambient interior of this modern café, where you can stand at the bar or relax on one of the cosy sofas while you enjoy one of the speciality coffees – different flavours, different toppings, many laced with cream – or get a vitamin fix in the form of a blended veggie juice or mixed fruit smoothie made to order. There are a range of tempting pastries, tarts and cakes also on offer, which are perfect with an *espresso* – a popular and relaxing place for a pause in this part of town.
✚ 201 E1 ✉ San Polo 3014, Campo dei Frari
☎ 041 3 03 21 59
⊙ Mon–Sat 6–8, Sun 8–1 🚤 San Tomà

Cantina Do Mori €
Do Mori, one of Venice's historic *bàcari*, is more than 500 years old. Located in a slip-through between two narrow streets, it has a vast

wine list, and you can choose from beautiful array of *cicheti* (snacks) at the long counter. Try a delicious stuffed *francobollo* (literally, postage-stamp) sandwich with a glass of fine Prosecco. There are no seats here but it's usually packed.
✚ 202 B2 ✉ San Polo 429, Calle dei do Mori
☎ 041 5 22 54 01 ⊙ Mon–Sat 8:30–8:30.
Closed 2 weeks in Aug 🚤 San Silvestro, Rialto

Insider Tip

OSTERIE, TRATTORIE AND RISTORANTI

Antiche Carampane €€/€€€
This off-the-beaten-track, laid-back restaurant specializes in serving beautifully cooked, elegantly served seafood and fish dishes in attractive surroundings. The style is a modern take on tradition, seen at its best in dishes such as *spaghetti alla granseola* (pasta with spider crab), *cassopipa* (spaghetti with a spicy fish sauce) or *branzino in salsa di peperoni* (sea bass in a sweet pepper sauce). The wine list is long and desserts are light elegant and imaginative. Booking essential.
✚ 201 F1 ✉ San Polo 1911, Ponte delle Tette
☎ 041 5 24 01 65; www.antichecarampane.com
⊙ Mon 7:30–10:30, Tue–Sat 12:20–3, 7:30–10:30
🚤 San Silvestro/Rialto Mercato

Il Refolo €/€€
Beautifully set beside a canal just off one of Venice's most atmospheric *campi*, Il Refolo has to be one of the city's great *pizzerie* – and a fashionable one at that. It serves *pizze*, salads and some straightforward meat and fish *secondi*. There are outside tables.

✚ 201 E2 ✉ Santa Croce 1459, Campiello del Piovan (off campo San Giacomo dell'Orio)
☎ 041 5 25 00 16 🕐 Tue–Sun 12–2:45, 7–11
🚊 Riva di Biasio, San Stae

La Zucca €/€€

"The Pumpkin" is a friendly, easy-going *trattoria* where home-style cuisine centres primarily 🏷Insider Tip around vegetables – with some exotic accents. Sit next to a romantic window overlooking the canal, or at an outside table, and sample peppers with balsamic vinegar, Sicilian-style pasta, or grilled chicken with tzatziki sauce. Desserts are imaginative.
✚ 201 E2 ✉ Santa Croce 1762, Ponte del Megio, San Giacomo dell'Orio
☎ 041 5 24 15 70
🕐 Mon–Sat 12:30–2:30, 7–10:30 🚊 San Stae

Muro Venezia Frari €/€€

Dark wood and minimalist design bring a feeling of space and modernity to this all-day bar-cum-eatery, where the menu offers a good range of *pizze* as well as standard Italian dishes. It's convenient after a morning's sightseeing in the area with the bonus of having outside tables. There are other branches at the Rialto and Campiello dello Spezier in Santa Croce.
✚ 201 E1 ✉ San Polo 2604B/C, Rio Terà dei Frari ☎ 041 5 24 53 10
🕐 Fri–Wed 11–10:30 🚊 San Tomà

Trattoria Da Ignazio €€

For more than 50 years, this *trattoria* has served home-cooked, genuinely Venetian specialities. Seasonal seafood from the lagoon includes fresh *granseola* (spider crab), *caparozzoli* (clams) and *capesante* (scallops). Home-made pastas are dressed with *seppie* (squid), or with mixed seafood. The wine features the whites of Friuli and the Veneto. In summer, eat outside in the courtyard.
✚ 201 E1 ✉ San Polo 2749, Calle dei Saoneri
☎ 041 5 23 48 52; www.trattoriadaignazio.com
🕐 Sun–Fri 12:30–2:30, 7:30–10
🚊 San Tomà

Where to...
Shop

The Rialto food and fish markets are at the heart of this lively district, and fun to explore – even if you won't be cooking. The surrounding streets are packed with superb specialist food shops, where you may easily pick up take-home gifts, while the streets stretching south towards the Frari are home to some of Venice's best middle-range fashion, leather and houseware shops. Northwest from the Rialto, Santa Croce is one of the least-visited areas of the city, where shops mainly cater for locals and prices are correspondingly lower.

Among the best food shops in the streets surrounding the market is the wonderful **Drogheria Mascari** (San Polo 381, Ruga Spezieri, tel: 041 0 22 97 62), a traditional grocer and spice merchants, where dried fruits, teas, spices and nuts are piled high beside jars of truffles, beautiful biscuits and mouth-watering chocolates – the ideal place to shop for gifts. 🏷Insider Tip
If something savoury appeals, head for the **Casa del Parmigiano** (San Polo 214/215, Erberia, tel: 041 5 20 65 25; www.aliani casadelparmigiano.it), a family-run, long-established speciality *salumeria*, which sells top-quality ham, *salame* and cheese from all over Italy; they will vacuum-pack goods for taking home.
Traditional Venetian cakes and pastries are on offer at **Premiata Pasticceria Rizzardini** (San Polo 1415, Campiello dei Meloni, tel: 041 5 22 38 35); you can sample them on the spot with a cup of coffee at the bar. Serious foodies will enjoy a browse in **Aliani** (654 San Polo,

San Polo & Santa Croce

Ruga Vecchia San Giovanni, tel: 041 5 22 49 13, www.aliani-casadelparmigiano.it), a high-quality, high-price *gastronomia* selling a wide range of prepared dishes, hams, oils, vinegars and breads – a great place to put together a delicious picnic.

For something other than food, head south towards San Polo on the Ruga Rialto, home to leather shops such as **Francis Model** (San Polo 773A, Ruga Rialto, tel: 041 5 21 28 89, www.francismodel. it), a family concern producing bags, purses and briefcases, perfect foils for the elegant knitwear on offer at **L'Erbavoglio** (San Polo 777/A, Ruga Rialto, tel: 041 5 23 03 64).

There are more easy-to-wear clothes at **Hibiscus** (San Polo 1061, Calle dell'Olio, tel: 041 5 23 74 86), where Indian silks and fine wools are made up into stylish jackets, coats and accessories; these would go well with the vivid *friulane* (Venetian slippers) in sumptuous velvet, brocade and felt from **Parutto** (669 San Polo, Ruga Rialto, tel: 041 5 23 14 55).

If you're looking for something to wear to the Carnival, check out the nearby **Balocloc** (Santa Croce 2134, Calle Lunga, tel: 041 5 24 05 51). They've been creating fine-quality handmade Venetian masks and costumes for the last three decades using historically accurate, traditional methods.

Those Venetian touches for the home can be found at **Colorcasa** (San Polo 1989/1991, Calle della Madonneta, tel: 041 5 23 60 71), which is a treasure-house of fabrics, cushions, linens, drapes and tassels.

Some of the city's best masks are to be found at **Tragicomica** (San Polo 2800, Calle dei Nomboli, tel: 041 72 11 02; www.tragicomica. it) near San Tomà

Just opposite there's a fine range of clean-lined Italian and oriental ceramics at **Sabbie e Nebbie** (San Polo 2768, tel:

041 71 90 73), while round the corner, on Calle Seconda dei Saoneri, **Gilberto Penzo** (San Polo 2681, tel: 041 71 93 72; www. venice boats.com) creates Venetian boats in miniature, including gondola kits to take home.

Where to...
Go Out

San Polo and Santa Croce are far from quiet after dark, with a wide range of entertainment to be found. In summer, much centres on the two main campi, San Giacomo dell'Orio and San Polo.

The area has some beautiful concert venues, showcasing 18th-century Venetian music. The best of these are the **Scuola Grande San Giovanni Evangelista** (San Polo 2545, Campiello della Scuola, tel: 041 71 82 34, www. scuolasangiovanni.it), whose offerings include winter concert opera, and the **Scuola Grande di San Rocco** (Campo San Rocco, tel: 041 5 23 48 64, www.scuola grandesanrocco.it) where baroque music is played.

Near by, the **Basilica dei Frari** also holds concerts – some-times free, as does the ancient and atmospheric church of **San Giacomo at the Rialto** (Campo di San Giacometto, tel: 041 4 26 65 59).

Blues and jazz can be heard at **Bagolo** (Santa Croce 1584, tel: 041 3 47 36 65 06), in lovely Campo San Giacomo dell'Orio, or at **Easy Bar** (Santa Croce 2119, Campo Santa Maria Mater Domini, tel: 041 5 24 03 21), which pulls in students and a young crowd for regular rock and jazz nights.

Dorsoduro & The Giudecca

Little Treats

Keep it Under Your Hat…

Anna Netrebko, Sarah Jessica Parker, Jan Delay… they all love the **creations** of young Viennese **hat maker Julia Cranz** ("Julia Cranz Hats, Hat pieces and more", Dorsoduro 564, Zattere, www.juliacranz.com).

Gianduiotto

No one makes a Gianduiotto ice-cream creation quite like **Nico** (Fondamenta Zattere al Ponte Longo, Dorsoduro 922, www.gelaterianico.com).

Cannoli & Co.

Sweet-toothed foodies will happily queue outside the **Pasticceria Tonolo** to get their hands on the crispy cannoli (Calle San Pantalon, Dorsoduro 3764, tel:5041 5 23 72 09).

Getting Your Bearings

Dorsoduro, the "backbone", gets its name from the solid subsoil on which it is built. Bounded to the north by the Grand Canal and to the south by the deep-water Giudecca canal, it is one of Venice's most compelling sestieri (wards), packed with historic buildings, fine churches and picturesque squares and canals, as well as three superb and contrasting art collections, the glorious Gallerie dell'Accademia, the Collezione Peggy Guggenheim and the Punta della Dogana.

The eastern point of Dorsoduro tapers with a flourish to the superb church of the Salute and the Punta della Dogana, once the Republic's customs house and now an important and contemporary art centre. The long *fondamenta* stretches south from here, beside the Giudecca canal, backed by quiet squares and pretty *rii* (little canals). This is a popular and smart residential area, with neighbourhood food stores and a clutch of excellent restaurants. West lies the Accademia and its bridge, one of the four crossings of the Grand Canal. The main route from here heads west again to emerge at the Campo Santa

Campo Santa Margherita 45

Palazzo Foscarini

Ca'Foscari

Santa Maria dei Carmini

Ca' Rezzonico 42

Angelo Raffaele

Canal Grande

Ospedale G B Giustinian

Gallerie dell' Accademia 5

Stazione Marittima

San Basilio

Squero di San Trovàso 43

44 **Zattere**

Zattere

Canale della Giudecca

Mulino Stucky

Palanca Giudecca

Ex Covento delle Convertite (Penitenziario Femminile)

Ex Chiesa d. S. Cosmo e Damiano

La Giudecca 48

The island of Giudecca

Il Redentore,
on La Giudecca

Margherita, Dorsoduro's town square, a glorious, bustling *campo* that's
the hub of the *sestiere*. From here, it's less than five minutes stroll to
Ca' Rezzonico, a glorious Grand Canal *palazzo*, whose interior gives a
true taste of 18th-century Venice.

Perfect Days in ...

The Perfect Day

If you're not quite sure where to begin your travels, this itinerary recommends a practical and enjoyable day exploring Dorsoduro and the Giudecca, taking in some of the best places to see. For more information see the main entries (➤ 136–145).

🕗 8:30am

Beat the crowds by arriving as the doors open at the ☆**Gallerie dell'Accademia** (➤ 136), Venice's great picture gallery and top of most people's must-see list after San Marco. Once inside, take your time, concentrating on what interests you.

🕚 11:00am

Walk along the Rio di San Trovàso to the **43** *squero* (boatyard, ➤ 144) before taking a break to relax and enjoy coffee at one of the bars on the Fondamenta Zattere with great views across to the Giudecca.

🕦 11:30am

Walk west along the **44 Zattere** (ill. above, ➤ 144), then cut through along the Rio di San Sebastiano and find your way to **San Nicolò dei Mendicoli** (➤ 185), one of the city's oldest and most charming churches. Spend time exploring the quiet surrounding streets.

🕧 12:30pm

Catch the end of the market in lively **45 Campo Santa Margherita** (ill. opposite above, ➤ 144). Grab an outside table at one of the *campo's* restaurants for lunch, right, and follow it up with an ice cream at Causin.

⏰ 2:00pm

Walk along the Rio di San Barnaba, with its vegetable barge by the Ponte dei Pugni, to visit **42 Ca' Rezzonico** (➤ 142), Venice's museum of 18th-century life, a superbly opulent window into the city's former wealth.

⏰ 3:30pm

Catch the *vaporetto* down the Grand Canal to the Salute stop, where you can alight to admire the interior of **46 Santa Maria della Salute** (➤ 144).

⏰ 4:00pm

For a shot of modern art, head for the ⭐**Collezione Peggy Guggenheim** (➤ 140), or hit the collection of 21st-century contemporary art displayed in the superbly converted **47 Punta della Dogana** (➤ 145).

⏰ 6:00pm

Stroll back towards the Accademia bridge, pausing for a quiet moment's rest in the Campo San Vio, one of the few *campi* right beside the Grand Canal.

⏰ 7:00pm

Cross the Giudecca canal for a stroll with a view before dinner at Mistrà (Giudecca 212/A, Fondamenta San Giacomo; tel: 041 5 22 07 43), on the **48 Giudecca** (➤ 145); then take a boat back and have a night-cap at a waterfront bar.

⭐5 Gallerie dell'Accademia

Known as the "Accademia" for short, this gallery contains the most significant collection of Venetian painting from the Gothic to the Rococo in the world.

The museum is housed in three buildings: the Convent of the Lateran Canons, designed by Palladio in 1561, the church of Santa Maria della Carità, built by Bartolomeo Bon from 1441–52, and the Scuola that bears the same name. The buildings were secularised in *c*1800, and art lovers soon set up a "collection point" for works of art that had become "homeless" after the abandonment of cloisters, churches and *palazzi*. This strategy created a collection for the gallery in record time. The works of art are hung more or less chronologically in 24 rooms today, giving a fascinating overview of more than five centuries of Venetian painting.

Paintings by Bellini and Giorgione displayed in room 23

Walking Route

The route begins upstairs in the Scuola's former assembly room with its beautiful coffered ceiling. The first display exhibits altarpieces by Gothic Masters from the 14th and early 15th centuries. Paolo Veneziano (active 1333–58), the first significant figure in Venetian painting, created the multi-part altarpiece (*Polyptych*, *c*1350) from the church of Santa Chiara. It shows the Coronation of the Virgin in the centre and four scenes from the Life of Christ on each of the side panels. Paolo's painting on the centrepiece is characterised by its delicate colours and static, icon-like figures, betraying the influence of Byzantine art. In contrast, the scenes from Christ's life show greater realism.

Room 2 contains altarpieces from the 15th and 16th centuries. One of the largest works of Early Renaissance painting in Venice, the *Pala di San Giobbe* (before 1480) by Giovanni Bellini (▶ 26), marks a clear shift from the small, multi-panel works of the Late Gothic to the large format altarpieces of the Renaissance. Bellini's representation of Saints gathered around the Mother of God (*Sacra Conversazione*) created a popular prototype for subsequent Venetian Renaissance altarpieces. His example was imitated on many occasions: see the *Mother and Child Enthroned* by Giambattista Cima da Conegliano

Works of art by Vivarini can be seen in room 24

CRÈME DE LA CRÈME

- Paolo Veneziano's polyptych of the *Coronation of the Virgin* – Room 1.
- *Pala di San Giobbe* by Giovanni Bellini – Room 2.
- *The Tempest* by Giorgione – Room 5.
- Veronese's *Feast in the House of Levi* – Room 10.
- *The Miracle of the Slave* by Tintoretto – Room 10.
- *La Pietà* by Titian – Room 10.
- *Translation of the Body of St Mark* by Tintoretto – Room 10.
- *Views and Genre Paintings* by Canaletto, Guardi and Pietro Longhi – Room 17.
- The cycle of *The Miracle of the Relic of the Cross* by Gentile Bellini, Carpaccio and others – Room 20.
- Carpaccio's cycle of *The Story of St Ursula* – Room 21.
- Titian's *Presentation of the Virgin* – Room 24.

Dorsoduro & The Giudecca

(c1459–1517) in Room 2, for instance, or the famous representation of *Jesus in the Temple* painted by Vittore Carpaccio (c1465–1526).

The subsequent rooms exhibit masterpieces from such artists as Giambattista Cima da Conegliano, Piero della Francesca (1416/1417–92), Andrea Mantegna (Bellini's brother-in-law; 1431–1506), and both Jacopo (1424–70/71) and Giovanni Bellini. Painted shortly after 1505, Room 5's famous *The Tempest (La Tempesta)* by Giorgione – Bellini's most important pupil after Titian – shows the potent atmosphere just before the outbreak of a storm. By building up layer upon layer of paint, Giorgione succeeded in creating a new synthesis of colour and space. In contrast, his portrait of an old woman, whose inscription literally means "look what Time has made of me", is marked by stark realism.

Room 10 displays various attitudes to painting in the Counter Reformation by inviting visitors to make a clear comparison between the work of Paolo Caliari (1528–88), called Veronese, and Jacopo Robusti (1514–94), called Tintoretto. A huge canvas by Veronese, *The Feast in the House of Levi*, hangs at one end of the room. It was originally a representation of the Last Supper, but the painter was accused of heresy for the work's content. Instead of changing the painting as commanded, however, he merely altered its title (in agreement with his Dominican paymasters) – avoiding punishment by referring instead to a passage in the fifth chapter of Luke ("then Levi held a great banquet for Jesus at his house"). Tintoretto's images are characterised by drama and surreality. *The Miracle of the Slave*, painted for the Chapter Room of the Scuola Grande di San Marco in 1548, represents a miracle from the life of Saint Mark. In the scene, the Evangelist intervenes to stop the blinding and crushing of a pious slave who had come to worship the Saint's relics against the wishes of his master. Also in Room 10 is Titian's incomplete final work, the harrowing *Pietà*, which depicts the descent from life to death in muted colours. The same artist's *Presentation of the Virgin at the Temple* (1534–38) in Room 24 – both the former guesthouse of the Carità confraternity and the last room in the collection – still hangs in the spot for which it was painted to this day.

Giovanni Bellini's *Pala di San Giobbe* was painted before 1480 – possibly in gratitude for surviving the plague of 1478. It shows the Madonna and Child enthroned above three musical angels. The figures are flanked by Saints Francis, John the Baptist and Job on the left, and Saints Domenic, Sebastian and Louis of Toulouse on the right

TAKING A BREAK

Insider Tip

Head to the Rio di San Trovàso to **Al Bottegon** (Dorsoduro 2104, Fondamenta Nani, tel: 041 5 22 79 11), where you'll find a great atmosphere, excellent *panini* and a huge wine list.

✚ 205 E3 ✉ Campo della Carità
☎ 041 5 22 22 47; guided tours: 041 5 20 03 45;
www.gallerieaccademia.org, www.palazzogrimani.org
🕐 Mon 8:15–2, Tue–Sun 8:15–7:15 � 1, 2, Accademia
🎟 €9 (combined ticket with Palazzo Grimani)

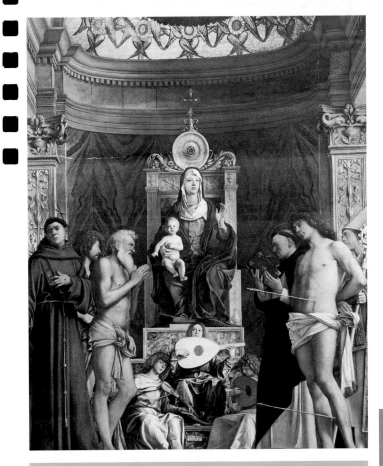

GIOVANNI BELLINI: OFFICIAL PAINTER OF THE VENETIAN REPUBLIC

Giovanni Bellini (c1430–1516), called "Giambellino", is famous for his altarpieces and devotional images. The scion of a Venetian family of painters (father, Jacopo Bellini; brother, Gentile Bellini), he was educated by the likes of his father and his brother-in-law, Andrea Mantegna. He himself went on to teach such important figures as Giorgione and Titian. One of the artist's major works is his triptych of the *Mother and Child Enthroned with the Four Evangelists* (1488) housed in the sacristy of Santa Maria Gloriosa dei Frari. This was the work that inspired Albrecht Dürer, who considered Bellini to be the best painter of his age, to paint his own *The Four Apostles*. Bellini's art is characterised by his use soft forms, warm, glowing colours and balanced figural compositions placed in front of atmospheric landscape backgrounds. Particularly impressive is his altarpiece (ital. *pala*) taken from the second chapel on the right in the church of San Giobbe. Hanging in the Accademia today, it is thought to be one of the first Venetian paintings to represent the interior of an imaginary church. Bellini was named Official Painter of the Venetian Republic in 1483, and died in his home city in 1516.

⭐ Collezione Peggy Guggenheim

The American heiress, patron and art dealer bought the unfinished *palazzo* on the Grand Canal in 1949 to house her collection of 20th-century art. Since then, the Guggenheim Foundation has been responsible for running the collection and the top-flight temporary exhibitions.

"I always did what I wanted and never cared what anyone thought. Women's lib? I was a liberated woman long before there was a name for it." Peggy Guggenheim (1898–1979) both lived and collected art in the same tempestuous style. At the start of the 1920s, the *enfant terrible* got involved with Parisian Bohemianism and married painter and writer Laurence Vail – an arrangement that didn't stop her having a great deal of close relationships with such artists as Marcel Duchamp, Samuel Beckett and Max Ernst. In 1938, she opened her first gallery in London with an exhibition of Cocteau's work. Her meeting with the author and art historian Herbert Read was a decisive moment in her life – with his help, she planned to found a museum similar to the Museum of Modern Art in New York. The outbreak of the Second World War put a stop to her plans, however.

Instead, she returned to Paris and – living by the motto "buy a picture every day" – quickly gathered together the foundations of her collection. She returned to New York in 1941, and moved to Venice in 1947 when her marriage to Max Ernst broke down. She achieved a breakthrough in 1948 when she filled a Biennale pavilion with works from her collection, gaining her recognition as a collector. She bought the Palazzo Venier dei Leoni – which had stood

The museum borders the Grand Canal

INSIDER INFO

- The Guggenheim is is one of the most visited museums in Venice, so make sure to **get there early**.
- Use an **audio-guide** (available at the ticket office) to get the best from your visit to the collection.
- Photos on the walls of the summerhouse and the museum café show scenes from the life of this extraordinary patroness.
- The Guggenheim has an excellent **book and gift shop**.
- Look for **Peggy Guggenheim's grave**, tucked away in the west corner of the Sculpture Garden.

The collection's interior spaces are light and airy

unfinished since 1748 – in 1949. The palace still houses her collection to this day.

The Collection

The collection on the Grand Canal boasts excellent pieces from the most important proponents of modern art: Braques, Dalí, Chagall, Duchamp, Ernst, Kandinsky, Mondrian, Picabia, Picasso, Pollock, Arp, Brancusi, Moore, Calder and many more. Max Ernst and Pollock – whom she discovered and promoted – are particularly well represented. Brancusi's *Maiastra* is one of the most beautiful sculptures on display.

The top crowd-puller is probably Marino Marini's *Angel of the Citadel*. The piece, a powerful figure of a horse and nude rider, stands on the terrace overlooking the Canal.

TAKING A BREAK

Pause for refreshment at the convenient **Museum Café**.

🕂 205 F3 ✉ Palazzo Venier dei Leoni, Fondamenta Venier
☎ 041 2 40 54 11; www.guggenheim-venice.it
🕐 Wed–Mon 10–6; Sat 10–10, in summer 🍴 Café, restaurant on site
🚢 1, 2, Accademia 🎫 €14

42 Ca' Rezzonico

The Museo del Settecento Veneziano gives an impression of the ostentatious lifestyle enjoyed by the nobility in 18th-century Venice during the last days of the Republic. The museum is housed in one of the most impressive palaces of the era, the Ca' Rezzonico. The building's staterooms are full to overflowing with furniture, textiles, glass and large paintings, and offer wonderful views of the Canal.

The palace was initially built for the Bon family from 1667 to 1682 by Venice's most important Baroque architect, Baldassare Longhena. Giorgio Massari completed the stately home a century later for the Rezzonico family, who bought their way into the nobility in the mid-17th century. A scion of this family, Carlo Rezzonico, would later rise to become Pope Clement XIII (1758–69). In the mid-19th century, the palace came into the possession of English poet Robert Browning, who lived there until his death in 1889. The palace has served as a museum since the 1930s.

Walking Tour
The palace's 40 or so rooms display salon art at its very finest, with silk wall coverings, Flemish tapestries, fanciful cabinets and dressers, and sumptuous Baroque furniture by Andrea Brustolon (1662–1732), who enjoyed carving Moorish figures out of ebony. This is accompanied by the chinoiserie, lacquer furniture, Venetian porcelain, ceramics and bronze work that was so popular during the age. An open staircase leads up to the massive ballroom, the ceiling of which was painted by G. B. Crosato (1755). The main treasures on this floor include the marriage allegory by Giambattista Tiepolo in the adjoining room – a work that immortalised the lavish wedding ceremony between Ludovico Rezzonico and Faustina Savorgnan in 1758 – and the

A view of the Baroque palace (left of the picture) from the *vaporetto* stop opposit

**Above top:
Section of
Tiepolo's
Mondo Nuovo
fresco (1791);
Below: The
throne of
Pius VI**

humorous genre scenes of Venetian daily life by Pietro Longhi (1702–85; second floor), including *Early Morning Chocolate, The Pancake Seller, and The Rhinoceros.*

TAKING A BREAK

Take a break from the opulently decorated rooms and enjoy a drink or snack in the **ground floor café**.

➕ 205 E4

✉ Dorsoduro 3136, Fondamenta Rezzonico

☎ 041 2 41 01 00; carezzonico.visitmuve.it

🕐 April–Oct Wed–Mon 10–6, Nov–March Wed–Mon 10–5

🚏 1, Ca' Rezzonico 💶 €8.50

INSIDER INFO

- If the **water entrance** is open, use it to arrive as 18th-century visitors would have done.
- Use the multi-lingual **information cards** provided in each room to help you get more out of your visit.
- Ca' Rezzonico has some of the best museum services in Venice – an **excellent gift and bookshop**, pleasant snack bar, **good toilets**.
- The **courtyard garden** is a haven of peace – leave time to enjoy it.
- **If your time is short,** avoid the third-floor **Egidio Martini picture gallery**; it's huge and mediocre, though the 18th-century apothecary's shop is worth a look.

At Your Leisure

43 Squero di San Tròvaso

Insider Tip

One of Venice's few remaining *squeri* (gondola boatyards) stands on Rio di San Tròvaso; it's a picturesque corner, with its yard sloping down to the edge of the canal and the geranium-hung, chalet-style owner's house on one side. Maintenance keeps the

Men at work: Squero do San Tròvaso

yard busy (gondola hulls need to be regularly cleaned), and they still build 3–4 new gondolas a year.

🕀 205 D3 ⊠ Rio di San Trovaso
🚤 51, 52, 61, 62, Zattere; 1, Accademia

44 Zattere

Built in 1519, the Zattere's wide quays were named after the *zattere* (rafts) once moored here. The waterway runs from the fine *palazzi* in the west to the old salt warehouses and the Punta della Dogana in the east. The **Officina delle Zattere** has served as an exciting second exhibition space for contemporary art on the promenade for the last few years (www.officinadellezattere.it; times/prices vary for different exhibitions). The busiest section is in the middle, from where *vaporetti* leave for the Giudecca (➤ 145) and where you'll find **Nico** (➤ 146), home to some of the city's best ice-cream.

🕀 205 D2 ⊠ Fondamenta delle Zattere
🚤 2, 51, 52, 61, 62, Zattere

45 Campo Santa Margherita

This oddly shaped but pretty *campo*, with its market, tree-shaded benches, shops, bars and restaurants, is one of Venice's liveliest and most beguiling squares, buzzing till late with partying university students and tourists. It is ringed by ancient *palazzi*, Santa Margherita's church, which is now a busy conference hall, and the odd little building in the centre is the Scuola dei Varoteri (Tanners' Guild).

🕀 205 D4 ⊠ Campo Santa Margherita
🚤 1, Ca' Rezzonico

46 Santa Maria della Salute

This Baroque church, which stands at the entrance to the Grand Canal, depicts the Madonna as "Ruler of the Sea" (Capitana del Mar): a statue of the Virgin bearing the staff of a Venetian High Admiral stands atop the building's 55m (180ft) high dome. The church was built in thanks for the end of the plague that tore through Venice in the summer of 1630, claiming 40,000 lives (almost a third of the population). The project was given to 33 year-old Baldassare Longhena, who began work on a foundation of exactly 176,627 wooden stakes (according to one calculation) in 1631. The church wasn't completed until 1687, five years after the architect's death. Eight mighty pillars support the dome in the interior, and there are six chapels on each side of the building. The floor is very beautiful. Flemish sculptor Giusto Le Court's figural group on the high altar (before 1674) is the most significant of the church's many statues: the Mother of God is shown answering the Venetians' prayers and driving away the plague. Venice commemorates being rescued from the plague at the annual Salute festival, for which a pontoon bridge

Santa Maria della Salute

was built over the Grand Canal from Santa Maria del Giglio.
➕ 206 B3 ✉ Campo della Salute ☎ 041 5 22 55 58 🕐 9–noon, 3–5 🚏 1, Salute 💶 Free

47 Punta della Dogana

Once Venice's customs house, the Punta della Dogana today serves as a museum for contemporary art. It houses part of the collection belonging to French multimillionaire François Pinault, which includes fantastic works by such modern and contemporary artists as Sigmar Polke, Richard Serra, Cy Twombly, Thomas Schütte, Jeff Koons and Cindy Sherman. In order to exhibit his collection, Pinault invested

20 million Euros to restore the building following plans by Japanese architect Tadao Ando, who is known for his minimalistic style.
➕ 199 D2 ✉ Dorsoduro 2, Campo di Salute ☎ 041 5 23 16 80; www.palazzograssi.it 🕐 Daily 10–7 🚏 1, Salute 💶 €15, combined ticket with Palazzo Grassi €20

48 La Giudecca

Across the water from Dorsoduro lies the island of Giudecca, the place where patricians built their elegant summer palaces and beautiful pleasure gardens in the Middle Ages. Later, the island was home to factories and low-cost housing, and today it's an increasingly desirable residential area that attracts such stars as Sting and Elton John, who owns a house here. Ever since the opening of the Molina Stucky Hilton Hotel in an old, brick-walled mill (➤ 43), this former workers' island has been caught up in a whirlwind of gentrification. As well as the luxury hotel on its western point, Giudecca is also home to the headquarters of the historic Fortuny textile house. There are two churches by Palladio: **Le Zitelle**, and the plague church of **Il Redentore** (1577–92). Its feast is celebrated in July (➤ 23), when a pontoon bridge spans the water from Dorsoduro.

The **Casa dei Tre Oci**, built by Mario De Maria in the early 20th century, hosts a changing selection of contemporary art and photography exhibitions (www.fondazionedivenezia.org).
➕ 204 B1–207 D2 ✉ Giudecca 🚏 2, 41

Where to...
Eat and Drink

Prices
Expect to pay per person for a meal, excluding drinks.
€ under €35   €€ €35–€55   €€€ over €55

BÀCARI, BARS AND GELATERIE

GROM €
Established in the early 2000s, GROM gelaterie has made a big impact on customers with their excellent and upmarket ice creams, made from impeccably sourced and fine ingredients. The range of flavours changes monthly, and depends entirely on what produce is in season, so don't expect to order strawberry ice cream in December or mandarin in July. The flavours are clear and true; coffee and salted caramel flavours are particularly good.
✚ 204 C3 ✉ Dorsoduro 2761, Campo San Barnaba ☎ 041 0 99 17 51; www.grom.it
Ⓓ Daily 10–10 ⛴ Ca' Rezzonico

Internet Café Noir €
Internet Café Noir is a fun place to hang out while you perhaps check your e-mails: listen to the music, have a beer and a sandwich, and relax. They serve more than 20 varieties of tea, iced coffee, hot chocolate and fresh juice and stay open till late. The atmosphere here is laidback and friendly.
✚ 204 D5 ✉ Dorsoduro 3805, Crosera San Pantalon ☎ 041 71 09 25 Ⓓ Mon–Sat 7am–2am, Sun 9am–2am ⛴ San Tomà

Insider Tip
Nico €
On the waterfront, with an ice-cream, what could be better! Nico is famous for its *Coppa Gianduiotto*, a rich and sinful frozen chocolate and hazelnut concoction (very filling), but the *crema* and fruit flavours, such as lemon or straw-

berry, are equally good. Bar service also available. Treat yourself to an evening stroll along the Zattere, or sit at the *gelateria's* romantic pontoon overlooking the Giudecca.
✚ 205 D2 ✉ Dorsoduro 922, Fondamenta Zattere al Ponte Longo ☎ 041 5 22 52 93; www.gelaterianico.com Ⓓ Fri–Wed 7am–11pm. Closed end Dec ⛴ Zattere

OSTERIE, TRATTORIE AND RISTORANTI

Al Bottegon (Cantinone gia Schiavo) €
Set on the same canal as the famous *squero* (➤ 144), this *bàcaro* is among the best in the city, packed inside with crowds spilling out on to the *fondamenta*. It's a great place for lunch, when bulging panini, delicious *cicheti* of all sorts and basic *secondi* are served at the bar and at tables in the back. Everything is prepared by three generations of the same family, who know their wines and will sell you a ready-chilled bottle to take away.
✚ 205 E3 ✉ Dorsoduro 992, Fondamenta Nani ☎ 041 5 23 00 34 Ⓓ Mon–Sat 8–2:30, 4–9:30 ⛴ Zattere, Accademia

Antica Locanda Montin €€/€€€
Jimmy Carter, Mick Jagger, David Bowie und Brad Pitt: Montin's has been pleasing well-heeled visitors and tourists for more than 50 years. The cooking remains reliable – and can be superb – and the atmosphere and service are traditionally Venetian. The menu includes all the specialities such as *spaghetti alle vongole* (with clams) *risotto*

nero (black squid risotto), crisp and light *fritto misto* (mixed fried fish) and locally sourced vegetables. The wine list is impressive, and the house wines excellent, and there are tables in the charming courtyard garden.

🚼 205 D3 ✉ Dorsoduro 1147, Fondamenta di Borgo ☎ 041 5 22 71 51; www.locanda montin. com ⊙ Thu–Mon 12–3, 7–10; closed 2 weeks Jan and 2 weeks Aug 🚢 Accademia, Zattere

Antica Osteria al Pantalon €€

On the main route to the Frari, this long, narrow restaurant tempts diners with its eye-catching window display of fresh fish and seafood. This, and the excellent pasta and rice dishes, are cooked to order and served with simple elegance at the plain wooden tables. It's wise to be guided in your choice by the staff and, unless you're eating early, to book ahead during the busy months – it's popular with students from the nearby university.

🚼 205 D5 ✉ Dorsoduro 3958, Crosera San Pantalon ☎ 041 71 08 49 ⊙ Mon–Sat 12:30–3, 7–10 🚢 San Tomà

Dona Onesta €/€€

Tucked away near the Frari, the "Honest Woman" has been a neighbourhood favourite for many years. Some of the classic Venetian dishes stand out – try the seafood risotto, the *insalata di mare* (seafood appetizer), the *sarde in saor* (sour sweet sardines) or the *seppie alla veneziana*, rich squid cooked in its ink and served with polenta. Delicate *bresaola* (air-cured beef) and veal escalopes are cooked in a variety of styles and will please meat-lovers.

🚼 205 E4 ✉ Ponte della Dona Onesta, Dorsoduro 3922 ☎ 041 71 05 86 ⊙ Mon–Sat 12:30–2:30, 7:30–9:30 🚢 San Tomà

La Rivista €€

An offshoot of the trendy Ca' Pisani (►36), the stylish 1930s-inspired décor of this laidback wine and cheese bar gives a foretaste of its general style. Food here is light and healthy, featuring delicious fresh salads, imaginative main courses and beautiful and well-balanced cheese platters. There's a good selection of wines both bottled and by the glass. This is an excellent place for a relaxing dinner.

🚼 205 D3 ✉ 979/A Dorsoduro, Rio Terà Foscarini ☎ 041 2 40 14 25; www.restaurant larivista.com ⊙ Tue–Sun 12–3, 7–10:30 🚢 Accademia

Mistrà €/€€

Off the beaten track, but well signposted, on the south side of the Giudecca, Mistrà is housed on the upper floor of an old warehouse surrounded by boatyards. Packed with locals, who come to enjoy fresh fish, seafood and Ligurian specialities, the airy dining room has spectacular lagoon views. Lunchtime sees lower prices and a more straightforward menu.

🚼 205 F1 ✉ Giudecca 212/A, Fondamenta San Giacomo ☎ 041 5 22 07 43 ⊙ Wed–Sun 12–3, 7:30–10:30, Mon 12–3 🚢 Redentore

Osteria 1518 €/€€

Situated just off the west end of the Zattere, is where you'll find the 1518, whose tables spill outside in throughout the year. Straightforward and unassuming, it prides itself on traditional Venetian cuisine served at honest prices. Expect impeccable fish from the market, a few meat dishes and look out for the good-value set lunch and dinner menus served, which are an improvement than those served in busier parts of town.

🚼 204 C4 ✉ Dorsoduro 1518/A, Calle del Vento ☎ 041 5 20 57 99 ⊙ Tue–Sun 12–10 🚢 San Basilio

Pizzeria Alle Zattere €/€€

If you are in the mood for an affordable pizza with a priceless view, this is the place! Sit on the pier overlooking the Giudecca for the cost of a modest margherita. The main menu is a bit touristy but the location is fabulous and the views make this a superb place for an affordable dinner.

✚ 205 E2 ✉ Dorsoduro 791/a, Fondamenta delle Zattere ai Gesuati ☎ 041 5 20 42 24; www.allezattere.com ⏰ Wed–Mon noon–3, 7–10. Closed Dec 1–Jan 10 🚏 Zattere, Accademia

Where to...
Shop

Dorsoduro has excellent shops for visitors and its wealthy locals, and is a great place to find unusual accessories.

Going west from the Salute, is **Antiquariato Oggetistica Claudia Canestrelli** (Dorsoduro 364A, Campiello Barbaro, tel: 041 5 22 70 72), a tiny shop specializing in 18th-century-style drop earrings.

There's more jewellery at **Susanna & Marina Sent** (Dorsoduro 669, tel: 041 5 20 81 36) on the Campo San Vio; they also sell glass in chunky shapes, scarves and accessories. Opposite is **Bac Art Studio** (Dorsoduro 862, tel: 041 5 22 81 71) with photos of Venice, framed prints and original art.

Further along the street, **Risuola di Giovanni Dittura** (Dorsoduro 871, Calle Nuova Sant'Agnese, tel: 041 5 23 11 63) is a shoe store selling cheap *friulani*, brilliantly coloured velvet slippers.

West from the Accademia calle Toletta is home to **Libreria Toletta and Toletta Studio** (Dorsoduro 1175/A, tel: 041 5 23 20 34), an excellent source of Venice-related picture and books at keen prices.

Campo San Barnaba is home to **Pantagruelica** (Dorsoduro 2844, tel: 041 5 23 67 66), the city's finest food shop. Nearby **Annelie** (Dorsoduro 2748, Calle Lunga Santa Barbara, tel: 041 5 20 32 77) sells affordable fine linens.

Mondonovo (Dorsoduro 3063, Rio Terà Canal, tel: 041 5 28 73 44), across Ponte dei Pugni, has been making masks for over 20 years.

Where to...
Go Out

Campo Santa Margherita is the hub of Dorsoduro's nightlife.

These include **Round Midnight** (Dorsoduro 3012, Fondamenta dello Squero, tel: 041 5 23 20 56), an intimate DJ bar with a nightly disco, and the more restrained **Piccolo Mondo** (Dorsoduro 1056, Calle Corfu, tel: 041 5 20 03 71) near the Accademia.

If you want to spend all evening in the *campo*, **Il Caffè Rosso** (Dorsoduro 2963, tel: 041 5 28 79 98; www.cafferosso.it) is perhaps the most popular bar which often hosts live music, or try **Margaret Duchamp** (Dorsoduro 3019, tel: 041 5 28 62 55), a chic place with plenty of outdoor tables for seeing and be-ing seen, or **Chet Bar** (Dorsoduro 3026, tel: 041 5 28 66 79), a lively newcomer on the scene with live DJs on Thu, Fri and Sat.

Classical music is sometimes on offer in the staggering surroundings of the **Scuola Grande dei Carmini** (Dorsoduro 2617, tel: 041 5 28 94 20; www.scuolagrandecarmini.it); programmes include 18th-century music and occasional concert per-formances of opera, and there's more music – usually organ recit-als – at the **Salute** (tel: 041 5 22 55 58) and **San Trovaso** (tel: 041 2 96 06 30).

For the ultimate musical ex-perience in a breath-taking setting, catch a concert at **Ca' Rezzonico** (➤ 142), where chamber music is performed in the ballroom.

The Lagoon Islands

Little Treats

Culinary Delights

Embark on a culinary adventure with Mauro Stoppa on board a *bragozzo* – one of the last flat bottomed sailing boats in Venice. (Mobile tel: 034 97 43 15 52, www.cruisingvenice.com).

Dark Days in the Serenissima

Venice detained the mentally ill on the island of San Servolo. This fact is kept alive by the **Museo del Manicomio** (visits by appointment, tel: 041 5 24 01 19, Mon–Thu 9.30–5pm, Fri 9.30-3.30pm, €3).

"Little Venice"

With its canals and palaces, Chioggia is reminiscent of Venice – minus the hustle and bustle of the crowds.

Getting Your Bearings

A number of small islands lie like enchanted oases in the shallow waters of the Venetian lagoon. With a touch of poetic licence, British poet Lord Byron described them climbing out of the waters, as if bewitched by a fairy. Apart from Burano, Murano and Torcello, only a few of these islands are inhabited today – it's almost impossible to imagine the history of Venice beginning here around 1,500 years ago.

Some of these islands once served as strongholds and hiding places, leper colonies and military hospitals, cloisters and kitchen gardens for the city. Others have played host to handicrafts for centuries: Burano is famous for its delicate lace, Murano for its exquisite glass. The only true pleasure island is the Lido, where people have lived the Dolce Vita on the golden beach since the Belle Époque. The larger islands are connected by *vaporetti*, but you can only reach the outlying islands on guided tours or under your own steam.

The fascinating landscape of the Venetian lagoon stretches from the mainland across to the Adriatic and from the estuary of the Sile river in the north right down to the Brenta in the south. The lagoon is a large, flat bay of around 212mi² in size. It has just three connections to the sea, known as the Bocche di Porto (Lido-San Nicolò, Malamocco and Chioggia). The lagoon is a wonderfully diverse world of water and mud, submerged marshes and sandbanks. Artificially deepened canals and creeks, known as *ghebi*, create navigable routes between the sea and the bay's 117 islands. Some of these islands still act as bulwarks against the tide, while others are floating gardens that supply produce to the markets in the Rialto. Most of the islands are only a stone's throw away from the city, while others lie isolated out in the far reaches of the lagoon.

The picturesque reflections of Burano's colourful houses on the surface of the water

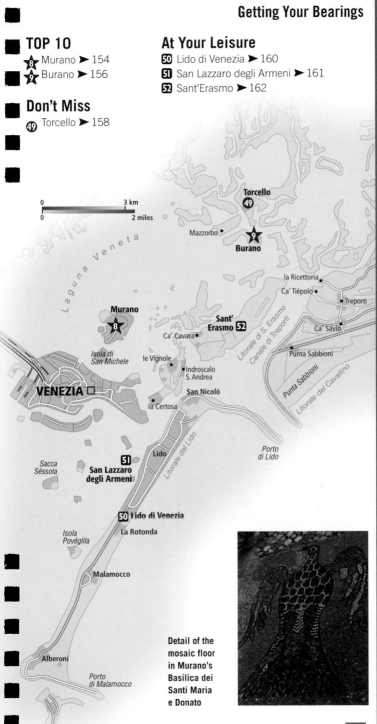

0   3 km
0   2 miles

Laguna Veneta

Torcello
49

Mazzorbo

⭐ 9
Burano

la Ricettoria

Ca' Tiépolo

Treporti

Murano
8

Sant'
Erasmo 52

Ca' Cavara

Litorale di S. Erasmo
Canale di Treporti

Ca' Sávio

Isola di
San Michele

le Vignole

Indroscalo
S. Andrea

Punta Sabbioni

VENEZIA □

la Certosa

San Nicolò

Punta Sabbioni

Litorale del Cavallino

Porto
di Lido

Sacca
Séssola

51
San Lazzaro
degli Armeni

Lido

Litorale del Lido

Isola
Povéglila

50 Lido di Venezia

La Rotonda

Malamocco

Alberoni

Porto
di Malamocco

Detail of the
mosaic floor
in Murano's
Basilica dei
Santi Maria
e Donato

Perfect Days in...

The Perfect Day

For time away from central Venice, this itinerary recommends a practical and enjoyable day exploring the Lagoon Islands, taking in some of the best places to see. For more information see the main entries (➤ 154–162).

⏱ 9:00am

Take the *vaporetto* from the Fondamenta Nuove for the 15-minute hop to ⭐**Murano** (➤ 154), alighting at the Museo stop. Head for one of the glass factories to watch a demonstration of glass-blowing and browse in one of the many showrooms.

⏱ 11:00am

Stroll across the Ponte Vivarini and enjoy coffee or an ice-cream beside Murano's own Grand Canal before visiting the lovely Basilica dei Santi Maria e Donato (ill. below, ➤ 155), a 12th-century Venetian-Byzantine jewel with glowing mosaics. Then head for the Museo dell'Arte Vetraria (Glass Museum, ➤ 154), which tells the story of Venice's ancient glass industry.

⏱ 12:15pm

Catch the *vaporetto* for ⭐**Burano** (ill. opposite, ➤ 156) from the Faro stop and sit back and enjoy the 40-minute journey across the northern lagoon.

⏱ 1:15pm

At Burano, head straight for the Via Baldassare Galuppi, the island's main street, where you'll find a good choice of fish restaurants for lunch – try family run Da Romano (Burano 221 Via B Galuppi, tel: 041 73 00 30).

⏱ 2:30pm

Work off your lunch with a gentle stroll through the gaily painted streets, or relax on a bench in the shade over-looking the water, before paying a visit to the Museo del Merletto (Museum of Lace, ➤ 157) to learn more about Burano's lace-making, a traditional industry that is still practised here today.

🕓 4:00pm

Get back on the boat for the five-minute ride to **49 Torcello** (➤ 158), the northern lagoon's most evocative island. Here you can saunter along to the grassy *piazza* to visit two of Venice's most extraordinary churches, the lofty 7th-century Basilica di Santa Maria Assunta (➤ 158) and, next door, the lovely 11th-century church of Santa Fosca, right. You could stop for a drink in the garden of the Locanda Cipriani (➤ 163), one of Venice's most famous restaurants, in front of the basilica.

🕕 6:00pm

Take the *vaporetto* back to Venice via Treporti and Punta Sabbioni, a peaceful lagoon sail which takes you past the monastery island of San Francesco del Deserto and **52 Sant'Erasmo** (➤ 162), a sparsely inhabited island where most of Venice's vegetables are grown.

🕗 8:00pm

All that sea air will have given you a good appetite, so choose a restaurant in the San Marco area, near where the boat terminates, for dinner. This could be the evening to splash out on an aperitif or nightcap at **17 Caffè Florian** (➤ 70) or Caffè Quadri (➤ 73) in the Piazza San Marco, whose ambience will round off the day perfectly.

⭐8 Murano

If you can fit in only one island visit, make it Murano, a short hop across the water from the Fondamenta Nuove. The network of small canals leading to a main waterway make the "Isle of Glassmakers" reminiscent of Venice.

Murano was one of the earliest islands to be settled in the lagoon. Until 1291, its inhabitants made a living from fishing and the salt trade. Murano's fortunes changed after glass production was moved there from Venice. In the 16th century, when Murano was home to around 30,000 people (there are fewer than 5,000 here today), it became the preferred summer retreat of rich Venetian patricians. These nobles owned palaces and pleasure gardens on Murano, and Italy's first botanical garden was planted on the island.

View of the Basilica dei Santi Maria e Donato

Museo del Vetro

The Glass Museum in the **Palazzo Giustinian** (17th c.) boasts one of the world's largest collections of Venetian glass. It also displays glassware produced by ancient Roman, Bohemian and Moorish glass blowers. One of the best-known showpieces is the Coppa Barovier (Room 1), a wedding chalice from the 15th century. It's probably the work of the daughter of Angelo Barovier, a member of Murano's most famous glass blowing family. The exhibition of modern blown glass art is also worth a look.

Insider Tip

San Pietro Martire

This church was rebuilt in 1511 after being burned down in a fire. It boasts some precious artistic treasures: Giovanni Bellini's *Barbarigo Altarpiece* (1488) and *The Virgin in Glory with Eight Saints* (1505–13) in the right-hand aisle, and Veronese's *St Jerome in the Desert*, and *Saint Agatha in Prison* in the aisle to the left.

Basilica dei Santi Maria e Donato

Built between the 7th and 12th centuries, Murano's most beautiful church is one of the oldest sacred buildings in the lagoon. Its east façade is particularly fine: the apse with two rows of arcades combines elements of Venetian-Byzantine and Early Romanesque architecture. Inside, the side aisles are separated from the nave by columns in Greek marble topped with Venetian-Byzantine capitals. The beautiful 12th-century mosaic floor looks like an oriental carpet decorated with lively animal figures and artistic ornaments.

TAKING A BREAK

Have a snack at the bar or enjoy a leisurely lunch in the garden of the **Antica Trattoria** (Fondamenta Cavour 18, tel: 041 73 96 10) overlooking Murano's own Grand Canal.

Masterful hands at work – glassmaking is still the island's bread and butter to this day

Basilica dei Santi Maria e Donato
⊠ Campo San Donato 🕔 Mon–Sat 9–noon, 3:30–7, Sun 3:30–7
🚢 12, 13, 41, 42 🖐 Free

Museo del Vetro
⊠ Fondamenta Giustinian 8 ☎ 041 73 95 86; museovetro.visitmuve.it
🕔 April–Oct Thu–Tue 10–6; Oct–March 10–5
🚢 DM, 41, 42 🖐 €5.50

INSIDER INFO

- Don't accept a "free" boat trip from the city centre to Murano. These are funded by the glass factories and you'll be under **considerable sales pressure** to buy something once you get to Murano.
- To **avoid the touts** from the big glass showrooms, don't get off the *vaporetto* at Colonna or Faro; wait instead for Museo or Venier, which are closer to what you'll want to see.
- **The cheaper the glass**, the less likely it is to have been made in Murano itself; all genuine Venetian glass is marked with the *Vetro Artistico Murano* trademark, an official, legally-supported guarantee of authenticity.

★9 Burano

Burano is the most picturesque isle in the Venetian lagoon. Lying around 9km (5½mi) away from Venice's main island, it can be reached in 40 minutes by boat.

This lively fishing community is famous for its array of colourful houses. According to legend, these one- and two-storey buildings were painted in such striking tones to help fishermen find their way home in poor conditions. The fishing boats in the narrow canals are also painted in vibrant shades, and look enchanting against the colour of the houses reflected in the water. You can cross a small wooden bridge to get to the neighbouring island of Mazzorbo (350 inhabitants), where wine production and agriculture shape the landscape.

Burano is renowned for its brightly coloured buildings

Lacework

The island, inhabited by around 3,100 people today, doesn't have much to offer art aficionados apart from the **Chiesa di San Martino Vescovo** (16th c.) with its leaning tower. Instead, Burano is famous for its lace. According to legend, a love-drunk Captain once left his sweetheart behind on Burano before making a voyage to sail past the island of the Sirens. Although the crew were overcome by the magical song and leapt from the ship, the lover withstood the test, just like Odysseus and Orpheus had done before

BALDASSARRE GALUPPI

The Buranese are proud of their native composer Baldassarre Galuppi (1706–85) who set many of the comic plays of Carlo Goldoni (1717–93) to music. The main street and the *piazza* are named after him and you can see his statue in the square.

him. Apparently impressed by the steadfastness of the Captain, the Queen of the Sirens made a crown of foam rise up from the sea. This transformed into the finest lace when it touched the seafarer's hands. The material later became the wedding veil for his beloved back on Burano.

Aside from the legends, Burano lace does have a special connection with the sea: its stitches are said to come from the manufacturing techniques used to produce fishing nets. Only a handful of people still master the craft today, and real Burano lace has long been a luxury item. In the **Museum** of the **Scuola di Merletti** (founded in 1872), you can learn a great deal about lacemaking techniques and see beautiful examples of lacework, including sumptuous fans, veils and gowns. If you want to round off your visit with a trip to one of Via Galuppi's fabulous fish restaurants, make sure to try a Burano ring *(bussola)* for dessert – they're best dunked in sweet wine.

The complicated "air stitch" *(punto in aria)*, the trademark of Burano lacemaking, was invented as early as the 16th century

TAKING A BREAK

Burano's best known restaurant **Trattoria Da Romano** (➤ 163) is good for lunch.

Museo del Merletto
✉ Piazza Galuppi 187
☎ 041 73 00 34; museomerletto.visitmuve.it
🗓 April–Oct 10–6; Nov–March 10–5 🚉 LN 🖐 €5.50

INSIDER INFO

- A nice way to approach Burano is to **get off at Mazzorbo** and walk across the wooden bridge connecting the two islands. You'll get to enjoy some great views of Venice from the bridge.
- If you're here in the morning, **visit the fish market** on the Fondamenta della Pescheria.
- To see Burano lace being made, ask at the **Scuola dei Merletti** whether lace-makers will be working when you visit.
- **Neighbouring Mazzorbo** is a great place for a picnic or a walk through its vineyards and smallholdings.
- Pop into **Chiesa di San Martino Vescovo** on Piazza Galuppi to see Tiepolo's huge and disturbing *Crucifixion*.

Insider Tip

㊾ Torcello

Torcello, the island of the "small tower", was the first settlement in the lagoon. For a few centuries, it was also the most powerful. It could boast its own bishop, a great deal of churches and palaces, a large harbour and shipyards, its own laws and over 20,000 inhabitants. The unstoppable rise of Venice and the constant threat of malaria due to swamps forming around the island meant that people gradually moved away from the start of the 16th century.

The **Basilica di Santa Maria Assunta**, the oldest building in the lagoon, is a reminder of the island's great history. According to an inscription to the left of the high altar, the basilica was built in 639 in a Venetian-Byzantine style. The crypt, the portico and the two side apses were built in the 9th century. The aisles were raised and the **Campanile** was added at the start of the 11th century. You can still see the foundation walls of a 7th-century baptistery in front of the church. The triple-aisled basilica's flooring comes from the 11th century; mosaics found beneath this date to the 9th century. The oldest mosaics can be found on the crossed vault in the right-hand apse. The angel bearing a medallion of the Lamb of God (on the apse vault) shows strong Byzantine influences and is reminiscent of the famous 6th-century mosaics in Ravenna – it's thought that the Ravenna mosaicists were also involved on Torcello.

A bird's-eye view of the Basilica di Santa Maria Assunta

Next to the Basilica stands the small church of **Santa Fosca**, which consists of an 11th-century central structure surrounded by 12th-century arcades. The square interior space with its oblong choir serves as a memorial to Saint Fosca, a martyr from Ravenna. The marble block in the form of a seat on the square outside is said to be the 5th-century throne of Attila the Hun. The nearby **Museo di Torcello** deals with the island's long history.

TAKING A BREAK

On the way from the *pontile* to the Basilica, you'll find the low-key **Osteria Ponte del Diavolo** (➤ 164), which offers good-value home-cooking and a cool shaded terrace – it's a cheaper alternative to the neighbouring Cipriani.

HOW MOSAICS ARE MADE

Large sheets of different coloured glass are first shattered into tiny pieces. Gold and silver pieces are made by applying leaf, then sealing it with a thin layer of clear glass. The laying surface is covered with cement, on which the outline of the image is traced. Next comes a thin layer of mortar; on this, a detailed painting of the final design is made. The pieces of glass, set at different angles to refract the light, are then pressed into the wet mortar.

The iconostasis (icon screen), common in Greek Orthodox churches, is used as a rood screen in the Basilica di Santa Maria Assunta to divide off the chancel

Basilica di Santa Maria Assunta
☎ 041 2 70 24 64 🕐 March–Oct daily 10:30–6; Nov–Feb 10–5
🚻 T 💶 €5

Campanile
ℹ closed due to renovations.

Santa Fosca
🕐 Daily 10:30–12:30, 2–5 🚻 12 💶 Free

Museo di Torcello
✉ Palazzo del Consiglio ☎ 041 2 70 24 64 🕐 March–Oct Tue–Sun 10:30–5:30; Nov–Feb Tue–Sun 10–5 🚻 T 💶 €3

INSIDER INFO

- Plan to make your visit visit as **early or late** in the day as possible to avoid the worst of the crowds of tourists.
- Ask for an **audio-guide** to help you understand the Basilica's history and the mosaics' story. The bell tower provides fine views of the lagoon.
- Note that **the last boat** leaves Torcello at 8.15pm.
- Don't bother with the **Museo di Torcello** if you've only got limited time.

At Your Leisure

Beach living on the Lido di Venezia

50 🚻 Lido di Venezia

Every Lido gets its name from Venice's version; it simply means "sandbank". This long, sandy strip of an island was once a bulwark against the Adriatic, a sparsely inhabited, desolate place with pine woods and

le Vignole
• Indroscalo
  S. Andrea
VENEZIA San Nicolò
  la Certosa
**San Lazzaro
degli Armeni 51** Lido
  *Isola
  Lazzaretto
  Vécchio*
  Litorale del Lido

50 Lido di Venezia

*Isola
Povéglila*

0 ___ 1 km
0 ___ 1 mile

long sandy beaches. It was "discovered" by Romantic writers in the mid-19th century, and the Edwardian cult of the seaside saw the construction of grand hotels as well as private houses on the seaward side. Today, the Lido is more a suburb than a resort. The hotels are still there, coming into their own during the Film Festival (➤ 48), and it's a popular and accessible place to escape the heat of the centre. The short hop into Venice makes it an excellent base for families; prices are lower, and there's the bonus of the beach. The Lido also has cars and buses, quite a shock if you're unprepared. Most people come here to enjoy a day sunbathing on the beach – a more popular pastime since strides have been made to clean the water surrounding Venice. Each grand hotel has its own immaculate beach, complete with first-class service and prices to match, and there are private beaches that charge less and provide changing cabins, loungers, umbrellas and bars. The *comune*, the local council, runs free beaches, or you could take the bus down to the neighbouring sandy island of **Pellestrina** to escape the crowds.

South, too, still on the Lido, is the pretty village of **Alberoni**, **Insider Tip** where there's a golf course and horse-riding stables. Evenings are the time for enjoying Italy's traditional evening stroll, the *passeggiata*, as well as shopping before having a leisurely dinner in a restaurant.

There's also the historic church of **San Nicolò**, founded in 1044, at the northern end of the island. The Doge traditionally came here on Ascension Day after the ceremony of marrying Venice to the sea. Art nouveau fans will find a good smattering of Liberty-style buildings which went up as the Lido developed as a resort. The Hotel Excelsior and Hotel des Bains are both splendid examples of this style of architecture; the perfect background for the *fin-de-siècle* melancholy of Thomas Mann's novel *Death in Venice*.
✉ Lido 🚤 1, 2, LN, 51, 52, 61, 62

51 San Lazzaro degli Armeni

It takes the best part of an afternoon to make the return trip to the island of San Lazzaro degli Armeni, one of the world's most important centres of Armenian culture and learning. Once a leper colony, the island was given by the Doge in 1717 to an Armenian abbot, Mekhitar, seeking refuge from the Turks. A monastery was built which became a focus for this displaced nation; it holds over 40,000 Armenian codices and has a museum run by the 12 resident monks. Guided tours are given of the church and monastery in a variety of languages.

Armenian itself is among the world's most difficult tongues, as the poet Byron found when he tried to learn the language while staying in Venice: you will be shown the room where he studied. San Lazzaro is the only place left where you'll hear the city referred to as the *Serenissima*.
✉ San Lazzaro degli Armeni
☎ 041 5 26 01 04 🕐 Guided tours only daily 15:25 (tours coincide with arrival of Zaccaria, ACTV line 20 3:10 boat)
🚤 20 💶 €6

The shady cloisters of the monastery on San Lazzaro degli Armeni

The Lagoon Islands

👫 TRAVELLING WITH KIDS

- Most **Murano glass-workers**, if slipped a fairly generous tip, will blow an animal or small figure and present it to your child to take away.
- A **day on the beach** is the perfect antidote to excess culture (and adults will love it, too!).
- Children will enjoy a **bike ride** around the Lido; keen cyclists can tackle Pellestrina as well, by putting their bikes on the ferry. You'll find rental outlets near the ferry (Bruno Lazzari, Gran Viale Santa Maria Elisabetta 21/B, tel: 041 5 26 80 19).

Vineyards in Sant'Erasmo, Venice's market garden

52 Sant'Erasmo

Sant'Erasmo has been Venice's market garden for centuries, boasting miles of fertile land where asparagus, artichokes *(castruare)*, onions, potatoes and wine are grown in large fields before being

GOLDEN WINE

Dorona: You won't find a more exclusive wine anywhere in the lagoon. A small 0.375 litre bottle costs €170, while a black Moretti hand-blown magnum adorned with a label made from gold leaf will set you back €1,300.

Once the favourite of Doges, this precious grape variety thrives on **Mazzorbo**. That's where the Battiloro family have replanted the oldest vines taken from Torcello and Sant'Erasmo. They've also opened **Venissa**, a little gem of a restaurant right next to the vineyard with six elegant bedrooms (Ostello Fondamenta Santa Caterina 3, Isola di Mazzorbo 30170, tel: 041 5 27 22 81, www.venissa.it, ferry terminal: Mazzorbo).

Insider Tip

sold at the Rialto market. The ferry makes its first stop at the isle of Le Vignole, which used to be known as the Isola delle Sette Vigne ("Isle of Seven Vineyards"). Wine with a slightly salty taste is still produced here today (wine festival: first Sun in Oct). Sant'Erasmo is the lagoon's largest island and is great for extended hiking trips.

✉ Sant'Erasmo 🚢 13

Where to…
Eat and Drink

Prices
Expect to pay per person for a meal, excluding drinks.
€ under €35   €€ €35–€55   €€€ over €55

MURANO

Trattoria Busa alla Torre €/€€

This lively *trattoria* is situated in the little square below the high red-brick tower that is easy to spot at the northern end of Fondamenta dei Vetrai. In fine weather you can enjoy a sunny lunch at an outdoor table, or sit in one of the two wooden-beamed dining rooms that are frequented by local glass-workers and their customers. The best dishes are usually the simplest – a bowl of mussels in a lightly piquant sauce, spaghetti with lobster or clams, fresh local fish *ai ferri* (grilled) with polenta and grilled vegetables. The wine list is not particularly long but it offers some of the stars of Friuli and the Veneto.
⊠ Campo Santo Stefano 3, Murano ☎ 041 73 96 62 ⑨ Daily 12:30–2:30 ⛴ Colonna, Faro

BURANO

Trattoria al Gatto Nero €/€€

Insider Tip

A terrace on a picturesque canal lined with multi-coloured houses, overlooking the old fish market, is the setting for this friendly *trattoria*. Inside, the walls are decorated with attractive paintings. The kitchen offers traditional Venetian specialities as well as more modern dishes, with seafood a principal ingredient. Here you can try the grilled *anguilla* (eel). The wine list includes a range of local varieties.
⊠ Fondamenta della Giudecca 88
☎ 041 73 01 20; www.gattonero.com
⑨ Tue–Sun 12:30–2:30, 7:30–9:30.
Closed 10 Nov–9 Dec ⛴ Burano

Trattoria Da Romano €€

This *locale storico d'Italia* (historic Italian eating place), formerly an artists' *trattoria*, is full of atmosphere, with an enormous dining room decorated with myriad paintings in many styles. Its red, white and green exterior is the main attraction in the town centre. The food is classic *trattoria* fare: good pastas, seafood risotto, fried fish and vegetables.
⊠ Via Baldassare Galuppi 221
☎ 041 73 00 30; www.daromano.it
⑨ Wed–Mon 12–3, 6–9.
Closed mid-Jan to end Jan ⛴ Burano

TORCELLO

Locanda Cipriani €€/€€€

You can't miss the Locanda Cipriani on Torcello: the long, low, yellow building is just in front of the Byzantine basilica. The dining rooms inside, and out in fine weather, are surrounded by a beautiful flower garden, with the church as a backdrop. It is a romantic setting for a peaceful lunch or dinner; set-price menus are available for both. The Locanda is popular with affluent visitors – and the service is correct without being stuffy. The food includes some local specialities as well as Italian classics, such as *tagliolini* noodles with tomato sauce, vegetable risotto and fish ravioli – but save room for one of the sinfully creamy desserts. The Locanda also has six hotel rooms.
⊠ Torcello
☎ 041 73 01 50; www.locandacipriani.com
⑨ Wed–Mon noon–3, 5–9:30. Closed evenings on weekdays in winter ⛴ Torcello

The Lagoon Islands

Osteria Ponte del Diavolo €€

Eat outside under a pretty *pergolato* in a bucolic atmosphere at this rustic *trattoria*. The fish here is fresh and well prepared – try the *granseola* (spider crab) or *schie* (tiny prawns) in season – but you will also find meat dishes such as cannelloni or carpaccio. Venetians come for the popular *fritto misto* (mixed fried fish), washed down with local wines. Finish with a home-made dessert or tart.

✉ Fondamenta Borgognoni, 10/11, Torcello
☎ 041 73 04 01; www.osteriapontedeldiavolo.com
🕐 Tue–Sun noon–3:30, Sat 7–10:30.
Closed 15 Dec–15 Feb 🚏 Torcello

Bar Gelateria Maleti €

This large, popular bar on the Lido's busiest avenue offers good home-produced ice creams, drinks and snacks until late at night. Delicious and good-value made-to-order sandwiches include Umbrian *porchetta* (herbed roasted pork). The bar serves cocktails, wine and 30 types of bottled beer.

✉ Gran Viale Santa Maria Elisabetta 45–47, Lido
☎ 041 5 26 14 55 🕐 Thu–Tue 7am–3am
(11 in winter) 🚏 Lido

Cri Cri €
Insider Tip

You'll find this friendly corner bar-cum-*cicchetteria* right on the Lido's long waterside main street. It's open all day and busy with locals popping in for a glass and a selection of the excellent range of snacks, such as *panini, tramezzini, pizzette* (sandwiches, filled rolls and miniature *pizze*), and tiny dishes of seafood and fish kebabs. At lunchtime, tables spilling out on to the pavement are packed with people enjoying lunchtime classics, such as *spaghetti alle vongole* (spaghetti with clams) and simply grilled fish with salad. This is a good-value eating place – ideal after a few hours on the beach.

✉ Via Sandro Gallo 159a ☎ 041 5 26 54 28
🕐 Mon–Sat 7am–9pm 🚏 Lido

Da Valentino €€

The Rosadas have owned Da Valentino for over 20 years; it is as popular with locals as with the cinema personalities that come for the Film Festival. The menu is divided between fish and meat, with lagoon seafood a speciality. After a choice of *antipasti*, try a home-made pasta, such as *tagliatelle* with *capesante* (scallops) or *gnocchi* with meat sauce. Grilled or fried fish follows, or veal *scaloppine* prepared any number of ways. The unusually good wine list is a very personal selection from some of Italy's finest small producers, lovingly assembled by the Rosada's *sommelier* son, Michele.

✉ Via Sandro Gallo, 81, Lido
☎ 041 5 26 01 28; www.ristorantevalentino
venezia.com 🕐 Wed–Mon 12–3, 6:45–10:30.
Closed Jan 🚏 Lido

La Tavernetta €/€€

Riccardo comes from Tuscany, Adriana is from Venice. In the kitchen of La Tavernetta – their small, upmarket restaurant – the pair draw on their culinary roots to produce creative, modern Italian cuisine that's trendily styled, healthy and quite simply delicious. The cellar boasts 150 Italian wines.

✉ Via F. Morosini, 4 ☎ 041 5 26 14 17;
www.latavernettalido.com 🕐 15 March–
1st week in Nov 12:30–2:30, 7–10 🚏 Lido

Gelateria Le Magiche Voglie €

Located right on the main drag, this very popular *gelateria* is the perfect stop-off on your way back from the beach. Choose a cone or tub filled with one of a wide range of creamy or seasonal fruit flavours, or branch out with one of its specialities – ice-cream cake, soft and unctuous *semifreddo* or *panna in ghiaccio* (frozen cream).

✉ LidoGran Viale Santa Maria Elisabetta, 47g
☎ 041 5 26 13 85 🕐 April–Sep 10am–11pm;
Sep–April Fri–Sun noon–6 🚏 Lido

🍴 Trattoria Favorita €

La Favorita has long been a favourite on the Lido: a bustling, family-run, *trattoria* that is perfect for families who want to eat and drink well. Its large garden veranda is always packed on summer evenings, the long tables filled with Italian diners of all ages, listening to the live music and enjoying platters of some of the freshest lagoon fish you'll find. There's a great assortment of hot and cold seafood *antipasti*, served with the classic polenta accompaniment. Seafood risotto is another speciality, as is *pasta con le vongole veraci* (clams) or *capesante* (scallops). Main-course fish are grilled or deep-fried in a light batter. For dessert, you could try a *sgroppino*: lemon, ice, vodka and Prosecco – it's very refreshing.

✉ Via Francesco Duodo 33, Lido
☎ 041 5 26 16 26 ⏰ Tue 7:30–10, Wed–Sun 12:30–2:30, 7:30–10. Closed mid-Jan to mid-Feb
🚢 Lido

Where to...
Shop

Leave early for your day trip to the lagoon islands. First stop will be Murano: pay attention to the identification label. Move on to Burano for lunch, browsing in the lace shops.

MURANO

Glassmakers include world-famous names, whose work is sold in stores everywhere, and tiny workshops producing extraordinary objects for sale only on the island. Among the former are **Archimede Seguso** (Fondamenta Serenella 18, tel: 041 5 27 13 68), known for quality and design. **Barovier e Toso** (Fondamenta Vetrai, tel: 041 73 90 49, www.barovier.com) is another historic firm whose designers collaborate closely with the *maestri* who produce the glass; their work is striking and technically complex. These criteria also apply to the glass at **Venini** (Fondamenta dei Vetrai, tel: 041 2 73 72 11, www.venini.it), which offers some modernist pieces by named designers, as does **Carlo Morletti** (www.carlo moretti.com). These three makers have a joint showroom on the Fondamenta Manin (tel: 041 73 62 72), known as the **Murano Collezioni** (Fondamenta Manin 1D, tel: 041 73 62 72; www.murano collezioni.com). **Fratelli Toso** (Fondamenta Colleoni 7, tel: 041 73 90 60; www.fratellitoso.it) specializes in striking multicoloured spiral designs to produce handsome vases and glasses. Beautiful table glasses, in the antique style, are made by **Vetreria Colonna** (Fondamenta dei Vetrai 10/11, tel: 041 73 93 89, www.vetreriacolonna. com); other good houses to try for table glass include **Mazzega** (Fondamenta da Mula 147, tel: 041 73 68 88, www.mazzega.it) and **Ferro e Lazzarini** (Fondamenta Navagero 75, tel: 041 73 92 99, www.ferrolazzarini.it). The latter two both welcome visitors to watch the glass-blowers at work. **Flora Gatto** (Fondamenta Giustinian 12/13, tel: 041 73 66 54), is where clean-lines jostles with multicoloured glass, ornaments, figurines and animals, lamps and mirrors. **SALIR** (Fondamenta Manin 77/79, tel: 041 73 90 33; www.salir.it) is noted for decorating and engraving traditionally styled Venetian mirrors. For the best of 21st-century glass, take a look at **Manin 56** (Fondamenta Manin 56, tel: 041 5 27 53 92), home to the Salviati collection, technically perfect glass, or head for **Nason e Moretti** (Calle Dietro degli Orti 12, tel: 041 73 90 20, www.nasonmoretti.com), or its other outlet, **Elle**, on Fondamenta Manin (No 52, tel: 041 5 27 48 66;

www.ellemurano.com), which sells a wide range of modern glass. There's more work of the highest standard at **Luigi Camozzo** (Fondamenta Venier 3, tel: 041 73 68 75; www. luigicamozzo.com), where the glass is incised and etched to resemble stone and marble. For another take on modern glass, visit **Rossana e Rossana** (Riva Lunga 11, tel: 041 5 27 40 76). Murano has produced *perle*, Venetian glass beads, for centuries, and the tradition continues at **Arte Nova** (Fondamenta dei Vetrai, tel: 041 5 27 44 56) and **CriDi** (Fondamenta dei Vetrai, tel: 041 5 27 53 79).

BURANO

Among the imported and machine lace there's still the genuine Buranese articles to be found, though expect to pay high prices. One of the best outlets is **Dalla Lidia** (Via Galuppi 215, tel: 041 73 00 52; www.dallalidia.co), where local ladies are often found bent over their lace pillows; the back of the shop is home to a lace museum. Nearby, at Piazza Galuppi 205, **Emilia** (tel: 041 73 52 99; www.emiliaburano.it) uses local lace to trim table linen, underwear and handkerchiefs. Cheaper by far are Burano's other speciality, *bussolai*, crisp biscuits – find them at **Dai Fradei** (Piazza Galuppi 380, tel: 041 73 56 30) and **Carmelina Palmisano** (Via Galuppi 355, tel: 041 73 04 85; www. palmisano carmelina.com).

Insider Tip

LIDO

The Lido's main street, Gran Viale Santa Maria Elisabetta, has food, clothing and souvenir shops, but the main draw is the **Tuesday morning market** (8:30–noon), which sells fruit, vegetables, food products, shoes, clothes and household goods. It's a 15-minute walk from the *vaporetto* stop or take the Alberoni bus to Riviera B Marcello.

Where to... Go Out

There is no nightlife to speak of on Murano or Burano, but if you are in the mood for an after-dinner outing on the Lido, try the piano bar in one of its grand hotels, or have a late ice-cream at a lively gelateria.

The Grand Hôtel des Bains at Lungomare Marconi 17 was where Thomas Mann was inspired to pen *Death in Venice*, his 1911 novella that was adapted for the silver screen by Luico Visconti. It also provided the backdrop for Anthony Minghella's telling of Michael Ondaatje's *The English Patient*. Unfortunately, the hotel is now closed, and is being transformed into a complex of luxury apartments offering "hotel-style service".

Situated right on the beach in front of the Film Festival's headquarters, the **Hotel Excelsior** is another gem. The piano bar has a romantic terrace on the sea that has long been a favourite of film stars; it, too, is open to non-residents (Lungomare Marconi 41, tel: 041 5 26 02 01; www.hotel excelsiorvenezia.com).

To complete this historic trio, an art nouveau piano bar can be found at the **Grande Albergo Ausonia & Hungaria (**Gran Viale Santa Maria Elisabetta, tel: 041 2 42 00 60; www.hungaria.it).

Gran Viale Santa Maria Elisabetta, the main street running from the Lido's *vaporetto* stops to the sea, hosts the evening *passeggiata*, or promenade. Its bars are all open after dinner, some till late, so stop in for *gelati* or a drink. **Il Gelatone** has home-made ice-creams, plus a vast selection of flavoured hot chocolates in winter (Gran Viale 63, tel: 041 5 26 56 46).

Excursions

Excursions

If you've had enough of water-girt glories and want to sample a taste of other historic cities, there's plenty of choice across the causeway. Take the train from Santa Lucia and head off through the fertile and tranquil flatlands to explore some of northern Italy's finest towns.

Easiest and quickest to reach is Padova (Padua), to the west. Northwest lies Vicenza. Verona (further west) and the lovely harbour town of Chioggio on the lagoon's southern edge are also worth a visit on the mainland.

On a boat bound for the mainland

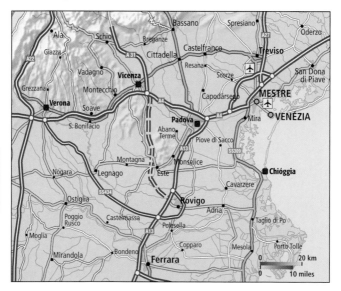

Padova (Padua)

It's an easy half-hour train ride from Venice to historic Padova, the Veneto's most important economic centre and a major university city where Galileo Galilei taught for twenty years. Its combination of spacious squares and streets, monuments and tempting shops make it the obvious place for an excursion.

Padua's medieval town hall, the Palazzo della Ragione, boasts many loggias that open onto the Piazza delle Erbe and the Piazza della Frutta on its southern and northern sides

The two most important sights in Padua are the **Cappella degli Scrovegni** with its magnificent cycle of frescos and the **Basilica di Sant'Antonio**, one of the best-loved pilgrimage sites in Italy. Between the generously sized **Cavour**, **dell'Erbe** and **della Frutta** piazzas, Padua's central cityscape is characterised by long arcades and impressive buildings. The **Pedrocchi coffeehouse**, built in a classical style in 1831, is a city institution.

Insider Tip

The **Cappella degli Scrovegni** was built from 1303 to 1305 on the site of the Roman Amphitheatre. It was constructed to be the domestic chapel for a palace that was later torn down. Enrico Scrovegni, son of Reginaldo Scrovegni, wanted to build the chapel to atone for his father's sins: according to Dante's "Inferno", Reginaldo grew rich through usury and is currently burning in Hell. For the interior, Giotto painted a moving fresco cycle representing the story of Mary and Jesus. Every year, southern Padua's Basilica di Sant'Antonio (known as "Il Santo" for short) sees hundreds of thousands of believers flock from all over the world to make the pilgrimage to the grave of Saint Anthony. A Franciscan and a Doctor of the Church, Anthony was born in Lisbon in 1195. He lived in Padua, and died in the city in 1231. His memorial church was begun just one year after his death. With its wide entrance façade, six domes, minaret-like towers and delicate blind arcades, the building is a fascinating mix of Romanesque, Gothic and Byzantine architectural styles.

Excursions

Tourist Information Office
✉ Stazione Ferroviaria ☎ 049 8 75 20 77; www.turismopadova.it
🕒 Mon–Sat 9:15–7, Sun 9–12
✉ Galeria Pedrocchi ☎ 049 8 76 79 27
🕒 Mon–Sat 9:30–6, Sun 9–12

Cappella degli Scrovegni (Giotto Chapel) and Musei Civici
✉ Piazza Eremitani ☎ 049 2 01 00 20 (Mon–Fri 9–7, Sat 9–6)
🕒 Daily 9–7; from 7pm–10pm on "Giotto Under the Stars" evenings
(Tue–Sun); max. 25 visitors may enter at a time; max. visit: 20 minutes;
Musei Civici: Tue–Sun 9–7 🎟 €13, includes entrance to the Museo Eremitani
and the Palazzo Zuckermann. Booking essential.

Palazzo della Ragione
✉ Piazza delle Erbe ☎ 049 8 20 50 06 🕒 Feb–Oct 9–7; Nov–Jan 9–6 🎟 €4

Caffè Pedrocchi
✉ Piazetta Pedrocchi ☎ 049 8 78 12 31; www.caffepedrocchi.it
🕒 First-floor rooms: Sun–Sat 9:30–12:30, 3:30–6. Bar: daily 8–11

Basilica di Sant'Antonio
✉ Piazza del Santo ☎ 049 8 78 97 22; www.basilicadelsanto.it
🕒 April–Oct 6:30–7:45; Nov–March 6:30–7 🎟 Free

Once a Roman theatre square, Padua's Prato della Valle, surrounded by a canal, is lined with statues of the city's famous citizens

Below: Padua's Botanical Garden is a UNESCO World Heritage Site

INSIDER INFO

- All trains heading southwest from Venice **stop at Padua** (travelling time 25–30 minutes). Alternatively, take a bus from Piazzale Roma bus terminus.
- You can **take a cruise boat along the River Brenta** from Venice to Padua and vice versa between March and early November (Battelli del Brenta, via Porciglia 34, Padova, tel: 049 8 76 02 33, www.battellidelbrenta.it).
- **Pick up a city plan** from the tourist information office at the station.
- Buy a **PadovaCard combined entrance ticket** if you're planning some extensive museum-visiting (€16/48hrs., €21/72hrs.; padovacard.turismopadova.it).
- Peace and quiet can be found in the **Orto Botanico (Botanical Gardens)**, laid out in the 1540s and the first of its kind in Europe.

Chioggia

The hard-working and salty port of Chioggia makes a great day-trip destination, with the chance to sample the many delights of the Lido and Pellestrina, en route.

Chioggia is often referred to as "Little Venice"

Chioggia lies on the southern lagoon mainland, facing seawards. Fishing has always been the major industry, with families setting huge store by their boats, the *bragozzi*, flat-bottomed, colourful craft about 12m (40ft) long. Ferries from Venice dock at the north end of the **Corso del Popolo**, Chioggia's main drag, a wide street with plenty of shops and cafés sheltering under gracious arcades.

The old town, its picturesque and tiny lanes leading off to the lagoon, spreads out from here over two islands, split by the Canale della Vena. Don't miss the glorious 14th-century **Granaio**, or the church of **San Domenico**, on its own little island, reached by bridge. The **Museo Storico della Laguna (Lagoon History Museum)** will fill you in on the story of lagoon life.

If you want to experience everyday life in Chioggia, walk along the Canale Domenico – where fishermen repair their nets and unload their boats – before strolling down one of the narrow alleys back to the Corso del Popolo.

Tourist Information Office
✉ Lungomare Adriatico 101, Sottomarina Lido ☎ 041 40 10 68
🕐 May–Sep Mon–Sat 10–5

Musei Civico della Laguna Sud
✉ San Francesco fuori le mura, Campo Marconi
☎ 041 5 50 09 11; www.chioggia.org/museochioggia 🕐 Tue, Wed 9–1, Thu, Sun 9–1, 3–6; 12 June–31 Aug Tue–Sun 9–1, 9–11 💶 €3.50

INSIDER INFO

- From the Lido, catch the **No. 11** bus from opposite the pontile. This runs down the Lido, boards the ferry at **Alberoni** and continues to **Pellestrina** to connect with the Chioggia ferry. In summer, the ACTV also offers a **direct connection** from San Zaccaria Pietà to Chioggia Vigo (No. 19).
- Alternatively rent a bicycle on the Lido and cycle there.
- **Buses** run hourly to Chioggia
- To sample Italian beach life, head for Chioggia's resort of **Sottomarina**.

Verona

Verona and its environs make up the western part of the Veneto. The landscape here rises from the river Adige into the hills of Valpolicella. Cradled in a riverbend, Verona's old town is home to one of the world's most famous open-air concert venues, the nearly 2,000 year-old Roman amphitheatre on the Piazza Bra.

Verona was already a significant city in Roman times (from 89BC) – its location at the end of the important Brenner Alpine pass predestined it for greatness. Three Roman roads met here to take advantage of its location: the Via Claudia, the route to the north, and the Via Postumia and Via Gallia, which led to the east and west. The Arena, Verona's best-known building, dates back to the Roman era. The mighty Roman city, built on a chessboard pattern inside a bend in the river Adige, was later occupied by the Goths. In c500AD, Theoderic the Great – a figure immortalised in the German sagas as Dietrich von Bern – made Verona his royal city during the Barbarian Invasion. The Scaliger took hold here in the 13th century before being displaced by the Visconti of Milan in 1387. The Serenissima took Verona in 1405, remaining in power for over 400 years. It was during this time that the lion of St Mark, the symbol of Venice, also came to be the emblem of Verona.

View of the Arena di Verona from the Piazza Bra

Worth a Look

The Roman **Amphitheatre**, built outside the Roman city in the 1st century, was damaged by earthquakes in the 12th century; only four arcades from its imposing outer wall still stand today. If you follow the **Via Mazzini**, the hottest shopping street in town, you'll arrive at Juliet's house in the **Via Cappello**. Officially called the **Casa Capuletti**, the building is a patrician palace from the 14th century. A vegetable market with lots of souvenir stalls is held daily on the **Piazza delle Erbe**, which also boasts some nice restaurants. You'll get a beautiful view over the city from the **Torre dei Lamberti**, the watchtower of the Palazzo del Comune. The **Piazza dei Signori** is Verona's secular centre. The Dante monument there stands as a reminder that the poet found refuge at the Veronese court of the Scaliger when he was

An atmospheric event in antique surroundings: The Opera Festival

driven out of Florence. The **Arche Scaligere** – the tombs of the Scaliger dynasty – are crowned with a life-size equestrian statue of Cangrande I (the original is in Castelvecchio). The Dominican church of **Santa Anastasia** at the end of its eponymous Corso was built from 1290 to 1481. It contains such treasures as the fresco of Saint George of Pisanello. The **Via del Duomo** leads to the monumental **Santa Maria Matricolare Cathedral**. Falconetto's frescos (1503) and Titian's *The Assumption of the Virgin* in the first side chapel on the left are particularly worth a look. Summer concerts are held in the Teatro Romano (early 1st c. BC) on the opposite bank of the Adige. The mighty Scaliger fortress of **Castelvecchio** sits further west along the river. The largest structure of its era, it was built in 1354.

MUSIC AND LITERATURE IN THE CITY OF ROMEO AND JULIET

Verona's Arena is the stunning venue for a summer **opera season**, running from the end of June to the end of August. It's best to book tickets for Opera performances and the annual **Lyric Festival** well in advance – the cheapest and most reliable option is **get service**, the Arena di Verona's online booking service (www.geticket.it/en_us). Tickets can also be reserved over the phone by calling 045 8 06 46 85 from 9–9, Mon–Sat. You can get information about performances and visits to the Arena by phoning the call centre on 045 8 00 51 51.

Excursions

Tourist Information Office
✉ Via degli Alpini 9, (Piazza Brà) ☎ 045 8 06 86 80; www.tourism.verona.it
🕐 June–Sep daily 8–8; Oct–May Mon–Sat 9–6, Sun 9–1

Arena
✉ Piazza Brà ☎ 045 8 00 32 04 🕐 Mon 1:30–7:30pm, Tue–Sun 8:30–7:30,
except during opera season (July–Aug) 9–3:30 💶 €6

Casa di Giulietta
✉ Via Cappello 23 ☎ 045 8 03 43 03 🕐 Tue–Sun 8:30–7:30, Mon 1–7:30
💶 €6; 1st Sun Oct–May: €1

Torre dei Lamberti
✉ Piazza dei Signori, Cortile Mercato Vecchio ☎ 045 92 73 02
🕐 Oct–March 8:30–7:30, April–Sep until 8:30, Fri until 10 💶 €6

Duomo
✉ Piazza del Duomo ☎ 045 59 28 13; www.cattedralediverona.it
🕐 March–Oct Mon–Sat 10–5:30, Sun 1:30–5:30; Nov–Feb Mon–Sat 10–4, Sun
1:30–4 💶 €2.50

Chiesa di Santa Anastasia
✉ Corso Sant'Anastasia ☎ 045 5 92 813; www.chiesaverona.it
🕐 March–Oct 10–6, Nov–Feb Mon–Sat 10–1, 1:30–5, Sun 1–5 💶 €2.50

Castelvecchio and Museo d'Arte di Castelvecchio
✉ Corso Castelvecchio 2 ☎ 045 8 06 26 11; www.comune.verona.it
🕐 Mon 1:30–7:30, Tue–Sun 8:30–7:30 💶 €6

The statue of Juliet in the Casa Capuletti brings the most famous fictional love story in the world to life.

INSIDER INFO

■ Catch an **Intercity train** from Venice (approximately hourly): the journey takes around one-and-a-half hours.
■ **Buses to the city centre** (nos 11, 12, 13 Mon–Sat; 91, 92 Sun) leave from outside the station; buy your ticket in the station before boarding, and validate it on the bus.
■ The **VeronaCard** (www.veronacard.it) is valid for two (€15) or five days (€20) and covers admission to museums, churches and monuments.

Vicenza

Vicenza is known for its magnificent goldsmiths' workshops and it's culinary speciality, *baccalà* (salted cod). Vicenza owes its true fame, however, to the work of the last great Renaissance architect, Andrea Palladio, whose buildings in the city have been named UNESCO World Heritage Sites.

Founded by the Venetians, Vicetia (Vicentia) became a Roman municipality in 49AD. Today's **Corso Palladio** follows the route of the Roman Decumanus Maximus. The city saw multiple changes of occupancy, becoming, for example, the seat of a medieval Langobard Duke, the property of a Frankish Count, and a protectorate of Verona. In 1404, Vicenza was subsumed into the Venetian Republic, under whose rule the city experienced its heyday.

Getting There and Sightseeing

Trains travel from Santa Lucia station to Vicenza every hour (a 55 minute journey). You can reach the city centre by bus. Start by going to the information office on the Piazza Matteotti and picking up a map showing the location of all of Palladio's buildings. The magnificently elongated **Piazza dei Signori** has been the centre of public and private life here since Roman times. The square is dominated by the **Basilica Palladiana**, which proved a real breakthrough for the young Palladio; the 12th-century **Torre di Piazza** at the northern corner stretches 82m (269ft) into the sky. The original Gothic basilica served as the assembly hall of the Great Council (Palazzo della Ragione). Palladio won a competition to beautify the building with his plan to cover the central structure with a two-storey columned portico made of marble. One of Palladio's most beautiful buildings – and

An elegant open-air salon and one of the most beautiful squares in Italy: Vicenza's Piazza dei Signori sits on the site of the earlier Roman Forum

Excursions

PALLADIO: THE PERFECTION OF FORM

Heavenly architecture on a human scale: Andrea di Pietro della Gondola was born the son of a stonemason in Padua in 1508. He moved to Vicenza in 1524, where he caught the attention of the humanist Count Gian Giorgio Trissino. The Count recognised the illiterate Andrea's extraordinary artistic talent, took him to Rome, had him educated and gave him the name that would eventually go down in architectural history: Palladius – after Pallas Athene, the Greek goddess of wisdom. Palladio lived in Vicenza for most of his life, shaping the city into a real centre of Renaissance architecture. Perhaps his most significant masterpiece is the Villa Rotonda outside Vicenza. Palladio also helped transform the face of Venice. The last sacred building he worked on in the city on the lagoon was the Tempietto Barbarano, a chapel designed for the family of his patron, Marcantonio Barbaro. Palladio didn't live to see the completion of this church: he died on the 19th of August, 1580.

also his last in the city – is the **Teatro Olimpico**. The stepped seating in the auditorium rises into a half-oval form, and the three gates on the stage (designed by his pupil Scamozzi) give a false sense of depth. The Teatro Olimpico used to be built entirely out of wood and stucco; it is thought to be the first covered indoor theatre in Europe. Concerts are held there today. The best-known of all Palladio's villas – "**La Rotonda**" (the "Round Villa"), also known as "Villa Capra Valmarana" – is located outside the city.

Andrea Palladio's buildings (above: The Villa Rotonda near Vicenza) bear witness to an intense engagement with antique architecture

Tourist Information Offices
✉ Piazza Matteotti 12 ☎ 044 4 32 08 54; www.vicenzanews.it
🕐 Mon–Sat 9–1, 2:30–6
✉ Piazza dei Signori 8 ☎ 044 4 54 41 22

Basilica Palladiana
✉ Piazza dei Signori ☎ 044 4 32 36 81 🕐 10–6 🎟 Free

Teatro Olimpico
✉ Piazza Matteotti 11 ☎ 044 4 22 28 00; www.teatrolimpicovicenza.it
🕐 June–Aug Tue–Sun 10–7; Sep–May 9–5 🎟 €5

La Rotonda
✉ Via Rotonda 29 ☎ 044 4 32 17 93; www.villalarotonda.it
🕐 Mid-March–Oct Tue–Sun 10–noon, 3–6, until 5 rest of the year 🚌 8
🎟 Interior: €10 € (Wed, Sat only); Exterior: €5

Walks & Tours

1 AROUND SAN MARCO
Walk

DISTANCE 2.5km (1½mi)   **TIME** 1.5 hours (start after breakfast
before it gets crowded)   **START POINT** Piazza San Marco ✚ 206 C4
END POINT Ponte dell'Accademia ✚ 206 C4

Squares and alleys, churches and
canals are among the attractions on
this walk through the quieter streets
of San Marco.

1–2

Stand in the **Piazza San Marco**
(➤54) with the **Basilica di San
Marco** (➤58) on your right and
head underneath the **Torre dell'
Orologio** (➤70) into the **Mercerie**
(➤71) – a chain of streets that
provide the oldest link between San
Marco and the Rialto, the politico-
religious and economic centres
of the Serenissima, respectively.
Follow the Mercerie all the way
up to the crossroads with the Via
2 Aprile and turn left to find **San
Salvador** on your left. This beautiful
mid-16th century church contains
two superb Titians, the *Annunciation*
and the *Transfiguration*, as well as
some fine sculpture and a vast
monument to Caterina Cornaro,
Queen of Cyprus.

The Renaissance church of San Salvador

2–3

Continue over the next canal then
turn left down Calle dei Fabbri.
Take the third turning right (Calle
del Magazen) and turn right into
Campo San Luca. Branch right
across the *campo* into Salizada
San Luca, which will take you
to Campo Manin. Turn left, and
follow the signs to the **Scala del
Bòvolo**, a flamboyant spiral staircase which twists up one corner
of the Palazzo Contarini. It was
built around 1499 and gets its
name from the Venetian dialect
for snail.

3–4

Continue down Calle delle Locande
to a T-junction and turn right along
Calle dei Fusèri and over a bridge.
You are now in the smart Frezzeria,
where arrows (*frezze*) were once
manufactured. Follow this right
down to its junction with Salizada
San Moisè, the main route from
San Marco to the Accademia. Turn
right and continue to **San Moisè**,

Baroque Angel, San Moisè

one of the most exuberant baroque churches in the city.

4–5

Cross the canal and walk down Calle XXII Marzo. Take the third (very narrow) turning on the right signed **"La Fenice"** (The Phoenix). Follow this to Campo San Fantin, home to one of Europe's most beautiful opera houses.

5–6

Walk straight across Campo San Fantin and down Calle della Verona. Cross a bridge then take the third left and first right. Continue to a T-junction then turn right into Campo San Benedetto. Walk straight through the square and down the **Calle del Traghetto**. This dead-end street provides a marvellous vantage point.

6–7

Retrace your steps to Campo San Benedetto, then turn right, cross a bridge, and turn left down Calle degli Avvocati into **Campo Sant'Angelo**, a spacious square named after a long-demolished church.

7–8

Turn right into the square and over a wide bridge into Calle dei Frati, which leads to **Campo Santo Stefano (►71)**.

8–9

Walk all the way through Campo Santo Stefano and follow the end of the square as it narrows and swings right by the flower stand. You will see the Accademia bridge ahead.

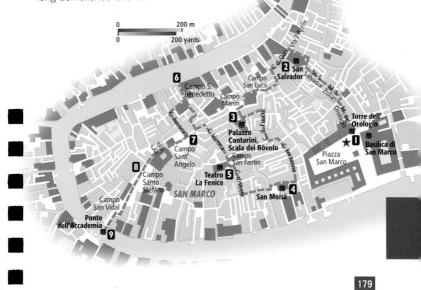

2 DOWN THE GRAND CANAL
Tour

> **DISTANCE** About 3.8km (2¼mi) **TIME** Allow about 40 minutes
> **START POINT** Piazzale Roma ✚ 200 B2 or Ferrovia Santa Lucia
> ✚ 200 C2 **END POINT** San Marco ✚ 206 C3 or San Zaccaria ✚ 207 D4

The trip down the Grand Canal is the big must-do in Venice, and the route of *vaporetto* No. 1 is the best and cheapest way to do it. The *palazzi* were built to be seen from the water, and the frequent stops give you plenty of time to take in this glorious parade of buildings on either side of what is still the city's main thorough-fare. There's an extra dimension in the constantly changing crowds of passengers, who provide a fascinat-ing glimpse of Venetians about their business.

❶–❷
Board the *vaporetto* at either Piazzale Roma or, a little farther down the canal on the opposite bank, at the Stazione Santa Lucia. There's been a station here since the causeway was built in 1846; the present one dates from the 1950s. Ahead, the stone-built Ponte degli Scalzi (1934) is one of four bridges crossing the Grand Canal. The domed church on the right is **San Simeon Piccolo**, built in 1738 and modelled partly on the Pantheon in Rome. A little farther down, on the left bank, is **San Geremia**, where the relics of St Lucy were taken when her church was demolished to make room for the station. The canal swinging in on the left is the **Canale di Cannaregio** (➤ 96), the former gateway to the city.

❷–❸
The boat calls next at **San Marcuola**, an 18th-century church whose name is a Venetian corruption of two

The Grand Canal is transformed into a colourful sea of lights in the evening

saints, Ermagora and Fortunatus. The cash ran out before it was completed, hence its unfinished brick façade. On the right bank you'll see the Venetian-Byzantine bulk of the **Fondaco dei Turchi**, unfortunately wrecked by heavy-handed 19th-century restoration. It was the headquarters of the Ottoman traders in the days of the Republic. The **Depositi del Megio** next door, a plain crenelated edifice with a splendid Lion of St Mark above the central door, was an important granary in the 15th century. Opposite, on the left bank, is the grandiose early Renaissance **Palazzo Vendramin-Calergi**, the

the same right-hand side, the *vaporetto* next stops at **San Stae**, a dazzling white baroque church which was constructed in 1709.

3–4
Look out on the right for an unforgettable view of **Ca' Pesaro** (➤ 126), Longhena's 1652 masterpiece, then to your left for your first glimpse of the **Ca' d'Oro** (➤ 102), Venice's

winter home of the municipal casino, designed by Mauro Coducci. It was here that the distinguished composer Richard Wagner died in 1883. Opposite, you can't miss the two fine obelisks on the roof of Baldassare Longhena's 1650 **Palazzo Belloni Battagia**, built for a nouveau-riche family who bought their way into the aristocracy. On

most famous Gothic *palazzo*. The historic palace of **Ca' Corner della Regina** is home to the Fondazione Prada today (www.prada.com). After the Ca' d'Oro stop, you'll see on the right the **Pescaria** (➤ 121) – the fish market; next to it is the long sweep of the **Fabbriche Nuove**, designed by Sansovino (➤ 27) in 1554–56 as a market Court, and later housing the Assize court. On the left, the **Fondaco dei Tedeschi** was once the German merchants' headquarters, complete with warehouse, club and lodgings; today, it's the main post office. Looming above is the **Ponte di Rialto** (➤ 118), with its *vaporetto* stop coming up on the left.

4–5

Below the Rialto Bridge, two *fondamente* run beside the canal: the left, the Riva del Ferro, where iron was unloaded, and the right, the **Fondamenta del Vin** (➤ 119), lined with restaurant and café tables. On the left bank, opposite the San Silvestro stop, Venice's city council occupies the Palazzo Loredan and **Ca' Farsetti**, both originally built around 1200; you can often spot official and police boats outside. Look out for the beautiful flower-hung Gothic **Palazzo Barzizza** next to the San Silvestro *vaporetto* stop, one of the few on the canal to preserve its precious 13th-century façade. Past the Sant' Angelo stop on the left you'll probably see the San Tomà *traghetto* in action – it's one of the oldest *traghetti* (gondola ferries), and the one most used by Venetians.

Ceiling detail in Palazzo Mocenigo

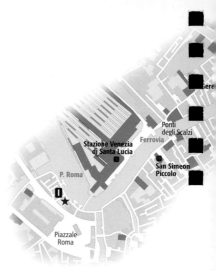

5–6

Hordes of passengers get on and off at San Tomà on the right, giving you time to take in the view of the beautiful **Palazzo Mocenigo** on the left, where the English Romantic poet Byron lived with his rather unruly mistress, Margherita Cogni. Today, the nation's first perfume museum tells the story of Italy's seductive fragrances. Its highlights include 2,500 perfume bottles spanning five centuries and a cosmetics study manual, *I Notandissimi Secreti de l'Arte Profumatoria* (G. Rossetti, Venezia 1555). Nearly 500 years old, it

contains more than 300 recipes. There's a big bend, La Volta, coming up. On the right, the 15th-century **Ca' Foscari** stands next to the massive **Palazzo Giustinian**, where Wagner composed the second act of *Tristan and Isolde* in 1858. A little farther down, the solid baroque **Ca' Rezzonico** (►142) faces the **Palazzo Grassi** (►20), Venice's finest example of classical 18th-century architecture.

6–7

After the Ca' Rezzonico stop, look out for the Gothic façade of the **Palazzo Loredan dell'Ambasciatore** and the former British Consulate *palazzo*, **Palazzo Querini**, both on the right, before the *vaporetto* halts at the **Accademia** (►136) and its eponymous wooden bridge.

7–8

A little below the bridge on the right lies the attractive **Campo San Vio**.

Part of the decorated Palazzo Cavalli-Franchetti is visible on the left; further on, the church of Santa Maria della Salute watches over the entrance to St Mark's basin

Beyond is **Palazzo Barbarigo**, its façade plastered with 19th-century mosaics. Next comes the bizarrely squat Palazzo Venier dei Leoni, home of the magnificent **Collezione Peggy Guggenheim** (➤ 140). On the left bank rises the huge 16th-century pile of the **Palazzo Corner della Ca' Grande**, designed in 1533 by Sansovino (➤ 23) for the hugely rich Cornaro family. Murky tales of murder, bankruptcy and suicide are associated with the charming **Palazzo Dario**, a little

The Palazzo Fondaco dei Turchi, whose origins date back to the middle ages, plays host to the city's Natural History Museum today

Gothic jewel, on the opposite bank, which you can admire from the Santa Maria del Giglio stop. Below, on the left, look out for deluxe hotels which cater to the rich and famous, such as the **Palazzo Pisani-Gritti** and the **Europa e Regina**, while, on the right, the great plague church of **Santa Maria della Salute** (➤ 144) dominates this end of the canal.

8–9

Below the Salute, Dorsoduro ends with a flourish at the 1677 **Punta della Dogana**, once the home of the Republic's customs offices, where all ships entering Venice were examined, and now housing the city's newest contemporary art space. The *vaporetto* crosses the canal from the Salute stop to the Vallaresso stop. **Harry's Bar** (➤ 72) is conveniently located right by the landing stage. Below here, on the left, you'll see the **Giardini ex Reali**, laid out by Napoleon, before the boat chugs past the **Piazzetta San Marco** (➤ 70) and the glories of **San Marco** (➤ 58).

3 FROM THE FRARI TO THE ZATTERE
Walk

DISTANCE 3.5km (2mi)
TIME 2.5 hours; start at 3:30 when the churches are open and aim to finish on the Zattere in time for a pre-dinner drink
START POINT Santa Maria Gloriosa dei Frari ✚ 201 D1
END POINT Fondamenta delle Zattere ai Gesuati ✚ 205 E2

Explore some of the hidden corners of Dorsoduro on this walk, which takes you along quiet residential canals to one of the longest settled parts of Venice. The route then twists through the heart of the sestiere to the Zattere, a long water-front with sweeping views across to the island of Giudecca.

1-2

From the side entrance of the **Frari** (➤ 122) turn right and walk round into Campo San Rocco, where you turn left immediately before the **Scuola Grande di San Rocco** (➤ 124) into the Calle della Scuola and over a bridge. At the T-junction, turn right, cross a bridge, then continue up Calle Vinanti until you reach a canal on your left. Take the second bridge on the left and continue straight down Calle della Misericordia and over another bridge. Turn immediately left on to the Fondamenta del Rio Nuovo, and follow the canal as far as you can, crossing one bridge en route. When you reach Campiello dell'Oratorio, turn right up the Calle dell'Oratorio, which brings you to **San Nicolò dei Mendicoli** (Mon–Sat 10–noon, 4–6, Sun 4–6; admission free). Nicolò was found-ed in the 7th century and retains its 13th-century Venetian-Byzantine layout and front loggia. Its serene interior has squat columns forming colonnades on either side of the

Sunlight on stone and water in Dorsoduro

apse. It's probably named after the *mendicoli* (beggars) who once lived in its shadow. Film fans may recognize it as the church in Nicolas Roeg's 1970s movie *Don't Look Now.* After the arrival

Walks & Tours

of the railway, the surrounding area was industrialized, the main employer being the cotton mill opposite (now part of the University).

2–3

Retrace your steps and turn right over the first bridge. This working-class enclave was one of the earliest parts of the lagoon to be settled. Many locals work for the port – you're within a stone's throw of the Stazione Maríttima

(Maritime Station), where Greek ferries and sleek liners dock while they're offloading. A left turn at the bottom of the bridge leads along the canal to the church of **Angelo Raffaele** (daily 9–12, 3–5; admission free), with its exuberant and light-filled panels by Guardi decorating the organ loft. Head right around the church and through a spacious square to **San Sebastiano** (Mon–Sat 10–5; admission €3). Paolo Veronese enthusiasts flock here to admire his superb 1555–65 paintings; the artist is buried here.

3–4

Cross the bridge in front of the church and turn left along the *fondamenta*, following it around to turn right at the third bridge into

Campo dei Carmini, with the church of **Santa Maria del Carmelo** and the **Scuola Grande** (▶ 124). Tiepolo fans should pause here.

4–5

The street gradually widens from the Carmini to open into the **Campo Santa Margherita** (▶ 144).

5–6

Leave Campo Santa Margherita down Rio Terrà Canal. The bridge at the bottom, with the vegetable boat moored beside it, is the **Ponte dei Pugni (Bridge of Fists)**, one of several of that name, recalling the

Vegetable producers supply the city by boat

Duck under the *sottoportego* opposite to the canal and follow this busy street, one of the main routes through Dorsoduro, over a bridge and along Calle della Toletta. The next canal you come to is the Rio di San Trovàso.

7-8

Cross the bridge and head right along the *fondamenta*. Across the water you'll see the church of **San Trovàso**. Pause to take in the **Squero di San Trovàso** (► 144), one of the last city-centre working gondola boatyards. A little farther brings you on to the Zattere (► 144).

You can walk beside the water all the way to the **Punta della Dogana** (► 145), or go left alongside the rococo church of **Gesuati** to cut through to the **Accademia** (► 136).

officially sanctioned punch-ups between rival gangs that took place on them until the 18th century. Two sets of footprints incised in the white marble of the bridge mark the starting point. Turn left off the bridge into **Campo San Barnaba**.

6-7

San Barnaba is used for a variety of exhibitions – its façade featured in the box-office movie hits *Indiana Jones and the Last Crusade* (1989).

> **TAKING A BREAK**
> Campo Santa Margherita is the obvious stopping place for refreshments, where there's a good choice of bars and cafés with outside tables.

4 THROUGH CASTELLO TO THE BIENNALE
Walk

DISTANCE 3.8km (2¼mi)   **TIME** 2 hours. Allow more time for stops.
Choose a weekday morning when street life throughout Castello is at
its liveliest   **START POINT** Arsenale *vaporetto* stop ✚ 207 F3
END POINT Riva dei Sette Martiri ✚ 208 B2

This walk takes you through eastern
Castello, a neighbourhood with
plenty of quiet residential streets,
historic churches, green spaces,
boatyards and shops.

0–2
From the Arsenale *pontile* turn
right along the *riva* and over
the Rio dell' Arsenale on to the
Campo San Biagio. From the
bridge there's a great view down
the canal to the 15th-century
gates of the **Arsenale** (▶ 88).
There are still naval links here; **San
Biagio**, once the Greek community
church, is now the naval chapel,
and next to it you'll find the **Museo
Storico Navale** (▶ 89). A few more
steps along the waterfront brings
you to another bridge; cross it to
reach Via Giuseppe Garibaldi.

2–3
Head up **Via Giuseppe Garibaldi**,
the widest street in Venice, which
was created in 1808 by filling in a
canal. It's the commercial hub of
eastern Castello, crammed with
alimentari (general stores), market
stalls (stands) and cheap-and-
cheerful bars and restaurants. The
first house on the right was home
to the Italian explorers John and
Sebastian Cabot in the late 15th
and early 16th centuries. Further
down is the entrance to the **Giardini
Pubblici**, marked by a statue of
Garibaldi, leader of the 19th-century
Risorgimento (Unification movement). Continue to the end of Via

Giuseppe
Garibaldi,
where the Rio di
Sant'Anna starts –
the vegetable barge here
is renowned as having some
of the city's best produce.

3–4
Head down the right-hand side
of the Rio Sant'Anna, then turn
left over the last bridge and walk
up Calle Crocera to emerge into the
Campo di Ruga. Walk through the
square and then into the Salizada
Stretta, taking the second turning
right towards the Canale di San
Pietro. From the vantage point of
the bridge you can see the boat
repair yards that line this canal as
you cross to **Isola di San Pietro**,
one of the city's oldest parts and
once its ecclesiastical centre.

Through Castello to the Biennale

4–5

The *sestiere* of Castello gets its name from the castle which once stood on this island. **San Pietro** (Mon–Sat 10–5; admission €3) was settled early, and by the eighth century a bishopric had been founded. In 1451, the first Patriarch of Venice was invested here and San Pietro remained the Patriarch's seat until 1807, when it was moved to San Marco. The present church dates from 1557. Inside, the chief treasure is St Peter's Throne (you'll find it halfway down the right aisle); this squat marble seat was carved in Antioch from an Arabic funeral stone engraved with verses from the Qur'an. Outside, a campanile looms drunkenly over the church green, the scene in late June of a jolly local festival in honour of San Pietro. You can peer into the cloisters of the old **Bishop's Palace (Palazzo Patriarcale)**; now disused, they're usually strung with washing and fishing nets.

5–6

Turn left behind the campanile and walk along the Fondamenta Quintavalle to cross the bridge and re-join the Fondamenta Sant'Anna, with the derelict ex-church of Sant'Anna on your left. Now take the first left to follow Calle GB Tiepolo and cross the Secco Marina.

Isola di San Pietro

C. larga S. Pietro **4**
San Pietro di Castello **4**

5 Ex Palazzo Patriarcale

C. Crociera

C. C. di San Pietro

C. Quinta Valle

3
Monumento a Garibaldi

Ex Chiesa di Sant'Anna

ELLO

6

San Giuseppe di Castello

Paludo S. Antonio

Giardini Pubblici

Biennale Internazionale d'Arte

7

Giardini

Via I Novembre

Rio dei Giardini

Viale dei Giardini Pubblici

QUARTIERE SANT'ELENA

Rio di Sant'Elena

Campo Sportivo

Sant' Elena

Parco delle Rimembranze

Via IV Novembre

8

9

Isola di Sant'Elena

Sant Elena

Viale Vittorio Veneto

| 0 | | 200 m |
| 0 | | 200 yards |

Statue of Verdi in the Giardini Pubblici, the setting of the Biennale since 1895

6–7

Corte del Magazen, opposite, brings you to the Fondamenta San Giuseppe. Turn right, cross the canal, and walk past the church of San Giuseppe. Cross the square, zigzag left, right and left to pick up the Paludo Sant'Antonio. At the end, cross the Rio dei Giardini and bear right through to the Viale IV Novembre.

7–8

This area is the island of the **Quartiere Sant'Elena**. It was enlarged during the Austrian administration as an exercise ground for their troops, whose last vestiges are now in the **Parco delle Rimembranze**. Follow the *viale* through the gardens, then turn left up the Calle Buccari and right towards the Rio di Sant'Elena.

8–9

Look across the canal to the 13th-century gothic church of **Sant'Elena**, founded after the acquisition of the body of Constantine's mother, and a glimpse of the home ground of

Venice's football team, **Campo Sportivo**,

9–10

Turn right and head down to the waterfront, then right through Parco delle Rimembranze. Cross the Rio dei Giardini to the **Giardini Pubblici**. Much of this space is occupied by the permanent pavilions built for the Biennale Internazionale d'Arte (➤ 20). It's been running since 1895 and still generates a great deal of razzmatazz. Just past the *vaporetto pontile* look out for a bronze statue of a prostrate woman on the waterline steps – the **Donna Partigiana (Partisan Woman)**, a memorial by Augusto Murer (1922–85) to the women who died in World War II.

TAKING A BREAK

There are plenty of bars and cafés in Via Giuseppe Garibaldi; try the **Osteria Da Pampo** near the soccer stadium, for real home cooking (Sant'Elena, Via Generale Chinotto 24, tel: 041 5 20 84 19; www.osteriadapampo.it).

Practicalities

Practicalities

WHAT YOU NEED

- ● Required
- ○ Suggested
- ▲ Not required

Some countries require a passport to remain valid for a minimum period (usually at least six months) beyond the date of entry – check before you travel.

	UK	USA	Canada	Australia	Ireland	Netherlands	Spain
Passport/National Identity Card	●	●	●	●	●	●	●
Visa (regulations can change – check before your journey)	▲	▲	▲	▲	▲	▲	▲
Onward or Return Ticket	▲	▲	▲	▲	▲	▲	▲
Health Inoculations (tetanus and polio)	▲	▲	▲	▲	▲	▲	▲
Health Documentation (► 196, Health)	○	○	○	○	○	○	○
Travel Insurance	○	○	○	○	○	○	○
Driver's Licence (national)	●	●	●	●	●	●	●
Car Insurance Certificate (if own car)	●	n/a	n/a	n/a	●	●	●
Car Registration Document (if own car)	●	n/a	n/a	n/a	●	●	●

WHEN TO GO

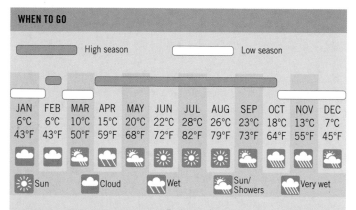

High season   Low season

JAN	FEB	MAR	APR	MAY	JUN	JUL	AUG	SEP	OCT	NOV	DEC
6°C	6°C	10°C	15°C	20°C	22°C	28°C	26°C	23°C	18°C	13°C	7°C
43°F	43°F	50°F	59°F	68°F	72°F	82°F	79°F	73°F	64°F	55°F	45°F

☀ Sun   ☁ Cloud   🌧 Wet   ⛅ Sun/Showers   🌧 Very wet

Temperatures are the **average daily maximum** for each month. Venice, like the rest of Italy and contrary to myth, is not bathed in perpetual sunshine but has a varied climate with well-defined seasons, and, because of its position, humidity is high throughout the year. January and February can be cold with freezing winds from the Alps, while March and April usually see warm sunny spells interspersed with heavy rain. May and June have plenty of sunshine and ideal temperatures, though these can soar into the 30s by mid-June. July and August are hot, with exceptional humidity when the scirocco is blowing, and regular thunderstorms. September, a good month, is followed by three months with a mixture of heavy rain and winds, fog and the occasional clear, cold day.

GETTING ADVANCE INFORMATION

www.veniceconnected.com
www.comune.venezia.it
www.veniceguide.net
www.hellovenezia.it
www.turismovenezia.it

In Italy
Venice Pavilion in Palazzina del Santi, near Piazza San Marco
☎ 041 5 29 87 11

In the UK
Italian State Tourist Office
1 Princes Street
London W1R 8AY
☎ 020 74 08 12 54

GETTING THERE

By Air Venice has one international airport, **Marco Polo**, on the northern mainland edge of the lagoon, handling scheduled flights. Charter, and some scheduled flights, land at **Treviso** to the north.

Direct flights arrive at Venice from all over Europe, New York and Philadelphia. Passengers arriving from other parts of the US, Canada, Australia, and New Zealand will have to route through either Rome or Milan.

Approximate flying times to Venice: London (2 hours), Dublin (3 hours), New York (9 hours).

Ticket prices are lower from October to March, excluding Christmas and Easter, and cut-price fares with budget airlines are available from the UK. Check with airlines, flight brokers, travel sections in the press and the internet for current special offers. Book well in advance for the lowest discounted fares.

By Train Venice is a significant hub on the European rail network, though so far it does not benefit from the high-speed express found elsewhere in Italy and Europe. There are direct services from adjoining countries, and easy connections at Milan and Bologna from many other international rail services.

By Road Venice is linked via the causeway to the Italian motorway system, which, in its turn, accesses the trans-European road system. If you decide to drive, remember to allow for high parking costs as part of your travel budget.

TIME

Venice is one hour ahead of GMT in winter, one hour ahead of BST in summer, six hours ahead of New York and nine hours ahead of Los Angeles. Clocks are advanced one hour in March and turned back one hour in October.

CURRENCY AND FOREIGN EXCHANGE

Currency The **euro** (€) is the official currency of Italy. Euro coins are issued in denominations of 1, 2, 5, 10, 20 and 50 euro cents and €1 and €2. Notes (bills) are issued in denominations of €5, €10, €20, €50, €100, €200 and €500.

Travellers' cheques These can be changed at banks or a cambio (exchange).

Credit cards are more widely accepted in Venice than in some parts of Italy, though not on the same scale as in Britain or the US and unwillingly, if at all, for minor purchases. Call your bank or card provider before travelling to confirm the dates you will be in Venice. Failure to do this may mean your credit card is refused.

Exchange You can exchange foreign currency and travellers' cheques at a bank or *cambio*. Banks generally offer better rates and lower commission charges, though always check the latter, as they vary considerably. You can also obtain money from a cash machine *(bancomat)*; most accept the major credit and debit cards.

In the US	In Australia	In Canada
Italian State Tourist Office	Italian State Tourist Office	Italian State Tourist Office
Suite 1565	Level 24	Suite 907
630 Fifth Avenue	44 Market Street	175 Bloor Street East
New York, NY 10111	Sydney NSW 2000	Toronto M4W 3R8
☎ (212) 2 45 56 18	☎ (02) 92 62 16 66	☎ (416) 9 25 48 82

Practicalities

NATIONAL HOLIDAYS

1 Jan	New Year's Day
6 Jan	Epiphany
Mar/Apr	Easter Monday
25 Apr	Liberation Day
1 May	Labour Day
29 Jun	St Peter and St Paul Day
15 Aug	Assumption of the Virgin
1 Nov	All Saints' Day
8 Dec	Feast of the Immaculate Conception
25 Dec	Christmas Day
26 Dec	St Stephen's Day

ELECTRICITY

 The power supply in Italy is 220 volts A/C.

Sockets two-pin round plugs, so British and US appliances need a two-pin adaptor. These are hard to find so bring one with you. US visitors should check if a voltage transformer is required also.

OPENING HOURS

○ Shops
● Offices
● Banks
● Post offices
● Museums/Monuments
● Pharmacies

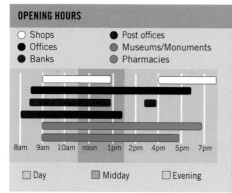

8am 9am 10am noon 1pm 2pm 4pm 5pm 7pm

☐ Day   ▨ Midday   ☐ Evening

Stores Many close Mon morning. Food shops often shut Wed afternoon.
Banks open Mon–Fri. Some also open on Sun.
Museums/Monuments Hours vary; many close Mon.
Pharmacies Many close Sat afternoons, but a rota ensures that at least one is open at all times. All pharmacies display the addresses of these.

TIPS/GRATUITIES

Tipping is not expected for all services.
As a general guide:
Restaurant/bar (service not included)   5–10%
Bar service (at bar)   10–25 cents
Tour guides   discretion
Taxis   Round up to nearest 50 cents
Chambermaids   €2.50 per day
Porters   charges are set by the porters' co-operatives. One piece of luggage costs around €10; two pieces €15; three to four pieces €20

VENICE CONNECTED

Venice Connected is an online, reduced-price booking service for all city services, including transport, museums, parking, WiFi and toilets, etc. Book 7 days in advance at www.venice connected.com, where you'll find more information about the scheme.

TIME DIFFERENCES

 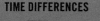

Venice (CET)	London (GMT)	New York (EST)	Los Angeles (PST)	Sydney (AEST)
12 noon	← 11am	→ 6am	→ 3am	→ 9pm

STAYING IN TOUCH

Post Main post office: San Marco 5554, Salizzada del Fontego dei Tedeschi, open Mon–Sat 8:10–7. *Poste restante* may be retrieved here and telegrams, telexes and faxes sent 24 hours a day (use the small door at San Marco 5552). Stamps can be bought at any *tabacchi*.

Public telephones Most telephone kiosks operate only with phone cards *(schede telefonica)*, available from post offices, *tabacchi* and some news-stands. To call the operator dial 182 for national calls or 170 for international. 12 will connect you with national directory enquiries, 176 with international directory enquiries. Dial 172 then the correct four-digit country code to connect with the operator in another country.

International Dialing Codes.
Dial 011 followed by:

UK:	44	Germany:	49
Ireland:	353	Netherlands:	31
Australia:	61	Spain:	34

Mobile phone providers UK, Australian and NZ mobiles work in Italy, but not US cell phones. The main providers are Tim, Vodafone and Wind; Tim and Vodafone have outlets in Venice. Check the rates from Italy with your provider before travelling. GSM phones can be used on 900 and 1,800 bands.

Wi-Fi and internet Much of Venice has wireless hot spots. You can buy access to these via the Venicia Unica (City Pass): it's cheaper to purchase it online than when you're there (www.veneziaunica.it). If you live, work or study in Venice, you can register for the city's WiFi network for free (not available to tourists; www.cittadinanzadigitale.it).

PERSONAL SAFETY

Venice is a safe city and crime against visitors is very rare. To be doubly sure, take obvious precautions and bear the following in mind:

- Don't carry too much cash.
- Keep an eye on your belongings in public places and crowded tourist areas, particularly around San Marco and the Rialto.
- Stick to main thoroughfares at night to avoid getting lost in ill-lit alleys; more for peace of mind than security.
- Lone women should avoid the Tronchetto car park at night.

Police assistance:
📞 113 from any phone

BY THE WAY...

When you're out shopping, don't be confused by the words Italians use for weights. Un chilo and *un mezzo chilo* ('a kilo' and 'a half kilo'), are as you'd expect. If you want 100g, however, say *un etto* rather than the more logical *cento grammi*. (200g is *due etti*).

EMERGENCY	113
POLICE	113 (Polizia di Stato) or 112 (Carabinieri)
FIRE	115
AMBULANCE	041 523 00 00 (ambulance boat) or 118

Practicalities

HEALTH

 Insurance EU nationals can see a doctor for free on production of the European Health Insurance Card. All foreign visitors can get free emergency treatment at the casualty department (*pronto soccorso*) of hospitals, but private medical insurance is strongly recommended for all.

 Dental treatment Dental treatment is expensive and may not be covered by medical insurance. In an emergency go to the Ambulatorio Odontostomalogico at the Ospedale Civile, Castello 6777, Campo Santi Giovanni e Paolo, tel: 041 529 4111.

 Weather High temperatures and humidity are common throughout the summer months. Take care against sunburn and dehydration by dressing suitably, applying sunscreen and drinking plenty of water – 1.5 to 2 litres daily in hot weather.

 Drugs Prescription and non-prescription drugs and homeopathic remedies, as well as advice on minor ailments, are available from pharmacies. Pharmacies operate a rota so one will be open 24 hours a day. If you think you may need to renew a prescription, ask your doctor for the chemical name of the drug, as it may be marketed under another name in Italy.

 Safe Water Tap water is safe. Mineral water is cheap and widely available. Unsuitable water is marked *Acqua Non Potabile*.

TRAVELLING WITH A DISABILITY

Venice is a difficult city for visitors with disabilities, owing to its large numbers of bridges and open water. Areas such as Piazza San Marco, some *campi* and stretches of the Zattere are relatively bridge free. Wheelchair routes are marked on the free tourist map and *vaporetti* and *motonavi* are easily accessible. Some bridges have automated ramps; get an access key from APT offices.

CHILDREN

Venice is not particularly child-friendly, and is hard if you have toddlers. Parents will need to work hard to avoid boredom. Most children are fascinated by this city built on water, and will enjoy many aspects of Venice. Special attractions for children are indicated with the logo shown above.

CONCESSIONS

Students/Youths Visitors between the ages of 14 and 29 can use the *Rolling Venice* programme, to get concessions on hotels, restaurants, shops, museum entry and travel passes. The card costs €4 from Vela and APT offices on production of your passport and two photos (www.hellovenezia.com).
Senior Citizens There are reductions on some museum entry charges on production of an identity document.

LAVATORIES

There are clean, public lavatories in museums, galleries, and bars, which make a small charge. Public lavatories throughout the city are marked with blue and green signs.

CONSULATES AND EMBASSIES

 UK ☎ 041 5 05 59 90

 USA ☎ 02 29 03 51

 Ireland ☎ 06 6 97 91 21

 Australia ☎ 02 77 70 41

 Canada ☎ 06 8 54 44 29 11/29 12

Useful Words and Phrases

SURVIVAL PHRASES

yes/no **sì/non**
please **per favore**
thank you **grazie**
You're welcome **Di niente/prego**
I'm sorry **Mi dispiace**
Goodbye **Arrivederci**
Good morning **Buongiorno**
Goodnight **Buona sera**
How are you? **Come sta?**
How much? **Quanto costa?**
I would like... **Vorrei...**
open **aperto**
closed **chiuso**
today **oggi**
tomorrow **domani**
Monday **lunedì**
Tuesday **martedì**
Wednesday **mercoledì**
Thursday **giovedì**
Friday **venerdì**
Saturday **sabato**
Sunday **domenica**

DIRECTIONS

I'm lost **Mi sono perso/a**
Where is...? **Dove si trova...?**
  the station **la stazione**
  the telephone **il telefono**
  the bank **la banca**
  the toilet **il bagno**
Turn left **Volti a sinistra**
Turn right **Volti a destra**
Go straight on **Vada dritto**
At the corner **All'angolo**
  the street **la strada**
  the building **il edificio**
  the traffic light **il semaforo**
  the crossroads **l'incrocio**
  the signs for... **le indicazione per...**

IF YOU NEED HELP

Help! **Aiuto!**
Could you help me, please?
  Mi potrebbe aiutare?
Do you speak English? **Parla inglese?**
I don't understand **Non capisco**
Please could you call a doctor quickly?
  Mi chiami presto un medico, per favore

RESTAURANT

I'd like to book a table
  Vorrei prenotare un tavolo
A table for two please
  Un tavolo per due, per favore
Could we see the menu, please?
  Ci porta la lista, per favore?
What's this? **Cosa è questo?**
A bottle of/a glass of...
  Un bottiglia di/un bicchiere di...
Could I have the bill?
  Ci porta il conto

ACCOMMODATION

Do you have a single/double room?
  Ha una camera singola/doppia?
with/without bath/toilet/shower
  con/senza vasca/gabinetto/doccia
Does that include breakfast?
  E'inclusa la prima colazione?
Does that include dinner?
  E'inclusa la cena?
Do you have room service?
  C'è il servizio in camera?
Could I see the room?
  E' possibile vedere la camera?
I'll take this room
  Prendo questa
Thanks for your hospitality
  Grazie per l'ospitalità

NUMBERS

0	**zero**	12	**dodici**	40	**quaranta**	400	**quattrocento**
1	**uno**	13	**tredici**	50	**cinquanta**	500	**cinquecento**
2	**due**	14	**quattordici**	60	**sessanta**	600	**seicento**
3	**tre**	15	**quindici**	70	**settanta**	700	**settecento**
4	**quattro**	16	**sedici**	80	**ottanta**	800	**ottocento**
5	**cinque**	17	**diciassette**	90	**novanta**	900	**novecento**
6	**sei**	18	**diciotto**	100	**cento**	1,000	**mille**
7	**sette**	19	**diciannove**	101	**cento uno**	2,000	**duemila**
8	**otto**	20	**venti**	110	**centodieci**	10,000	**diecimila**
9	**nove**	21	**ventuno**	120	**centoventi**		
10	**dieci**	22	**ventidue**	200	**duecento**		
11	**undici**	30	**trenta**	300	**trecento**		

Useful Words and Phrases

acciuga anchovy
acqua water
affettati sliced cured meats
affumicato smoked
aglio garlic
agnello lamb
anatra duck
antipasti hors d'oeuvres
arista roast pork
arrosto roast
asparagi asparagus
birra beer
bistecca steak
bollito boiled meat
braciola minute steak
brasato braised
brodo broth
bruschetta toasted bread with garlic or tomato topping
budino pudding
burro butter
cacciagione game
cacciatore, alla rich tomato sauce with mushrooms
caffè corretto/ macchiato coffee with liqueur/ spirit, or with a drop of milk
caffè freddo iced coffee
caffè lungo weak coffee
caffè latte milky coffee
caffè ristretto strong coffee
calamaro squid
cappero caper
carciofo artichoke
carota carrot
carne meat
carpa carp

casalingho home-made
cassata Sicilian fruit ice cream
cavolfiore cauliflower
cavolo cabbage
ceci chickpeas
cervello brains
cervo venison
cetriolino gherkin
cetriolo cucumber
cicoria chicory
cinghiale boar
cioccolata chocolate
cipolla onion
coda di bue oxtail
coniglio rabbit
contorni vegetables
coperto cover charge
cornetto croissant
coscia leg of meat
cotolette cutlets
cozze mussels
crema custard
crostini canapé with savoury toppings or croutons
crudo raw
digestivo after-dinner liqueur
dolci cakes/desserts
erbe aromatiche herbs
fagioli beans
fagiolini green beans
faraona guinea fowl
farcito stuffed
fegato liver
finocchio fennel
formaggio cheese
forno, al baked
frittata omelette
fritto fried
frizzante fizzy
frulatto whisked
frutti di mare seafood

frutta fruit
funghi mushrooms
gamberetto shrimp
gelato ice cream
ghiaccio ice
gnocchi potato dumplings
granchio crab
gran(o)turco corn
griglia, alla grilled
imbottito stuffed
insalata salad
IVA VAT
latte milk
lepre hare
lumache snails
manzo beef
merluzzo cod
miele honey
minestra soup
molluschi shellfish
olio oil
oliva olive
ostrica oyster
pancetta bacon
pane bread
panna cream
parmigiano Parmesan
passata sieved or creamed
pastasciutta dried pasta
pasta sfoglia puff pastry
patate fritte chips
pecora mutton
pecorino sheep's milk cheese
peperoncino chilli
peperone red/green pepper
pesce fish
petto breast
piccione pigeon
piselli peas
pollame fowl
pollo chicken

polpetta meatball
porto port wine
prezzemolo parsley
primo piatto first course
prosciutto cured ham
ragù meat sauce
ripieno stuffed
riso rice
salsa sauce
salsiccia sausage
saltimbocca veal with prosciutto and sage
secco dry
secondo piatto main course
senape mustard
servizio compreso service charge included
sogliola sole
spuntini snacks
succo di frutta fruit juice
sugo sauce
tonno tuna
uova strapazzate scambled eggs
uovo affogato/in carnica poached egg
uovo al tegamo/fritto fried egg
uovo alla coque soft-boiled egg
uovo alla sodo hard-boiled egg
vino bianco white wine
vino rosso red wine
vino rosato rosé wine
verdure vegetables
vitello veal
zucchero sugar
zucchino courgette
zuppa soup

Street Atlas

For chapters: see inside front cover

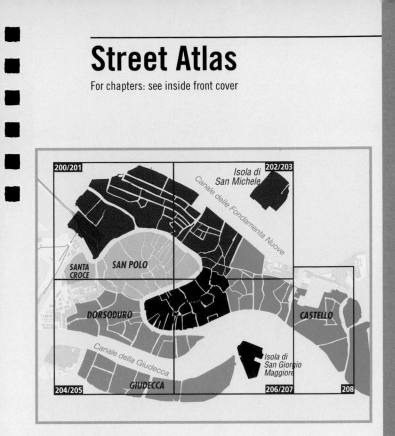

200/201
Isola di San Michele
Canale delle Fondamenta Nuove
202/203
SANTA CROCE
SAN POLO
DORSODURO
CASTELLO
Canale della Giudecca
Isola di San Giorgio Maggiore
204/205
GIUDECCA
206/207
208

Key to Street Atlas

ℹ	Information	★	Place of interest
M̂	Museum	— — —	Ferry, traghetti
🎭	Theatre / Opera house	▮	Public building / Building of interest
⚱	Monument		
⊕	Hospital		
✿	Police station	★	TOP 10
✉	Post office	26	Don't Miss
✝	Church	22	At Your Leisure

1 : 7.200

0   250   500 m

0   250   500 yd

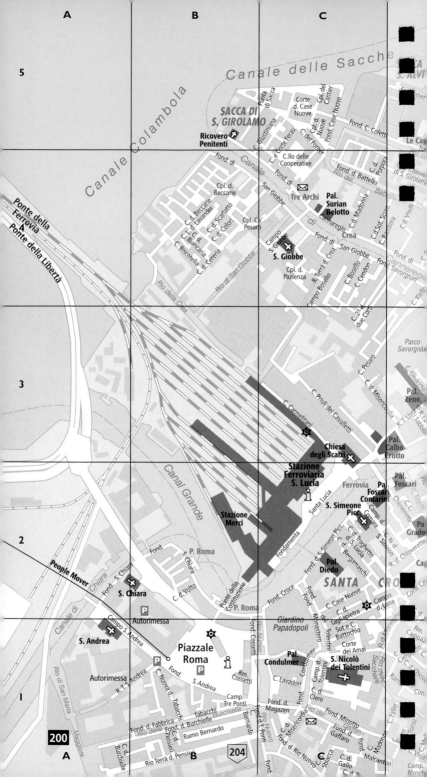

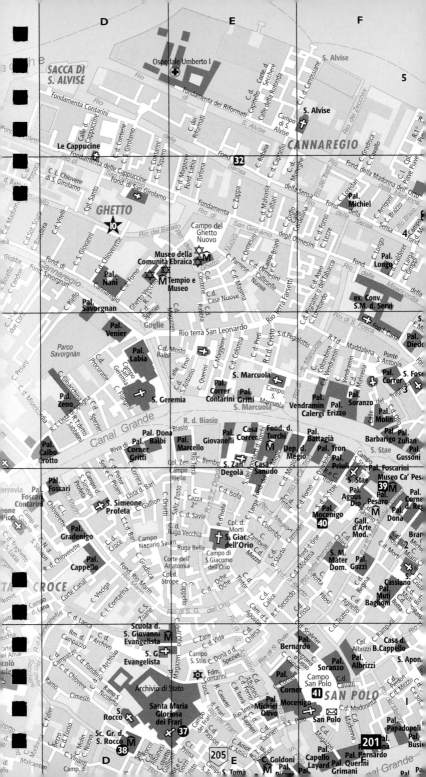

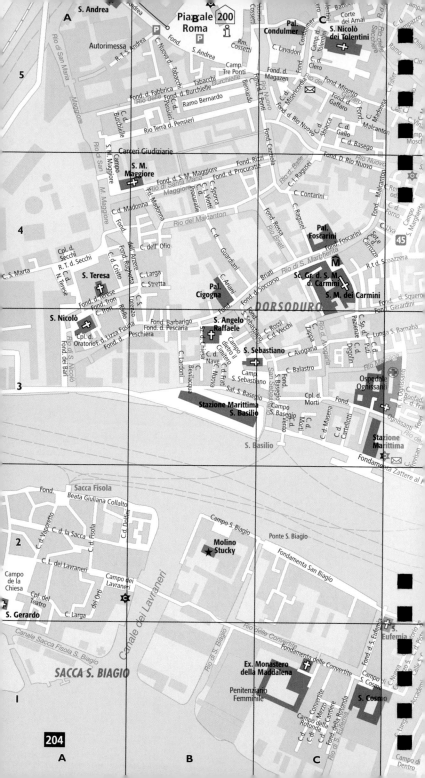

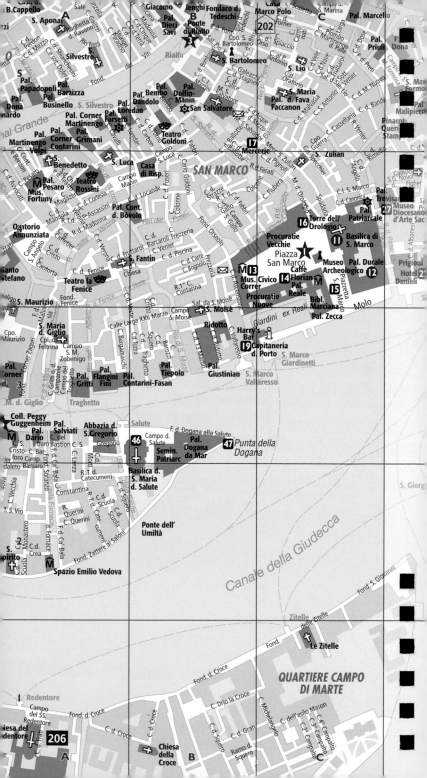

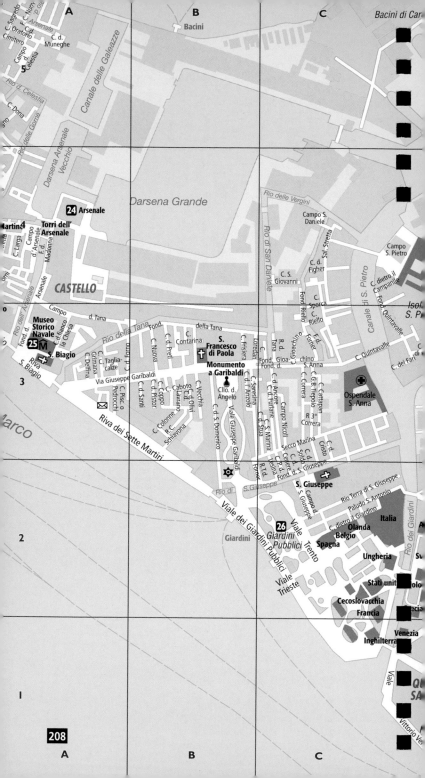

Street Index

Street Index

Street Index

Street Index

Index

Index

Index

Picture Credits

Impressum

1st Edition 2015

Worldwide Distribution: Marco Polo Travel Publishing Ltd
Pinewood, Chineham Business Park
Crockford Lane, Chineham
Basingstoke, Hampshire RG24 8AL, United Kingdom.
© MAIRDUMONT GmbH & Co. KG, Ostfildern

Authors: Sally Roy und Carla Capalbo, Hilke Maunder
Editor: Robert Fischer, www.vrb-muenchen.de
Revised editing and translation: Jon Andrews, jonandrews.co.uk
Program supervisor: Birgit Borowski
Chief editor: Rainer Eisenschmid

Cartography: © MAIRDUMONT GmbH & Co. KG, Ostfildern
3D-illustrations: jangled nerves, Stuttgart

Printed in China

Despite all of our authors' thorough research, errors can creep in.
The publishers do not accept any liability for this. Whether you
want to praise, alert us to errors or give us a personal tip –
please don't hesitate to email or post:

MARCO POLO Travel Publishing Ltd
Pinewood, Chineham Business Park
Crockford Lane, Chineham
Basingstoke, Hampshire RG24 8AL
United Kingdom
Email: sales@marcopolouk.com

FSC
www.fsc.org
MIX
Paper from
responsible sources
FSC® C020056

10 REASONS
TO COME BACK AGAIN

1. **Quick to reach by plane**, a visit to Venice whisks you off into a completely different world.

2. **Staying in hotels and eating out** in Venice have become much cheaper over the last few years.

3. Venice is packed with centuries of **artistic creation** that's just waiting to be discovered.

4. **With no cars to contend with,** Venice is the ideal place to drift along and stroll around!

5. Experience the never-ending romance between **Venice and the water.**

6. A short boat ride is all that separates **city living** from **fun at the beach.**

7. Enjoy **Venice's diverse cuisine**, cooked with the freshest produce from Rialto's market.

8. Napoleon's words still ring true: St Mark's Square is **Europe's "most beautiful living room".**

9. Venice loves taking to the stage and **getting dressed up** – and not just during the Carnival.

10. **Warning:** Venice is addictive!